the GARDEN BOOK

MURDOCH BOOKS

First published in 2006 by Murdoch Books Pty Limited

Murdoch Books Pty Limited Australia
Pier 8/9, 23 Hickson Road
Sydney NSW 2000
Phone: 61 (02) 8220 2000
Fax: 61 (02) 8220 2558
www.murdochbooks.com.au

Murdoch Books UK Limited
Erico House, 6th Floor North
93/99 Upper Richmond Road
Putney, London SW15 2TG
Phone: + 44 (0) 20 8785 5995
Fax: + 44 (0) 20 8785 5985

Chief Executive: Juliet Rogers
Publisher: Kay Scarlett
Design Manager: Vivien Valk
Design and illustrations: Alex Frampton
Editor: Ariana Klepac
Production: Megan Alsop

Text: Susan Berry, Steven Bradley, Val Bradley, Toby Buckland, Geoffrey Burnie,
Mark Edwards, John Fenton-Smith, Denise Greig, Margaret Hanks, Richard Key,
Meredith Kirton, Ariana Klepac, Chris Maton, Paul Urquhart

Printed by Midas Printing (Asia) Ltd
Printed in China

National Library of Australia Cataloguing-in-Publication Data:
The garden book. Includes index.
ISBN 9 78174045 8573.
ISBN 1 74045 857 5.

1. Gardening - Australia - Handbooks, manuals, etc.
2. Gardens - Australia - Design. I. Hill, Diana.

635.0994

the GARDEN BOOK

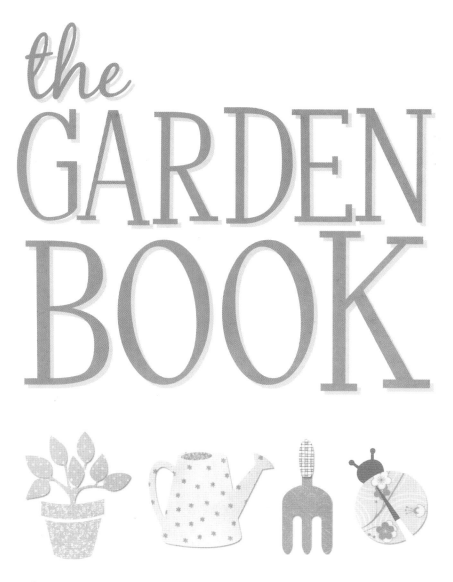

Thousands of practical tips for beautifying and maintaining your garden

contents

Design

It's all in the planning. If you get the opportunity to design a garden at any stage, you will need to think ahead. This way you can save yourself a lot of time and trouble down the track, as well as incorporate elements that will grow to make your garden a year-round delight.

Before you start

It isn't hard to design an attractive garden that will fit both your needs and your lifestyle, even if you know next to nothing about gardening. In working out a design, you should first consider how you and your family will want to use and enjoy your garden.

The first thing to do is to forget all about plants. Thinking of a garden only in terms of what plants to grow is like designing a house by first choosing the curtains. Just as you consider a house in terms of its rooms – living, dining, bedroom and so on – you can imagine your garden as a sequence of outdoor living rooms. Their 'walls' are made of trees and foliage, the floor is the earth, carpeted with grass or paving, the ceiling is the branches of trees or the open sky, and it's all decorated with flowers and such furniture as you might use. The particular plants you choose are not important at all at this stage. Instead, think about the overall look you want to achieve.

Assess your needs

Begin your planning by sitting back and daydreaming a little:

- Does the idea of breakfast in the sun on a Sunday morning appeal? Or what about dinner under the stars, in the cool of a summer evening? Then you probably need a sheltered and private patio.

- Do you need space to build a boat, work on the car, or pull the motorbike to pieces?

- Do you long for a swimming pool – maybe not now, but when you can afford it?

- Do you want to grow your own vegetables and fruit or do you want lots of flowers for cutting?

- If you enjoy entertaining then it might be time to think about whether you should build a permanent barbecue and whether you need extra parking space for your guests.

- If you, or the children, like kicking a football around in the garden or if you have a dog that likes to romp, then you are going to need unencumbered space surrounded by tough plants that are able to withstand the punishment.

- It pays to think ahead a few years. If the children are still at the tricycle-and-sandpit stage, you might want to create a special space for them, but one that can be transformed as they grow older. Planning for the future now will mean less disruption later.

- Finally, think about how much of your free time you want to spend at home. If you're a reluctant gardener, enthusiasm may develop as the garden grows and you begin to see results from your labours, but it's wise not to plan a garden that will demand more time than you're prepared to give it. All gardens are work and the more elaborate the layout and contents, the more work there is. If you enjoy gardening, you'll think of it as a hobby, but if you'd rather be sailing or golfing or doing other things, you won't have the time or the inclination to maintain big beds of flowers or vegetables, or to care for hedges or fruit trees that need pruning or regular spraying.

PLANNING CHECKLIST

When planning and designing your garden, consider these factors:

Which direction does the garden face and what will you use it for?

How much time can you realistically spare to work in the garden?

Will you use it to sit in and, if so, at what time of the day?

Will children use it? What age are they and how will they use it?

Will you want to entertain in the garden, and how many people?

Do you want flowers, and do you want them for cutting?

Do you want a lawn, and what will you do on the lawn?

Do you want one or more trees, and will you use them for shade?

Do you want a water feature, and if so will you want fish?

Do you want to grow vegetables and fruit?

SOFT AND HARD LANDSCAPING
The planting is known as 'soft landscaping', while constructed items such as paving, decks and walls are 'hard landscaping'.

Time-saving ideas

If you know you won't have time to work in the garden every day or each night when you get home from work, don't plant a high-maintenance garden. Planting roses, perennials such as dahlias that need regular dividing and lifting, and very fast growers might seem like a good idea at the time, but they will eventually make you a slave to your garden.

Choose low-maintenance plants that are cold, drought and wind tolerant (depending on the area you live) and cope with a bit of neglect. Include plenty of shrubs – all chosen especially for your conditions. Generally speaking, shrubs require the least amount of care. Avoid large areas of lawn, vegetables and flowers, as these plants require the most effort to cultivate and demand more of your time. Group together any demanding plants, such as fruit trees, so that feeding, spraying and watering can all be done in one go.

Paving is a good alternative to lawn. It is a good surface for entertaining, relaxation and children's play and, unlike lawn, it dries quickly after rain.

Assess your site

Before you start transforming your garden into what you would like, take stock of what you have. Whether you're faced with bare soil and the debris of a just-departed builder or an established or partially established garden, look around critically – it's surprising how this process will throw up ideas to get you going.

Start with the house. If you have big windows looking straight out onto the street or at the neighbour's windows, so that you have to keep your curtains

LITTLE AND OFTEN
The best tip for garden maintenance is to do a little work often. Just 10 minutes a day weeding and tidying up will save hours of work in the long run.

HIGH-MAINTENANCE FEATURES

As a word of warning, listed below are some of the more labour-intensive garden features:

Large areas of mown grass

Island flower beds

Fussy beds and borders with many different types of plants

Rose gardens

Large traditional perennial borders with staked plants

Fast-growing hedges that are trimmed into formal shapes

Vigorous climbing plants

Large vegetable plots, or many smaller ones

Fruit trees

Greenhouses

Hanging baskets

LOW-MAINTENANCE FEATURES

Listed below are some of the garden features that require less maintenance than average:

Long-grass areas

Naturalized bulbs

Ponds and bog gardens

Planting in gravel

Hard surfacing – decking, paving, gravel etc.

Evergreen groundcovers

Natural perennial plantings in drifts

Mulched borders (plastic and bark chippings)

Mixed informal hedges

Drought-resistant plantings

Raised beds

Mixed shrub borders

drawn for privacy, a screen of foliage might be called for. Not necessarily a dense mass – a clump of airy trees or shrubs will usually be enough to take away the fish-bowl feeling and allow you to look out.

A group of birches might lead you to a woodland theme for a garden, or palms may lead you to create a tropical wilderness through which you can wind a path to the door. Always try to position screening shrubs and trees as far away from the place to be screened as possible. This creates an area between you and the screen that can be gardened into a pleasant outlook, and it also minimizes any loss of light.

Sloping sites

A sloping site may call for some juggling of earth to create level areas for outdoor living, with retaining walls and steps to link it all together. But remember that earthworks will mean either money to a contractor or back-breaking work – a level site is easier to develop.

On the other hand, a strongly sloping hillside site might well have fine views, and you will want to ensure that your plants frame them while at the same time masking distractions such as the neighbours' houses and electricity or telephone poles. A two-storey house may have views from upstairs, too, so make sure the garden looks good from there.

Trees and paving

Nothing can give the garden a head start like established trees, and you should think very carefully before deciding to remove any that you already have. Even if a tree is a bit scruffy now, a few years' care will probably see it grow into a beauty, although judicious pruning may be needed to reveal handsome trunks and branches. If you have doubts about the safety of a tree, always get advice from a professional tree surgeon.

Paths and pavements are another matter. If they fit your purposes, fine, but if they don't, the cost of replacing them will be well spent.

The soil

If the soil is not the ideal deep, crumbly loam, don't worry – beautiful gardens have been made on all soil types. It's almost always better to work with what you have than to import topsoil (unless your builder has carried away your topsoil or buried it irretrievably under subsoil and rubble). Any soil can be improved out of sight by cultivation and the addition of as much organic matter, such as compost, as you can manage.

DESIGN FOR YOUR CLIMATE

It's always pleasant to sit in the sun in winter, but in summer a retreat to the shade is safer and more comfortable. A usable garden needs a balance between sun and shade, through the day and through the year, and once you know which way your property faces you can plan for it easily.

The ideal aspect

The ideal aspect for outdoor living is the sunny side of the house (north or north-east in the southern hemisphere, south or south-east in the northern hemisphere). Paving here reflects warmth to the house, but you'll need shade for the summer. You could rig up awnings or umbrellas but the shade of trees is cooler. Deciduous trees let the winter sun through their bare branches; plant them on the east to let through the early winter sun. Evergreens can go to the south in the northern hemisphere or to the north in the southern hemisphere. To avoid afternoon sun in hot areas plant them on the west side also.

Putting the plan on paper

Now that you've made an objective assessment of your needs and your site, it's time to think about what you want the garden to look like. Perhaps you'd like to look onto an English-style garden of flowers and lawns, or perhaps a slice of

SEPARATING SPACES

Different parts of the garden can be assigned different functions. You could have a play area for the children, an outdoor living area, a place to grow vegetables and flowers, and a utility area for the clothes line or compost heap. These separate spaces, or outdoor 'rooms', can be physically marked off, making the garden more interesting to look at and to be in. To divide space you can use:

- Shrubs: densely foliaged to the ground for total separation.
- Trees: which allow you to see under the branches.
- Low planting: for a gentle division, maybe with a climber-covered pergola overhead for added interest and decoration.
- A screen, fence or wall – perhaps softened with creepers, shrubs or tall flowers, or even hanging baskets.
- A change of level, with steps as a link, and associated planting creates a separate, upper room.
- A change of level, without dividing plants or structures, keeps the spaces separate but open.

SHADING THE HOUSE

Shading the roof can make quite a difference to your comfort inside, and large areas of glass simply cry out for shade. Remember that once the heat gets in, it's hard to get it out. If the addition of shade trees will dominate the garden too much don't forget the ancient climate-control device of the vine-covered pergola.

In sunny climates, it is better to err on the side of too much shade than too little; most trees will put up with a bit of judicious pruning and thinning if they get too dense.

woodland or bushland might be more to your liking. Japanese-style gardens are lovely, but maybe a more formal, European plan would suit you better. If you live in a warm area, a garden based on lush, tropical-looking plants can be attractive but you might prefer the stark lines of dry-climate plants. An old-fashioned cottage garden, with a delightful jumble of plants, might be your dream, or maybe you'd prefer an Italian Mediterranean-style garden.

Once you have decided on the type of look you want, it will be much easier to plan the garden layout and contents and that's the time to start drawing. It doesn't matter if you can't draw very well. As long as you can understand your own doodles, drawing a range of ideas, just roughly at first, will help you to gather your thoughts together.

Once you've decided which of your rough doodles you like the most, draw it up on a larger scale using graph paper, make an enlarged photocopy or lay a piece of tracing paper over your original site plan and transfer the doodle to it. Work out your ideas in detail, checking the measurements to make sure paths are wide enough, there is room for screening shrubs and you've allowed for steps between the patio and the lawn. Make sure you haven't forgotten anything important. Resist the temptation to elaborate the design – remember the art of all art is knowing when to stop.

Think of the third dimension

A plan can be deceptive, as it gives an exaggerated emphasis to things like paving patterns, and it flattens out the third dimension of height. We draw

DESIGN AND PLANNING CHECKLIST

Have you thought about:

- Summer shade, winter sun
- Windbreaks
- Blocking undesirable views, providing privacy
- Clothes line
- Compost heap
- Storage for garden equipment and furniture
- Steps and/or retaining walls where there are changes in level in pavements and lawn
- Lighting
- Mailbox
- House number
- Drainage
- Easements, overhead lines, drains and/or sewers
- Widths of paths, gates and steps
- Position of outdoor living areas
- Size of pavings and patios
- Shape of lawns and ease of mowing them
- The ultimate size of trees and the effect of their shade on your and your neighbours' properties
- Security, especially for swimming or other pools
- Space for children's games, herb and vegetable gardens and other special projects
- Access for the car
- Access to the garden during construction and afterwards
- Comfortable access to the house
- Enough space for planting, so that plants won't outgrow themselves and need constant cutting back
- Council approval for fences, structures and pools, and for planting on the street
- Building the garden in separate stages, if necessary

trees and shrubs as circles on a plan, but that's not how we see them in real life. You can plot perspective drawings, but remember that perspective does need considerable artistic skill. It's much easier to simply tilt the plan at an angle and draw in the trees and structures at their measured height. This gives you a sort of bird's eye view (it is technically known as an 'axonometric projection'), and though the heights tend to look a bit exaggerated, it can be a great help at all stages of making the design.

A safe, organic garden

Efforts to reduce your home's impact on the environment are particularly rewarding in the garden. There are many ways to reduce the amount of water you use; kitchen scraps and other biodegradable household waste can be composted and returned to your garden. With a little extra care and observation you can grow a more abundant, healthy garden without relying on pesticides and herbicides.

Taking health and safety measures seriously is especially important in the garden. Great care should be taken with the correct storage of the many dangerous chemicals that lurk in the shed or garage. In many places fences around pools are required by law. There's little point worrying about indoor pollution if you regularly pour toxic chemicals on your garden paths and flower beds and take no precautions when you use them. Regular cleaning and tidying outside also uncovers maintenance jobs that you can attend to, preferably before they become major undertakings.

The environmentally friendly garden

A carefully planned garden is an enticing haven for its inhabitants as well as environmentally friendly:

- Shrubs around the house will have a cooling effect on your home as plants don't absorb and retain heat as much as concrete.
- Trees provide shade, act as a windbreak and filter noise and air.
- Deciduous trees near north-facing windows in the southern hemisphere, and south-facing windows in the northern hemisphere, allow the maximum amount of sun in the winter when the branches are bare. In the summer they provide shade.
- Pergolas and trellises covered in trailing deciduous vines add shade in the summer while allowing light through in the winter.
- In some areas, native bushes between the house and road absorb noise and pollution as well as attract native birds to the garden.
- A compost heap and worm farm are used to recycle biodegradable household waste and garden clippings into a natural fertilizer and mulch that can be put back into the garden.

GARDEN SAFETY CHECKLIST

■ Make sure pool fences are maintained and gates securely closed when there young children about.

■ Keep your garages and sheds locked at all times.

■ Keep children's play areas well away from driveways.

■ Keep play equipment maintained and adhere to safety standards.

■ Trim back any branches that are at children's eye level.

■ Keep pathways clear from debris, toys and tools.

■ Mulch is used on garden beds to maximize water retention and to suppress weeds.

■ A rain water tank augments the local water supply.

■ Grey water is channelled onto the lawn rather than wasted.

■ A fixed watering system delivers water directly to where it is needed without wasteful run-off.

■ A small kitchen garden provides an abundant supply of fresh herbs and salad vegetables.

■ Carrying out companion planting helps to deter pests without the potentially harmful use of chemicals.

Allergies in the garden

Allergies strike outside as well as inside. Pollen from garden plants and trees may be a problem for those who suffer from hay fever. Some people are allergic to stings from insects that are attracted to gardens. Gardens may also be home to numerous moulds. Contact dermatitis – an allergic reaction caused by touching a trigger substance – can be activated by plants or chemicals. There are many ways you can reduce your exposure to allergens in the garden:

CLOTHING Wear sunglasses to protect your eyes. A mask made from a headscarf will protect your nose and mouth, while a headscarf or hat keeps pollen out of your hair. Long-sleeved clothing and trousers protect limbs from coming into contact with irritants and allergens as well as insects. Change your clothing after a spot of gardening or a spell outside, and wash it regularly to minimize pollen levels.

LAWN LORE Mowing the lawn frequently keeps the production of pollen down. Ideally, choose a low-pollen grass that does not need frequent mowing. Replacing lawn with a rock garden or patio reduces the pollen level even more, while also cutting down on the need for pesticides. Avoid using a string trimmer or whipper-snipper as sap can fly up onto your skin. Remove grass cuttings from the surface of the lawn.

POLLINATED PETS Pets bring pollen into the house on their fur. If you suffer badly from allergies and have pets, you might consider either keeping them out of the house or – more appropriately perhaps for dogs than cats! – rinsing them before letting them inside.

HAIR Washing or rinsing your hair after being outside for a while removes pollen and reduces longer-term exposure.

FLOORS In any room with access to the garden, use easy to clean, hard flooring, such as vinyl, linoleum, wooden floorboards or ceramic tiles. By doing so, you can remove dirt, pollen, mould spores and animal hairs that blow in or are walked in from the garden.

ENCOURAGE WILDLIFE INTO YOUR GARDEN

- To encourage birds, let a few plants go to seed, or install a birdbath, bird table or feeder in your garden.
- Ponds, and the plants around them, provide food and shelter for frogs, bees, dragonflies, birds and lizards.
- Rocky outcrops attract lizards.
- A small sunny spot is ideal for a patch of unmown grass that will attract butterflies and other insects.
- Moss-covered walls and old tree stumps provide shelter for numerous mini-beasts.

LOW-ALLERGEN PLANTS

- Annuals and biennials: begonia, forget-me-not, impatiens, love-in-a-mist, pansy, petunia, phlox, salvia and snapdragon

- Perennials: agapanthus, columbine, daylily, Jacob's ladder, Japanese windflower, oriental poppy, oyster plant and penstemon

- Groundcovers: bugle flower (*Ajuga reptans*), catmint, cranesbill, hosta, lady's mantle, lamium and periwinkle

- Climbers: clematis, 'Iceberg' rose, ornamental grape, passionfruit and Virginia creeper

- Shrubs: banksia, camellia, deutzia, escallonia, flax, hebe, hydrangea, photinia, viburnum and weigela

- Trees: bottlebrush, crab apple, Irish strawberry tree (*Arbutus unedo*), magnolia, ornamental pear and tupelo (*Nyssa*)

SHOES OFF A 'shoes off in the house' policy helps allergy sufferers as well as housekeepers by reducing the amount of dirt and other materials that leaves the soles of your shoes and enters your indoor living spaces. Try to make it easy for everyone to abide by this policy by placing shoe racks at the front and back doors to hold shoes, boots and slippers.

COMMONSENSE COMPOST If someone in the house is allergic to moulds, you need to take extra care with a compost heap. Using a closed system – for instance, some of the special boxes or bins that garden centres sell – will help prevent spores flying off into the surrounding air. Turning the compost regularly prevents fungus growing by bringing new material into contact with the air. Anyone who is prone to allergies should be let off compost-turning duties (or should wear a mask recommended by their doctor) and avoid areas of the garden where compost has recently been spread.

PLAYTIME For children with grass allergies, play areas can be covered with rubber tiles instead of grass, or artificial turf, both of which can be cleaned with a garden hose to remove dirt, pollen and spores. A sandpit is another alternative, but install a cover to keep out cats when it's not in use.

POLLUTION BUSTERS
Solid fences and walls block out the view of traffic, but they can also create an air vacuum behind the wall and suck in the sound. On the other hand, a combination of trees and shrubs of varying heights and leaf textures improves the view, increases privacy and filters pollution and traffic noise. Add some more pleasant noises, such as the sound of splashing water in a small fountain, and you'll be amazed by how much the traffic noise is reduced.

Stinging strategies

Insect bites and stings are always irritating and sometimes painful. But for those who are allergic to them, stings can be extremely painful and occasionally fatal. To help prevent stings, bear these factors in mind:

- Many scents attract wasps – for example, perfumes, hairsprays, strongly perfumed sunscreens and shampoos, and even sweat.
- Neutral, green or brown clothes are less likely to attract insects than brightly coloured ones.

The relaxed garden

If you are not the neat, obsessive type, then don't succumb to a clipped, manicured garden. Instead give your creativity free rein by planting a selection of spillovers, cover-ups and wild things.

FIRST AID FOR BEE STINGS AND WASP STINGS

- Bees: Remove the sting by scraping it sideways. This reduces the chance of more venom being released. Wipe the affected area clean. Apply a paste of bicarbonate of soda (baking soda) and water to the sting site. Wrap a bag of ice in a towel and hold it over the sting.
- Wasps: Daub the sting area with cider vinegar. Wrap a bag of ice in a towel and hold it over the sting.

Many annuals and even some perennials pop up in any little crevice, put on a show and then fade away as quickly as they came. This self-seeding process creates a delightful link with nature and can often produce chance associations that are far more effective than anything you could design. Often these little treasures are the plants that remain in old gardens. What are they, how can you obtain them and how are they best used in your garden?

If you want to create a relaxed, cottage feeling in your garden, try to encourage plants to self-seed. This may mean temporarily putting up with some messy plants as you wait for the seed heads to form fully. It also means weeding and disturbing the soil as little as possible, as the tiny new plants are hard to see and can easily be damaged. Try to keep the garden moist, and wait until spring before mulching so that young seedlings are large enough to be noticed and left undisturbed.

Annual favourites include forget-me-nots with their pink or eggshell-blue flowers, marvellous plants if kept in check; Johnny-jump-up, a self-seeding viola sometimes called heartsease; and columbines, also known as granny's bonnets. Other useful self-seeders include sweet Alice, primulas and cosmos. *Erigeron karvinskianus* – which goes by various names such as fleabane and babies' tears – can also be a lovely groundcover, but be warned, it will overtake everything if given the chance.

Many perennials propagate themselves asexually, spreading into massive clumps of rhizomes or tubers. These plants can be great for stifling weeds. The Japanese windflower (*Anemone* x *hybrida*) works well under established trees, as does the arum lily. The bugle flower (*Ajuga reptans*) is another vigorous grower in difficult semi-shaded areas and comes in lovely cultivars, including variegated and large-leaved types. Don't forget that old-fashioned violets can be used in these conditions as well.

For sunny spots, Easter daisies are reliable performers during the autumn months. The pick of the crop, *Aster* x *frikartii*, is certainly worth hunting out. One couldn't talk for too long about groundcovers without mentioning the unstoppable, indestructible campanula. There are many different types of campanula, ranging from mauve shades through pink and white, but all have delightful bell-shaped flowers and will spread anywhere.

The fragrant garden

One of the most glorious features of many plants is their scent, but we don't take advantage of this nearly enough. Consider the following tips for using fragrant plants more effectively in your garden:

Near the house

- In the area immediately outside the house, the places to concentrate on are around the windows and doors, especially the ones you open regularly during the summer.

- Fragrant climbers are ideal for training on the walls of the house, including wisteria, Chinese jasmine (*Trachelospermum*), roses and honeysuckle. The exact choice of plant, however, will be largely governed by the orientation of the house because different plants tolerate different conditions.

- Try to select the right plant for the location. For instance, if you are looking for a plant to fragrance the bedroom, choose one like honeysuckle. This produces most of its scent during the evening because it is pollinated mainly by moths, and is therefore ideal for growing near a room that is occupied mainly at night.

- In winter, when you may only use the main door to the house, plant a daphne or a viburnum near the door so that you can smell it each time you go in and out. This is particularly appealing if you tend not to venture out into your garden a great deal during very cold weather. Remember, there is always a way to benefit from fragrant plants, whatever the weather.

- If you enjoy cooking, keep a range of your favourite herbs within easy reach of the kitchen door so that you can enjoy the scent as well as easily and quickly cut some off for use, even if it is raining.

FRAGRANT CONTAINERS
The great attraction of growing fragrant plants in containers is that they are movable, so you can position them wherever they will give the best effect.

HERB AND LAVENDER DRY POTPOURRI

The following recipe is for a simple, fragrant potpourri.

Ingredients
1 cup lavender flowers (*Lavandula angustifolia*)
1/2 cup dried spearmint (*Mentha spicata*)
1/2 cup marjoram (*Origanum majorana*)
1/2 cup oregano flowers (*Origanum vulgare*)
2 tablespoons powdered orrisroot
2 teaspooons lavender essential oil

Method
Mix the ingredients together well, then place in a plastic bag for
2 weeks to mature, shaking regularly. Display in an ornamental bowl.

Other plants suitable for potpourri:

■ Scented flowers: honeysuckle, hyacinth, jasmine, lavender, lilac,
mock orange (*Philadelphus*), rose and violet.

■ Aromatic leaves: basil, bay, bergamot/bee balm (*Monarda didyma*),
lemon balm, mint, rosemary, sage, sweet cicely (*Myrrhis odorata*)
and thyme.

■ Fragrant spices, peels and roots: allspice, cinnamon, clove, ginger,
juniper, nutmeg and star anise; all types of citrus peel; roots of
cowslip (*Primula veris*), sweet flag (*Acorus calamus*) and valerian.

■ If your sitting room has doors opening onto the garden, aim for
a range of plants that will provide scent throughout late spring,
summer and autumn when the doors will be opened regularly. Use
every option in terms of climbers, groundcover and containers to
extend the season whenever possible.

Along pathways

Many pathways are attractive features in themselves, but even the dullest-
looking path can be enlivened with careful planting. Use an edging of fragrant,
low-growing plants that can be clipped back if they start to encroach on the
pathway itself – pansies, thyme, chamomile, swan river daisies (*Brachyscome*)
and lavender are all suitable.

AN EVENING-SCENTED GARDEN

There is nothing nicer than making the most of a warm summer evening by relaxing in the garden and if the air is perfumed as well, so much the better. There are many plants that are fragrant during daylight hours, but some plants are scented only during the evening because this is when they are pollinated by night-flying insects such as moths.

- Evening primrose (*Oenothera*)
- Flowering tobacco (*Nicotiana alata*)
- Four-o'clock (*Mirabilis jalapa*)
- Honeysuckle
- Lily (*Lilium*)

- Night-scented stock (*Matthiola bicornis*)
- Phlox
- Sweet mignonette (*Reseda odorata*)
- Sweet rocket (*Hesperis*)
- Climbing moonflower (*Ipomoea alba*)

If you are building a pathway from scratch, you could leave planting gaps at intervals along its length so that low-growing plants can be inserted to break up any hard lines even further. However, this may not be advisable if the pathway is regularly used to carry items such as trays of food or baskets of washing, which can obscure your view of the path.

Around sitting areas
Patios and decking may be treated in the same way as pathways, bringing the plants over the edges so that there are no hard lines on view and you get as much fragrance from the garden as possible. One of the most enchanting ways in which to enjoy fragrant plants is to turn the seating area into a scented arbour where you can sit, relax and appreciate the splendour of your garden. An arbour overhung with scented roses is a truly romantic setting.

Near the dining area
There are many reasons for using fragrant plants around an outdoor eating area, all of which will influence the plants used:

- If you often dine there during the day, when you need shade from the sun, plant a leafy perfumed climber on an overhead pergola.

- If you use the area in the evening, then the emphasis changes to plants that have scent at that time of day, such as honeysuckle, night-scented stock or flowering tobacco (*Nicotiana alata*).

- If you cook outdoors on a barbecue, you might need a range of fragrant and tasty herbs nearby. In the heat of the day, these smell wonderful as they release their essential oils into the air, and they are ready to use when you cook.

- Some plants are insect-repellents. Ants, for example, dislike the scent of mint and avoid it if they can, so low-growing pennyroyal (*Mentha pulegium*) can be used around the edge of seating areas.

The importance of boundaries

Boundaries are the key feature of a well-designed garden. They enclose its sides, separate one part from another, and define its focal points and views. Boundaries have a far-reaching influence which touches all aspects of gardening, from where the sunshine or shadows fall, to the position of entrances. They even define a garden's atmosphere and how it feels. The right hedge, fence or wall gift-wraps a garden, whereas a poor one detracts from it, like ripped packaging.

In garden design terms, boundaries have two major functions. One is that they physically stop you in your tracks and the other is that they block your view – or they do both. Most perimeter boundaries form a physical barrier, but that doesn't necesssarily mean that they obscure the view of the garden. Indeed, in front gardens the boundary is often low and exists simply to mark a change in property ownership and discourage trespassers.

Visual boundaries (boundaries that block your view) don't need to be solid and they can be achieved by planting a bushy evergreen in front of an attractive view. You can walk around the evergreen, but from behind its foliage you can't see out and, more importantly, no one can see in.

When planning a boundary, consider the following:

VIEWS Assess whether there are any features, distant or near, such as large trees or power stations, that you want to either emphasize or obscure.

MICROCLIMATES Boundaries can filter and enhance the weather, so a stone wall in the right place will hold the heat of the sun well into the evening, while a soil-filled willow wall will always feel cool, benefiting plants that perform best in shade. When it comes to buffeting winds, a solid wall is not as effective as one that lets some air through.

SECURITY Small gardens present the biggest problem when creating a secure boundary because you can't have a high, dominant surround. But even a low, see-through enclosure will discourage cats and dogs from straying onto your property and present a visual deterrent to entry. A tall boundary will not deter a determined thief, but it will stop them eyeing off valuables in your house and garden, and it will slow their access.

VERTICAL GARDENING Walls and fences can provide support for climbers and wall shrubs. In addition, tall, vertical plants can form a boundary in themselves.

INTIMACY Boundaries can shield seating areas and patios from the view of overlooking windows. In a small garden where space and light are limited, a close mini-boundary along one side of a patio is often all you need to make a seating area private.

NOISE BARRIERS The thicker the boundary, the greater its ability to deter noise. Soil-filled walls, dense hedges or thick wooden sleepers (railroad ties) combined with dense planting, all help to make your space quieter.

DETAILS Boundaries offer opportunities for detail, from copper cladding to trellis or detailed ironwork.

ENTRANCES Enclosures require at least one entrance and these can make focal points or vistas or views. A gate is a way of giving you that feeling of an enclosure in what would normally just be a thoroughfare.

SEATING Boundaries create backdrops and can be a perfect place to position a seat. These may be designed into the boundary, perhaps in the corner of a fence, under an arch or on the top of a low retaining wall.

TERRACING Boundaries are a way of retaining soil, transforming sloping gardens into levelled areas that are easier to maintain. They also offer ways of bringing in interest from steps, plinths topped with flowering urns and cascading water features.

DECORATIVE PRUNING TECHNIQUES FOR SMALL GARDENS

Topiary, standardizing and espalier are all pruning techniques that can be used on a wide range of plants to keep them smaller.

■ Topiary, or clipping plants into shapes, can be a way of introducing formality or even whimsy. You could prune your favourite hedging plant into a bird, watering can or simply an obelisk. Easy, fast-growing plants suitable for topiary include box, box honeysuckle (*Lonicera nitida*) and creeping wire vine (*Muehlenbeckia axillaris*).

■ For the traditional standard, or the 'ball on a stick' look, choose from the following plants: azalea, daisies, ficus, fuchsia, potato vine (*Solanum jasminoides*) and roses.

■ Espalier involves growing plants flat against a wall or frame. Try using bougainvillea, nasturtium bush (*Bauhinia galpinii*), pyracantha or sasanqua camellias.

Great ideas for small gardens

If you love visiting open gardens in spring, you may return home feeling as though you need a garden ten times the size of what you have to create a really satisfying garden. However, small spaces can be just as beautiful.

Confined garden spaces are becoming a fact of life for most city dwellers, and the courtyard or balcony can be a big challenge on a small scale. The contained garden can be intimate, with colourful creepers, evergreen hedges and scented screens. Small spaces can be converted into green, usable extensions of a living area, becoming outdoor rooms. The following tricks of the trade might make the difference at your place:

FOCAL POINTS Create a highlight such as a garden seat, potted urn or fountain – a focal point makes an outdoor space more inviting to explore.

ILLUMINATION Lighting helps create mood and gives a small garden depth.

CEILINGS AND WALLS Plant a tree, or build a pergola or raised garden beds to help enclose an area and convert it into an outdoor room.

PATTERN AND TEXTURE Decking and paving, unusual types of foliage and architectural shapes can add interest, definition and substance to small spaces.

TRICKERY AND ILLUSION Mirrors, hedges, trompe l'oeil and manipulation of perspective can all make a space appear larger than it is.

Using colour

Historically, the most successful garden designers have used colour in much the same way as artists do, selecting from their palettes and blending colours to create a harmony which results in a certain mood or effect. The result may be restful or flamboyant.

The three primary colours – red, blue and yellow – are the building blocks of all other colours. The three secondary colours – green, violet and orange – are mixtures of these. Together, the primary and secondary colours make up the colours of a rainbow. Shades or hues vary depending on the strength and

MEDITERRANEAN MAGIC

Blue skies, warm seas and balmy nights scented with orange blossom ... dreaming of another place? It's the Mediterranean and you can create your own in the back garden:

- Lime-washed walls, lots of terracotta pots, ceramic tiles and colonnades will give you an authentic start.
- Add a water feature – a simple wall fountain will do.
- Build your garden with plants. The Italian cypress is lovely. Plant formal hedges of box, lavender or rosemary for structure, then fill in with colourful geraniums and nasturtiums.
- Climbers can soften the effect. Use bougainvillea draped over columns for spectacular colour. The ornamental grapevine can shade pergolas and loggias.
- Large tubs will complete the look: hydrangeas in shady spots, cumquats in the sun and classic terracotta window boxes overflowing with red geraniums will give that finishing touch to your own Mediterranean paradise.

THE VALUE OF THE VERTICAL

Although a sea of colour can be spectacular, you could create a different look by punctuating the horizontal level with spear-like plants that spire into the sky, adding definition and accent. Flowers that give this effect in the garden include acanthus, delphinium, foxglove, larkspur and verbascum. Some, like hollyhocks, can flower up to 2 m (6 feet) skywards.

intensity of each primary colour, while tone is a measure of the black and white component in each colour. Black, white and grey are inert colours: they don't change the colour, only the brightness.

The colour wheel can usefully be divided into two halves: in one half you will find the 'cool' colours of green, grey, blue and mauve, and in the other the 'warm' colours such as yellow, red, orange and hot pink. Colours next to each other on the colour wheel, or nearby, are called harmonious colours, while colours opposite each other are called contrasting colours.

You can use this knowledge as a tool in garden design. For example, for a vibrant garden full of vitality, use contrasting colours from opposite sides of the wheel – red and green, purple and yellow, blue and orange. Start with a cool colour as a base and add the hot colour as a highlight to intensify the effect of both colours. Alternatively, hues next to each other on the colour wheel harmonize. If you're trying to create a tranquil haven, then select complementary colours – for example, pink and mauve – on the same side of the wheel. Gardens planted in one colour can also be very restful.

Some tips for using colour

- Colour outside should be used to back up the function and mood of the garden, the flower colour adding to the effect of the foliage, form and texture of shrubs, trees and groundcovers.

- Colour has a big effect on mood. Use bright colours in lively environments, and softer, subtle tones in restful areas.

- Locate the strongest colours in the foreground, and allow the colours to become paler with distance. Too much strong colour at a distance foreshortens the space.

- Work with any surrounding colour schemes, including the house as well as the boundary and distant views.

- Grey foliage 'cools down' bright colours, and white flowers help contrasting colours to blend effectively.

- Colour changes, depending on the intensity of sunlight. Pale colours look soft and gentle in the morning and evening, yet can appear bleached and washed out during the day, and colours that work in the heat of the day can look garish in softer light.

- When you want something to stand out and be noticed, a loud splash of colour nearby will capture and hold the eye.

- Select a range of colours that suits your home and personality, but try deviating from this range to allow contrast into your garden.

- Try working with foliage colour as the backbone of your garden's year-round interest. Darker foliage makes colours more pronounced.

- Large flowers are harder to blend successfully than smaller ones.

White gardens

A close examination of a white garden reveals creams, soft pink centres, pale yellows and off-whites blending with the greens of foliage in natural harmony. White is useful for night gardens, and for small gardens as it can make a small space feel larger. Here is a selection of beautiful white-flowering plants:

GARDENIA Gardenias not only smell divine, they also look fabulous with their glossy green foliage which highlights the stunning, double white flowers. Gardenias like rich, moist soil and will grow in semi-shade or full sun, although the flowers brown quickly if they're in strong sun. Apply Epsom salts every 2 weeks in the growing season.

'ICEBERG' ROSE 'Iceberg' has made a name for itself as a trouble-free, prolific flowerer that looks great as a shrub or a tree rose. The light green foliage is reasonably resistant to black spot. Other white roses well worth trying include 'Climbing Iceberg', 'Popcorn' (a mini), 'Wedding Day' and 'White Simplicity'.

WHITE HYDRANGEA Plant masses of white, shade-loving hydrangeas for summer-long bunches of flowers and a cool, vanilla-white garden.

Plant your own colour scheme

COLOUR	PLANT	MOOD
Red	Cineraria, nemesia, pansy, polyanthus, poppy, snapdragon, strawflower, viola, wallflower	Passion; makes time seem longer; excellent for the creation of ideas
Orange	Calendula, French marigold, pansy, poppy, snapdragon, strawflower, viola	Drama
Yellow	Calendula, linaria, pansy, polyanthus, poppy, snapdragon, stock, strawflower, viola, wallflower	Happiness
Green	Bells of Ireland, mignonette, Zinnia elegans 'Envy'	Calms and facilitates concentration
Blue	Cineraria, delphinium, forget-me-not, lobelia, love-in-a-mist, lupin, nemesia, pansy, statice, viola	Blue is cooling, and makes weight seem lighter and time even shorter
Purple	Alyssum, cineraria, lobelia, love-in-a-mist, pansy, polyanthus, primula, stock	Intrigue, mystery, power
Pink	Alyssum, Canterbury bells, cineraria, lobelia, pansy, polyanthus, poppy, primula, snapdragon, stock	Romance
White	Candytuft, cineraria, gypsophila, lobelia, nemesia, pansy, primula, snapdragon, stock, viola	Simplicity, peace, coolness
Black	Carnations, iris, scabiosa, tulip, violet	Sombre, mournful mood

WHITE MARGUERITE DAISY Plant these fast growers in any sunny spot and they will quickly form a bushy shrub.

PEACE LILY Mostly grown indoors, peace lilies do equally well in shady spots in frost-free areas. The flower makes a long-lasting, elegant cut bloom.

WHITE AGAPANTHUS There are now white miniature and standard agapanthus, perfect for clumps, lining paths and driveways or edging beds.

POTATO VINE Possibly the fastest, most prolific flowering vine you can choose for a warm, protected area. *Solanum jasminoides* 'Album' will grow in the sun or shade, and is seldom without flowers.

FRANGIPANI You can't talk about summer flowers in warm areas without including frangipanis. Perfect for picking or for lying under on a warm day.

WHITE ANNUALS If there are any gaps left in your white summer garden, cram the sunny spots with petunias and the shady areas with impatiens.

Black gardens

Much has been written about white, but rarely does black get a mention, although black flowers do exist. Carnations, columbines, cranesbills, hellebores, hollyhocks, iris, scabiosa, tulips and violets all have black or near-black varieties.

Some darker flowers rely on flies to pollinate and so have unpleasant odours, such as *Dracunculus vulgaris*. Chocolate cosmos (*Cosmos atrosanguineus*) doesn't fall into this category, however, as it has a delicious chocolate scent.

Another addition to a black garden is the globe artichoke 'Violetto', which has silver leaves and almost-black edible flowers.

Designing with foliage

The value of foliage is often forgotten. Foliage plants provide the garden with year-round interest – important in winter when most flowers have faded.

Silver foliage

As the colour of silver is elusive, it is often used as a background for other, brighter colours. Many silver plants are dazzling in the sunlight or visible at night, while others have rich textures that create a tapestry in the garden.

Silver and grey plants provide the imaginative gardener with many creative possibilities. They are a wonderful buffer between colours, holding together a diverse palette (even hot tones) with their neutrality, or adding to the harmonious feel of a pastel garden. When silver and grey plants are planted in the border they create a sense of extended perspective.

Wonderful in a thematic garden or when used as accent plants, silver foliage plants will highlight dull garden corners, add light to a dark green garden bed and provide a feeling of freshness to well-established areas in your garden.

Variegated plants

The ornamental value of leaves, as distinct from the more obvious attraction of flowers, has long been recognized. Often neglected as a tool in creating tonal interest year round, variegated foliage can lighten up dull corners, break up a solid mass of green foliage and even be a striking focal point.

The palette of variegated foliage ranges from the clear hues of smoky grey-greens through to acid yellows and milky whites and creams. There are also plants with purple, pink, orange and red markings. Leaves can have lighter coloured edges, which highlight the leaf shape, or the reverse, which make them look lacy.

The variety of variegated plants is increasing all the time as breeders respond to the demand for combining foliage effects in garden design. Try not to place all your variegated plants together, or the special effect will be lost. Instead, use variegated foliage to highlight areas of importance.

Choose variegated plants with care. If you place a sun lover in too much shade, the foliage will tend to revert to green, whereas shade dwellers in full sun are easily scorched. Some plants will still throw back to their parentage, so simply trim these rogue portions out as you spot them.

Purple foliage

Be adventurous and add some delicious plum and burgundy shades to your garden. Use purple foliage to gently warm silver-leaved plants and add lushness to greens. Muted purple can intensify reds and warm up cool tones, and works well with bagged finishes. Wine tones have a wonderful ability to harmonize with anything; they even work well with gold, lime and yellows.

PERFECT PASTELS
Mauve, soft blues, pale pinks and white are easy colours to use. This palette can be carried into autumn with well-known flowers such as aster, delphinium and phlox, but some lesser-known additions will also add great charm.

Soil

Start with the soil. If your garden plants aren't thriving, the problem may lie in the soil. It really pays to find out what kind of soil you have so you know if it will support the range of plants you hope to grow, or whether you need to help it along by adding amendments.

Soil types

Soil is the foundation of your garden and its quality makes a significant and vital difference to how your plants will grow. Generally, experts agree that the ideal soil is deep, crumbly, or friable, fertile, well drained and rich in organic matter – however, in reality, few garden soils fit that description.

Different types of soil have different properties and different regions have different soils depending on the type of rock from which they were formed. It is well worth finding out what type of soil you have in your garden.

CLAY SOIL This type of soil compacts when dry and becomes waterlogged with too much moisture, but it does have the ability to hold nutrients well. Drainage and aeration are both poor and it is very difficult for the roots of young plants to move through this type of soil.

SANDY SOIL Sand never compacts and it provides excellent aeration and drainage. However, it has no ability to hold nutrients or water.

LOAM This beautiful soil is a combination of clay and sandy soil and it has excellent properties for plant growth. However, unfortunately not many gardeners are blessed with this ideal soil type.

Identifying your soil type

Just feeling the soil can teach you a great deal about it. Take a handful of your topsoil when it is moist and squeeze it gently to form a lump. Soil with a high clay content will form a tight, sticky ball, while the sandy type will lose its shape and fall readily from the hand. Soil of good, friable texture will hold its shape but will break away easily when further squeezed or prodded.

SOIL IS NOT STATIC
Changes in physical, chemical and biological properties take place all the time, and are caused by both nature and human beings. In nature, the weather, the plants themselves, insects, worms, bacteria and fungi all change the nature of soil. The changes we make are numerous and far reaching: just digging over the soil can change its character. Adding fertilizers, chemicals and mulches can completely alter the type of soil.

▤ ADDING GYPSUM TO CLAY SOIL

Gypsum is a mineral that, when added to clay soil, can cause the fine particles to clump together into bigger particles, thereby opening up the soil and improving its drainage. However, it doesn't work on all clays and you should carry out the following test before you buy and apply it.

1 Drop a 6 mm (¼ inch) fragment of dry soil into a glass of distilled or rain water and let it stand for 24 hours. Don't shake or stir it.

2 If the water turns cloudy around the fragment, your soil will be improved by the addition of gypsum. The more obvious the discolouration, the greater the improvement will be.

3 If there is no discolouration, repeat the test with moist soil that has a plasticine-like consistency.

4 If the water then turns cloudy, adding gypsum will help prevent wet weather damage to your soil.

5 Add gypsum at the rate of 500 g per square metre (1 pound per square yard) but don't dig in.

Soil pH

The pH is a measure of acidity determined on a scale of 1 to 14. A pH of 1 would be extremely acid while a pH of 14 would indicate extreme alkalinity. Seven is neutral, being neither acid nor alkaline. Most plants prefer slightly acid soil and do well where the pH reading is between 6 and 7. Some plants, such as azaleas, camellias, magnolias and rhododendrons, like quite acid soil with a pH of between 4.5 and 5.5, but only a few plants could tolerate strongly acid soil of pH 4 or less. Those plants that prefer alkaline soils generally do best with a pH of between 7.5 and 8.

The pH of soil affects the level of nutrients available to plants. Thus, if you grow a plant native to alkaline soils in a more acid soil, it will have overdoses of some nutrients and shortages of others. The result will be poor growth, yellowing leaves and/or eventual death.

You can test the pH of soil with a simple electronic meter or a soil-testing kit. The latter, available from garden centres, is usually more reliable. Overly acid soil (less than pH 5) can be made less acid with the addition of lime. Excessively

Plants for various soil types

PLANTS FOR CLAY SOIL			
Aster	Hemerocallis	Phlox	Spiraea
Coreopsis	Ligularia	Rosa	Thalictrum
Escallonia	Ligustrum	Rudbeckia	Viburnum
Geranium	Mahonia	Solidago	Yucca

PLANTS FOR SANDY SOIL			
Anthemis	Cistus	Grevillea	Monarda
Callistemon	Echinops	Helianthemum	Papaver
Calluna	Fuchsia	Kniphofia	Potentilla
Centranthus	Genista	Lupinus	Tulipa

PLANTS FOR PEATY/ACID SOIL			
Acer	Epimedium	Kalmia	Pieris
Camellia	Eucryphia	Magnolia	Rhododendron
Daboecia	Fothergilla	Phyllodoce	Vaccinium

PLANTS FOR ALKALINE SOIL			
Allium	Bellis	Erysimum	Syringa
Alyssum	Brunnera	Gypsophila	Sempervivum
Anchusa	Buddleja	Phlomis	Thymus
Aquilegia	Clematis	Salvia	Verbascum

HYDRANGEAS AND PH

In acid soils hydrangea flowers are blue. In alkaline soils they are pink. If you want blue flowers, your soil should have a pH of between 5 and 5.5. For pink flowers, maintain a soil pH of 6 or more by adding lime to your soil if it is acid.

alkaline soil can be acidified with flowers of sulphur. Apply at the rate of about one handful per square metre (square yard) and lightly dig into the soil, then water the treated area deeply.

Don't try to make large changes in the pH suddenly or you may shock your garden to death. Instead, apply the appropriate remedy as described above. Let the soil lie for 2 months, test it again and make another application if necessary. Repeat at 2-monthly intervals until the correct pH is achieved.

TESTING SOIL pH

Purchase a standard soil-testing kit, which is readily available from garden centres. This will tell you the level of acidity of your soil and help you choose the right plants or take the appropriate action.

1 Remove a small handful of soil from the area to be tested and add it to the test tube provided. Then add the soil-test powder included in the kit.

2 Next, add distilled water to the soil and the test powder, filling up to the level marked on the side of the test tube.

3 Secure the lid and shake the test tube. Wait a few seconds for the liquid to change colour and then compare it with the pH colour chart supplied.

4 A yellow or orange liquid indicates an acid soil. A bright green liquid indicates a neutral soil. Dark green indicates an alkaline soil.

ADDING LIME TO ACID SOIL

Do this on a windless day and make sure you wear gloves, as lime is caustic. Apply at the manufacturer's recommended rates.

1 Wearing suitable protective clothing, shake the lime over the area of the soil to be covered, spreading it well to ensure even coverage.

2 Lightly fork the lime into the soil and cover. Do not add manure to the soil for at least 6 months following the application of lime.

COFFEE REDUCES pH
Coffee grounds (from real coffee, not instant) added to alkaline soil will bring down the pH.

Range of pH soil values supporting plant growth

pH VALUE	LEVEL OF ACIDITY	TYPICAL PLANT GROWTH
3.5–4.0	Extremely acid	None
4.0–4.5	Very acid, peaty soil	Coniferous trees
4.5–5.0	Very acid	Blueberries, cranberries, rhododendrons
5.0–5.5	Moderately acid	Potatoes, tomatoes, raspberries
5.5–6.0	Moderately acid	Grasses
6.0–6.5	Slightly acid	Most garden crops, most ornamental plants
7.0–7.5	Neutral to slightly alkaline	Most garden crops, slightly alkaline most ornamental plants

Tips for improving soil quality

Extremes of clay and sandy soils can be improved by adding organic matter, which can take several forms, such as old farmyard manure, compost, leaf mould or composted sawdust. These natural substances are further broken down by soil organisms such as bacteria, fungi and earthworms. In the process, humus is formed. With repeated applications, a booming population of soil organisms distributes the organic matter through the top layers of soil, opening up clays and making sands more water retentive and rich.

▓ MAKING STRAW COMPOST

Old straw makes bulky organic matter to improve soil drainage, moisture retention and fertility. It can also be used as an organic mulch, spread over the soil surface to preserve moisture and suppress weeds. This layer will be gradually incorporated into the soil by the activity of worms, bacteria and other soil-borne organisms.

1 Cover the base of the area chosen for the compost heap with 30 cm (1 foot) of loose straw. Soak the straw thoroughly with water.

2 Sprinkle a light covering of nitrogenous fertilizer over the straw. This will help to speed up decomposition.

3 Add another 30-cm (1-foot) layer of loose straw to the stack; again water it thoroughly, and add more fertilizer.

4 As the straw decomposes, it will become covered in white mould and will begin to resemble well-rotted manure.

Soil drainage

Only aquatic plants or those native to swamps or bogs survive sodden roots. Dry land plants must have air in the soil around their roots or they will drown.

If all or part of your garden is poorly drained, you can either grow plants that will tolerate it, build a raised bed or install subsurface drainage.

Testing your soil for drainage

Dig a few holes of about 50 cm (1³/4 feet) deep. Fill them with water, allow them to drain and refill them. If water remains after 24 hours, your soil is badly drained and the more water in each hole, the worse the drainage problem.

Another way to tell is to observe what happens after rain. Does water lie in pools or does the soil remain sodden? If so, subsurface drainage will allow you to grow a much wider range of plants. If the poor drainage is restricted to a small area, an alternative to drainage is to raise the area about 30 cm (1 foot) above the natural level using retaining walls. Fill the area within the walls with good quality, weed-free topsoil bought from a landscape supplier.

Raised beds

Raised-bed gardening is a compromise between garden beds and containers. It can also solve the problem of localized poor soils and drainage. Beds can be constructed from railway sleepers (railroad ties), rocks or a variety of other strong materials. Moisture levels should be monitored, as raised beds tend to dry out faster than normal ground-level beds.

NETTLES MEAN FERTILE SOIL
Stinging nettles are a sign of fertile soil. For an organic liquid fertilizer, fill a bucket with water and add a bunch of nettles. Allow the nettles to rot down for 2–3 weeks. Use the resulting liquid as a nutrient-rich foliar spray, which is also useful against aphids, blackfly and mildew.

INSTALLING A DRAINAGE SYSTEM

1 Using a garden line and canes, mark out where the drainage pipes are going to be. Dig a trench 60–70 cm (2–2¹/₂ feet) deep, and 30 cm (1 foot) wide. Keep the topsoil and the subsoil separate.

2 Place a 5-cm (2-inch) layer of gravel, ash and sand in the trench, and lay the drainage pipes on top. Place the pipes end to end.

3 Refill the trench with a layer of gravel, ash or sand over the pipes to within 25–30 cm (10 inches–1 foot) of the surface. Fill the trench with topsoil to leave a slight mound (this will settle down in 4 weeks). Don't press the soil into the trench, especially if it is wet. Spread the remaining soil over the site, where it will be incorporated into the topsoil in a few months. The drain should feed into a natural outlet, such as a ditch.

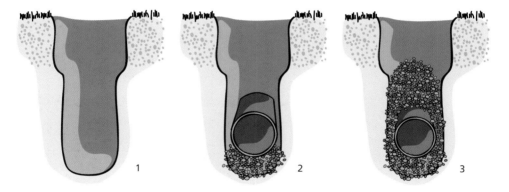

BUILDING A RAISED BED FROM TIMBER

1 Mark out the area of the raised bed and remove any vegetation. Level the soil along the lines where the timber sections are to be positioned. Lay out the first layer of timber to create a low 'wall' for the planting bed, and use a builder's square to check the right angles. Also, use a spirit level to check the timber sections are level. Repeat the process, stacking timber sections to raise the height of the wall. Drive 15 cm (6 inches) into the corner joints on each layer of timber in order to keep them stable.

2 When the wall has reached the required height, fix the top row by driving 15-cm (6-inch) nails at an angle through the vertical joints.

EARTHWORMS

Worms and other soil organisms transform organic matter into humus – nature's plant food and soil conditioner. Their tunnelling activities carry organic matter through the soil and allow for the easy penetration of air and water.

3 Dig over the soil inside the bed area. Add extra soil and organic matter and mix with the existing soil to aid drainage and water movement. Firm the soil to reduce uneven settling later when the plants are in place.

4 Finally, plant the vegetables and herbs into the new bed. These are usually planted slightly closer together than when growing plants in rows in regular garden beds.

Digging

Digging creates better growing conditions for your plants, and is the easiest and quickest method of creating a weed-free, fine layer of soil. Digging not only improves soil drainage, but it also opens up the soil to the air, allowing organic matter to break down more easily to release nutrients.

COLLECTING ORGANIC MATTER

Where can you get organic matter? If you live in a leafy area, you can sweep up bagloads of fallen leaves from the streets, and riding schools or stables will usually give you as much horse manure as your trailer will carry. You can buy bulk quantities of composted organic matter from landscape supply companies and some council tips. Best of all, make your own compost from your kitchen and garden waste.

Don't use fresh organic matter. When it comes to organic matter, the older and more rotten, the better. That's because the process of decomposition uses up nitrogen and, if green matter or fresh manure is dug into the soil, the nitrogen needed will come from the soil. Nitrogen is one of the most important plant foods, and so while you'll be improving your soil you'll be starving your plants. Get around this by using only rotten organic matter or composting fresh matter first.

RAINY WEATHER

If your plants die off suddenly in rainy weather, this is a strong indication that you may have drainage problems. Address wet spots and other drainage issues by installing drains. These can be either subsurface drains, such as agricultural pipe, or surface drains, such as swales or gravel trenches.

HOW TO DIG

Digging is a vital skill. Follow these steps to prepare your soil well:

1 Insert the spade vertically into the soil, with one foot pressing on the blade. Ensure that the handle is sloping slightly away from you.

2 If the topsoil is compacted, making it difficult to proceed, work the spade backwards and forwards to gain the depth required.

3 Pulling the handle towards you, slide your right hand down the shaft of the spade and bend your knees slightly for correct balance, prior to levering out the soil.

4 Lift the soil onto the spade, slowly straightening your legs so that they, rather than your lower back, take the weight. It is best to work in a rhythm, taking manageable loads.

Double digging

With double digging the soil is cultivated to a depth of two spade blades. This technique is most frequently used on land that is being cultivated for the first time or where a hard subsurface layer (called a pan) of soil has formed, impeding drainage and the penetration of plant roots.

EASY DIGGING

If at all possible, lay a drainage system when the soil is dry. This will produce much easier working conditions. If you are working in wet weather, use broad wooden planks to prevent the soil from becoming even wetter and more sticky from being walked on. Dig the trench on a slope, starting from the lowest point and working upwards, so that any water is draining away from you as you work.

SHRUBS AND TREES THAT LIKE POOR DRAINAGE

There are some plants that will thrive in poorly drained sites. Some large specimens will even drain the area for you.

Shrubs	Trees
Japanese aralia (*Fatsia japonica*)	Bull bay (*Magnolia grandiflora*)
New Zealand flax (*Phormium tenax*)	Evergreen alder (*Alnus jorullensis*)
Papyrus (*Cyperus papyrus*)	Liquidambar (*Liquidambar styraciflua*)
Swamp blueberry (*Vaccinum corymbosum*)	Poplar (*Populus* sp.)
Swamp wattle (*Acacia elongata*)	River birch (*Betula nigra*)
Sweet pepper bush (*Clethra alnifolia*)	Weeping willow (*Salix babylonica*)

This method of digging improves the friability of the subsoil without bringing it nearer to the surface, so the most biologically active layer of topsoil is always closest to the roots. It's important to avoid mixing subsoil with topsoil as the fertility of the topsoil will be diluted, instead of the fertility of the subsoil being improved. Although this is hard work and can be laborious, the benefits of double digging can last up to 15 years, provided the soil is managed correctly.

To double dig an area so that deeper-rooted plants such as roses, shrubs, trees or fruit bushes and trees can be grown, a number of gardeners favour adding a layer of well-rotted manure or compost into the bottom of the trench before the topsoil is reincorporated.

HOW TO DOUBLE DIG

1 Starting at one end of the plot, mark out an area 60 cm (2 feet) wide using a garden line and canes. Dig a trench the width, and the depth, of one spade. If it is very large, the plot may be divided in two.

2 Remove the soil from this first trench and take it to the far end of the plot, laying it quite close to the area where the final trench is to be dug. When the soil is removed from the first trench, fork over the base of the trench to the full depth of the fork's tines. If required, compost or manure may be forked into the lower layer of soil or scattered on top of it after cultivation.

3 When the base of the trench is cultivated and the compacted layer broken through, mark out the next area 60 cm (2 feet) wide with a garden line. Using a spade, start to dig the soil from this second area, throwing it into the first trench, while making sure that the soil is turned over as it is moved. This process will create the second trench at the same time as the base is forked over.

4 The process is repeated until the entire plot has been dug to a depth of about 50 cm (1^3/$_4$ feet).

USING A ROTARY CULTIVATOR

There are many different kinds of powered cultivators available and they all operate on the same basic principle, with rotating steel blades to turn over the soil. Most have a depth adjuster, which works by limiting the depth to

TIPS FOR BUYING HEALTHY PLANTS

- First of all, check that the plant's leaves are uniformly green.

- Look for a specimen that has well-balanced proportions, one that does not look lopsided or top-heavy.

- See if you can spot insect damage, weeds or fungus rots. Leave any contaminated plants alone.

- Never buy a pot-bound plant. You can tell these from the roots growing out of the base of the pot or circling the surface. Don't hesitate to remove the plant from the pot to have a good look at the root system, but remember to replace it!

- Don't be seduced just by the flowers, ask how long they last and try and picture what the plant will look like when they finish.

NO-DIG GARDEN

The Australian gardener Esther Dean first became famous in the late 1970s for a specialized form of sheet composting which became known as the 'no-dig' garden. This technique can be used anywhere, even on the worst and most compacted soils, or directly onto lawn, to provide a flourishing, fertile garden bed.

1 First provide an edging for the future garden. Then give the soil a good soak. Next, lay overlapping thick layers of newspaper on the ground (cardboard or even old carpet can also be used), and follow this with a layer of lucerne hay, a layer of organic fertilizer, a layer of loose straw, and another thin layer of organic fertilizer.

2 After watering well, make depressions in the surface and fill them with compost. Well-established seedlings, large seeds, tubers and bulbs can then be planted immediately. If there is sufficient compost available, it is an even better idea to place a layer of compost right over the top of the garden, rather than just in pockets. The contents of your no-dig bed will reduce in height quite rapidly, and it will allow you to grow excellent crops.

3 No matter how heart-breaking the original soil is, this method will result in a great improvement in the soil's texture and will encourage the presence of large numbers of earthworms.

which the rotating blades can penetrate the soil. The travelling speed of the machine and the rotating speed of the blades determine how finely cultivated the soil will become.

1 Start by setting the depth gauge. If the ground is hard, cultivate to a shallow depth before repeating, cultivating to the desired depth.

2 If a fine tilth is required, set the forward speed on a slow setting and the rotor speed fast. Allow the machine to travel at an even pace.

3 Allow the rear flap to trail out over the freshly cultivated soil just behind the rotor, to level the soil and leave an even surface.

4 Switch off the motor and disconnect the spark plug. Remove any soil with a scraper such as a piece of wood, then clean the blades with a hose.

Propagation

Save money and make your own new plants. Individually, plants aren't very expensive, but when you start a new garden the number of plants needed adds up and can cost big money. Propagating your own plants saves you cash, is fun to do and sometimes is often the only way to obtain a plant that's hard to find.

What is propagation?

There are two basic methods of propagation: raising plants from seeds and reproducing plants using vegetative propagation.

RAISING SEEDS This is the most basic form of propagation. A seed is a miniaturized plant, packed and stored within a protective coat, waiting for the perfect conditions that will give it its start in life. Some plants will easily self-seed, while others may need collecting, treating, sowing and transplanting. Seeds from dry seed heads can be shaken or rubbed from the plant, and any debris removed. In many cases, collecting seed heads in paper bags will help contain the seeds as they fall.

VEGETATIVE PROPAGATION Unlike seeds, which are the result of a combination of male and female flower parts, vegetative propagation doesn't involve sex. Plants reproduced vegetatively are an exact copy of one parent plant only – sort of like cloning. Vegetative propagation is done in one of three basic ways: by removing a part of the plant that already has roots (by dividing a clump of perennials or bulbs), by removing a part that hasn't got roots and inducing it to make roots (by taking a cutting or making a layer) or by uniting a rootless piece of plant with one that is already rooted and growing it (by one of the several forms of grafting).

Growing plants from seeds

Most of the plants that are grown from seeds are annuals (plants that grow from seed to flower in one growing season) or biennials (plants that grow from seed to flower over two growing seasons). Another group comprises plants that are frost tender, but that are actually perennials in warm climates.

Growing seeds is very simple in principle. Sow them in fine-textured soil, cover them to a depth equal to the size of the seed, and keep the soil moist until

PROPAGATION UNIT
For convenience, you can buy a ready-made propagating unit – this will help ensure successful seed germination. The unit consists of a tray with a hinged clear plastic lid.

they come up. When the seedlings are big enough to handle, they are transplanted (which is known as 'pricking out') into another pot or bed that will give them more room until they are large enough to plant out in the final positions you have chosen for them in the garden.

Seed-raising mix

The ideal growing medium for germinating seeds under cover is made up of two layers. The first, or base layer, comprises seed-raising mix and the upper layer comprises horticultural grit or vermiculite, which is free draining. The advantage of this two-layer system is that the seeds are sown in the free-draining layer of grit, but the seed-raising mix in the layer below provides the nutrients that are required once the rooting process begins. The alternative is to simply fill the container in which the seeds are to be sown with proprietary seed-raising mix. Soil-free mix is popular for this purpose.

Sowing seeds in containers

The great advantage of sowing seeds in containers is that it gives you complete control of their growing conditions. This is especially an advantage with seeds sown in spring, when cold snaps may be a problem.

WHERE TO SOW SEEDS You can sow in the greenhouse if you have one, or on a sunny windowsill indoors, and the seedlings will be ready for transplanting earlier than they would be if they had been grown outside.

WHAT TO SOW SEEDS IN The ideal container is wider and shallower than a flower pot. You need area rather than depth of soil, except for tree seeds for which depth is important. You can get wide, shallow seed trays from nurseries, or you can use egg cartons, flat plastic take-away food boxes or even waxed paper trays or polystyrene boxes from greengrocers. Just remember to make some holes in the bottom for drainage.

HOW TO SOW SEEDS Sow the seeds thinly into seed-raising mix, which is sold at nurseries. You can enclose small containers in a plastic bag, or spread plastic food wrap across the top of a bigger one to keep everything warm and moist, but be sure to uncover the containers as soon as germination is under way or the seedlings may go mouldy.

GERMINATION TIME The time needed for seed germination varies. Most annual and vegetable seedlings appear in 10 days to a fortnight after sowing,

STIMULATING SEEDS FOR BEST GERMINATION

Certain types of seeds need to be stimulated and shocked out of dormancy before they will germinate. Some cold-climate plants need an artificial cool time (called stratification) for germination to occur. This is an adaptation to prevent seeds from germinating until the last of the cold weather is over, so that late frosts or snow don't harm the young seedlings. Other seeds respond to heat and smoke (which is in effect the simulation of a bushfire) or drought. Hard seed coats can prevent plants from germinating by keeping out air and water – two vital ingredients in the process of germination – and the seeds will therefore need to be chipped or rubbed with abrasive paper (a process called scarification) before sowing.

but shrubs and trees may take much longer, so don't be in too much of a hurry to throw out a container of seeds that haven't yet come up.

TRANSPLANTING After germination, the seedlings will become overcrowded if you leave them too long in the sowing container or bed. Once they have grown 3–4 cm (1¼–1½ inches) tall, they are ready to be pricked out. Be very gentle – lift them with a small, pointed stick, and either relocate them to a new container or a fresh part of the nursery bed, setting them about 5 cm (2 inches) apart. Water them in, and give them some shade for a few days. When they have settled in, they can be given some slow-release fertilizer, and once they have made three or four sets of leaves they are ready to go in their final positions. You may want to pot up trees, shrubs or perennials for a few months or a year until they are big enough for the garden.

THE PROS AND CONS OF SEEDS

The advantages of raising plants from seeds are cost, access to interesting new genetic material, variation and variety, ready availability, and minimal storage and space requirements. However, this must be weighed against the possible loss of particular characteristics (such as flower colour), which may change in the second generation of plants, particularly in the case of annuals and biennials.

SOWING FINE SEEDS

When sowing very fine seeds, such as those produced by African violet, azalea, campanula, ferns, gloxinia, impatiens, lobelia, polyanthus and primula, add some fine, dry sand to the seeds to make spreading them easier.

SOWING SEEDS IN TRAYS

Germination depends on heat and many plants will not easily germinate without some additional warmth. A large number of the plants used for summer bedding are half-hardy annuals and their seeds will not germinate in garden soil until early summer, so sow them in spring under glass.

1 Fill a seed tray to the rim with a suitable seed-raising mix. Firm gently until the mix is 1 cm (1/2 inch) below the rim. If you are planting very fine seeds, it is a good idea to sieve another, thin layer of fine mix over the surface and firm it down lightly.

2 Sow the seeds as evenly as possible over the surface. Sow half in one direction, then turn the tray and sow the remainder in the opposite direction to ensure even distribution.

3 Sieve a thin layer of fine seed-raising mix over the seeds and firm gently. If you have very fine seeds, press them lightly into the surface of the mix, rather than covering them.

4 Lightly water the seed tray before covering it with a sheet of clear glass, and a sheet of newspaper for shade if required.

SEED-SOWING TIPS

- Don't plant seeds too deeply or they will never germinate.
- Fine seeds should be barely covered with very fine soil.
- Bigger seeds can be sown slightly deeper.
- Never allow the soil to dry out before seedlings have emerged.

Sowing seeds outdoors

Many seeds can be sown directly where they are to grow. Big, easy-to-handle seeds are usually sown this way. With direct sowing, it is important to have the bed cultivated to a fine tilth so that the soil won't cake over the emerging seedlings. You should also water very gently, with a fine mist. Put out snail bait so that you won't lose your seedlings as soon as they come up (but be careful if you have pets or young children as the baits are toxic). It's easiest to sow in rows, making a shallow furrow with a pointed stick. Big seeds can be sown at their final spacings, but smaller seeds are sprinkled along the furrow and the seedlings thinned to their correct spacings when they come up. For an even distribution of fine seeds, mix them with dry sand and sprinkle the mixture.

▦ SOWING SEEDS OUTDOORS (BROADCAST)

Broadcast sowing is a useful technique for hardy annuals, salad vegetables such as radishes and spring onions (green onions), and green manure crops such as comfrey or mustard.

1 Rake the soil, remove any stones and break down clods of earth to form a seed bed that is finely tilled. This will leave the soil with a fine layer on the top surface.

2 It's a good idea to pour a few of the seeds from the packet into the palm of your hand, so you will be able to sow carefully.

3 Sow the seeds by scattering them evenly over the soil surface. Sow from a height of about 30 cm (1 foot) above soil level.

4 Lightly rake over the bed in at least two different directions. This will ensure that the seeds are incorporated into the soil and that you avoid clustering. Label the seed bed.

 OPTIMUM TEMPERATURE FOR GERMINATION
All seeds have an optimum temperature range at which they germinate best. This range is generally between 15° and 25°C (60 and 75°F), so (depending on your climate) spring and the early part of autumn generally make the most appropriate times to sow seeds.

A GOOD PLACE TO GERMINATE SEEDLINGS
You don't need any fancy equipment to successfully germinate your seedlings. The top of the refrigerator is just the right temperature to give bottom heat for your trays of seedlings.

SOWING SEEDS OUTDOORS (DRILL)

Drill sowing is an excellent technique for growing various annuals and perennials, as well as most vegetables you are likely to grow. This technique allows you to see immediately when seeds have germinated and to easily remove weed seedlings from between the drills.

1 Rake the soil to form a seed bed that has been finely tilled – break up large soil clods and remove any large stones. Mark out the rows with a garden line (keeping it taut).

2 Then, using a draw hoe, or even just a simple piece of cane or a stick, make a long, straight groove in the soil. This will form the seed drill in which you will sow.

3 Sow the seeds thinly into the drill by hand, aiming for a set distance between them. Never sow the seeds directly from the packet.

4 Finally, carefully using a rake, draw the soil gently back into the drill, covering the seeds. Gently pat and firm the soil over the seeds using the back of the rake.

Division

Division is probably the simplest means of propagating – a plant multiplies itself into a clump and you simply lift it from the ground, separate it into several sections and replant each one.

You can simply cut the clump apart with a garden fork, secateurs or a sharp knife. The best propagations are almost always the young, strong growths from the outside of the clump. Don't try to break up the clump into smaller divisions than those that break off fairly easily.

Division is most appropriate with perennials and bulbs, but some thicket-forming shrubs can be divided too, or you can detach rooted suckers.

▪ HOW TO DIVIDE A PLANT

Many plants can be divided easily to provide you with new stock. This method also ensures plants remain vigorous and free-flowering.

1 Using a garden fork, lift the plant out of the soil and wash it clean with a hose to remove as much soil as possible.

2 Push two hand forks into the middle of the clump, back to back, and pull them apart to split the clump into smaller sections.

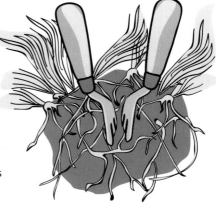

3 Break down each section into small individual plants with several roots and a few shoots or buds to each piece; these can be replanted.

SUITABLE PLANTS FOR DIVISION

Perennials
Achillea, Aster, Campanula, Geranium, Helianthus, Heuchera, Nepeta, Phlox, Primula, Ranunculus, Rudbeckia, Salvia, Stachys, Viola

Bulbs
Allium, Camassia, Chionodoxa, Erythronium, Fritillaria, Galanthus, Hyacinthus, Iris (reticulata and xiphium types), Leucojum, Muscari, Narcissus, Nerine, Ornithogalum, Scilla, Tulipa

Corms
Babiana, Brodiaea, Colchicum, Crocosmia, Crocus, Dierama, Freesia, Gladiolus, Ixia, Sparaxis, Triteleia

Tubers
Alstroemeria, Anemone, Arum, Corydalis, Dahlia, Eranthis, Oxalis, Rhodohypoxis, Roscoea

Shrubs
Buxus, Gaultheria, Hypericum, Kerria, Mahonia, Sarcococca, Sorbaria, Spiraea, Symphoricarpus, Vaccinium

Layering

Many trailing or running plants layer themselves, which means they form roots where their runners touch the ground. These rooted sections can be severed from the parent, dug up and then replanted.

Most shrubs with branches that can be bent low enough to touch the ground can also be layered – bend a suitable branch down, make a nick by cutting into but not through the lowest point, bury it, and when it has made roots in a few weeks or months, detach the new plant and transplant it. You need to hold the branch still, either by putting a brick on top of the buried section or, better, by staking the far end of your branch upright. Layering is particularly valuable with plants such as rhododendrons that root only slowly from cuttings, but any plant that will grow from cuttings can be layered.

SIMPLE LAYERING

The most basic form of layering is called 'simple layering'. This is where a soft, flexible shoot is bent down to touch the soil in the garden bed. If rooting is successful, this shoot can then be separated from the parent plant so that it can grow on independently.

1 Select a suitable shoot and gently bend it down to soil level to see where the hole should be dug. Remove any leaves 30 cm (1 foot) from the tip. Cut a 4-cm (1½-inch) nick halfway into the stem.

2 Dig a shallow hole, so that the side nearest to the parent plant slopes at 45 degrees and the other is vertical.

3 Lay the wounded section into the bottom of the hole. Peg into place with a wire hoop. Cover with soil.

▤ AIR LAYERING

If you can't bend a branch down to the ground you can take the soil to the plant, in what is called air layering or marcottage. Select the point where you want roots to grow, make a nick in the stem there and pack some moist sphagnum moss or peatmoss around it, tying it in place with a piece of clear plastic. When you see roots through the plastic, cut the branch off and plant it (taking the plastic away, of course). Air layering can be done with almost any shrub that will strike roots from a layering or a cutting. The only thing to watch is that the moss doesn't dry out, but if you seal it well inside clear plastic it won't.

Cuttings

Cuttings are made when you remove a part of the plant that has no roots and place it in soil in such conditions that it will be kept alive until roots develop and it can start to support itself. Normally, you take a piece of the stem, either one that is actively growing (softwood or tip cuttings), one that has stopped growing but is not quite mature (semi-ripe cuttings) or one that is quite mature and firm (it may be dormant and have lost its leaves – mature or hardwood cuttings).

Most cuttings, of whatever type, make roots best from a node in the stem, the point from which a leaf arises, and that is where to cut. Remove all leaves that will be buried and cut the remaining leaves in half to reduce moisture loss. Always take a few more cuttings than you think you will need to allow for

SERPENTINE LAYERING

This method is used for clematis or wisteria. Several cuts are made along the shoot and pegged down so that a number of new plantlets will form.

SUITABLE PLANTS FOR LAYERING

Simple layering
Abelia, azalea, barberry, birch, bittersweet, butterfly bush, clematis, cotoneaster, deutzia, euonymus, forsythia, holly, honeysuckle, juniper, lilac, magnolia, privet, pyracantha, rose, viburnum, weigela, wisteria

Air layering
Apple trees, azalea, camellia, citrus trees, dieffenbachia, holly, magnolia, rhododendron, rubber plant

some failures. If you have a choice, take cuttings from young, more vigorous plants rather than from old, sedate ones, or at least from vigorous shoots – and always take the cuttings from the choicest, healthiest plants you have. That way you have the best chance of success.

The length of time rooting takes varies with the species, but as long as the cutting hasn't died, the process is under way. You can speed it along by dipping the cut ends into fresh rooting hormone (the preparation loses its potency quickly, and an old or opened packet is useless).

Hardwood cuttings can be struck in the ground in the same sort of bed in which you would grow seeds, but soft and semi-ripe cuttings need some protection. The simplest way is to put them up in pots of very sandy soil (three parts sharp sand to one of regular potting mix/potting compost), and enclose each pot in a plastic bag to keep the cuttings moist and humid.

Types of cuttings
SOFTWOOD CUTTINGS These are the youngest shoots, from which cuttings are taken from the tips in spring and early summer. These cuttings tend to root more easily than other types, so this method is widely used for plants that are difficult to propagate from mature cuttings. Humidity, warmth and moisture are very important during the rooting period, and a closed propagating case is advised.

SEMI-RIPE CUTTINGS These are taken in late summer or early autumn from the current year's growth. They do not root as readily as softwood cuttings, but their survival rate is better.

HARDWOOD CUTTINGS These are taken in autumn or winter when the shoots are about a year old, and are rooted outdoors or in a cold frame. They will not root readily unless hormone rooting powder is applied to the wound, and root formation can be very slow, but most will have rooted by the following spring.

TAKING SOFTWOOD CUTTINGS

A wide range of plants will root very quickly and easily from softwood cuttings, many of them forming new roots in just a few weeks.

1 Cut a section of stem from the plant near the tip of a branch – which is the fastest-growing part – and store in a moist plastic bag.

2 Fill a container with an open, free-draining mix and firm it down, tapping the tray to level it.

3 Trim the stem base to below a node (leaf joint) and remove the lower leaves.

4 Dip the stem into rooting powder and insert into the mix to just below its lowest leaves. Water well.

GOOD PLANTS FOR CUTTINGS

Softwood cuttings
Argyranthemum, Buddleja, Chrysanthemum, Clematis, Dianthus, Fuchsia, Forsythia, Geranium, Hydrangea, Osteospermum, Pelargonium Penstemon, Weigela, and other tender perennials and greenhouse pot plants

Semi-ripe cuttings
Evergreen herbs, conifers, box, heather and most shrubs

Hardwood cuttings
Brambles, *Cornus*, fruit tree rootstocks, grapevine, hazel, rose, willow

COLLECTING CUTTINGS IN WARM AREAS

If you live in a warm area, remember that the best time to collect your cuttings is in the early morning before the sun heats up and the plants become fatigued.

TAKING HARDWOOD CUTTINGS

This technique is suitable for propagating a wide range of deciduous trees and shrubs, as well as bush fruits. It is the simplest and cheapest method of propagating from cuttings.

1 Prepare the ground by forking it over and then roughly levelling it – do this before adding a base dressing of a general-purpose fertilizer. Cover the soil with black plastic, making sure you bury the edges to secure it and prevent it flying away at the first sign of a breeze. Insert the tines of a fork vertically through the plastic into the soil.

2 Remove healthy current-season shoots from the plant you want to propagate. Trim the shoots into 25-cm (10-inch) lengths, making the top cut above a bud, and the bottom cut below the bud.

3 Gently push the cuttings, base first, vertically through the holes in the plastic into the soil below. Plant them so that the bottom two-thirds of the cuttings are in the soil.

Root cuttings

Some plants produce very short stems and shoots, which can make taking cuttings very awkward, so another part of the plant has to be used. The roots of many herbaceous plants and alpines, and a number of trees, shrubs and climbers, can be used for propagation.

FLESHY STEMS

Plants with extremely fleshy stems can be encouraged to root in water. Place the cut stem of the plant in a jar of water and wait for the roots to appear. When they start to emerge, pot up the stem in the normal way.

▦ TAKING ROOT CUTTINGS

1 After carefully digging up the roots of the plant that is to be propagated, wash them carefully to remove as much soil as possible.

2 Cut thick roots into sections of 5–8 cm (2–3¼ inches) long, and make a flat cut at the top, and a slanting cut at the bottom – this will become the planted end.

3 Insert the root cuttings by gently pushing the slanted ends into a pot of growing mix so the top of each cutting is level with the surface.

4 Cover with grit, which allows air to reach the top of each cutting without letting them dry out and also ensures good drainage.

Leaf cuttings

You can propagate some plants, such as African violets, begonias and Cape primroses (*Streptocarpus*) by cutting and planting their leaves in a pot of potting mix (potting compost). New plantlets grow from the base of the leaf or the veins that run across it.

ROOTING POWDER

When applied to the cut end, a rooting hormone preparation increases the rooting capacity of the cutting. Dip the base of the cutting in the powder and then blow away any surplus.

■ TAKING LEAF CUTTINGS

1 Lay the leaf upper-side down. Use a sharp knife to cut along the leaf close to the thick fleshy midrib, to leave two sections of leaf blade. Discard the midrib of the leaf.

2 If you are dealing with particularly long leaf strips, cut them into halves or thirds so that they will fit comfortably into a tray or pot of growing mix.

3 Insert the strips so that the cut surface is just below the top of the mix. Lightly firm the mix, water and leave on a warm windowsill or in a propagator.

Cut close to the midrib

Insert the leaf strips into the growing mix

Grafting

Grafting is the union of one plant (the scion) with the roots of another (the stock or understock). It is a more skilful process than other forms of propagation and most home gardeners will not need to master it. However, you may have a camellia that is too good to discard but has flowers that don't appeal – you can convert it to a plant you like by grafting, or you could try grafting several different varieties on it to create a multi-coloured tree. Grafting is also used to change varieties on grapevines. Most often, however, grafting is used to control the growth of the scion, either by giving it the benefit of more vigorous roots than it would make for itself (as when roses are budded on wild rose roots) or, conversely, by using a less vigorous, 'dwarfing' stock, a technique used especially with apples and pears to create smaller, more manageable trees.

Although grafting isn't difficult, it does call for some skill. What you are doing is making a wound on the stock plant and inserting into it a piece of scion (a cutting), in the hope that both stock and scion will callus together and grow as one. To do this, you must match the cambium layers (the green section of stem immediately below the bark) together perfectly. Use razor-sharp blades to make the cuts, and a steady hand to make the match precisely. Disinfect the blades after each cut so as to minimize the chance of transmission of infection.

Types of grafting

BUDDING (SHIELD GRAFTING) This is the simplest form of grafting. You lift a flap of bark on the understock (which has been grown from seeds or a cutting), and slip in a growth bud from the scion, trimmed to give just a sliver of bark to support it. Cambium matching is automatic, and you bind everything together with raffia or plastic tape. Around midsummer is usually the best time for budding, and after it's done you let the stock grow, cutting it off just above the bud the following winter. Come spring, the bud will grow away to start the branches of a new plant on the more desirable roots of another species.

CLEFT GRAFTING With cleft grafting, you cut off the stock first, cleave it with a sharp knife and insert a scion into the cleft (or make two clefts and insert two scions, one on either side), matching the cambiums exactly. All the wounded surfaces are then covered with grafting wax and the graft is enclosed within a plastic bag to keep the scion moist. The best time for this process is towards the end of dormancy (early spring). The understock can be a young plant or a mature branch, which will need several grafts.

REMOVE SUCKERS
Suckers occur when the rootstock of a grafted plant starts to produce shoots from the area below the graft union. If suckers are allowed to grow unchecked, they will compete with the grafted plant to which they are joined. Because the rootstock is usually more vigorous than the cultivar grafted onto it, the growth of suckers will outstrip that of the grafted plant, usually resulting in the death of the grafted plant. Suckers must therefore be removed at an early stage.

ROSE GRAFTING

1 Start hardwood cuttings, taken from 1-year-old shoots of a rose rootstock, in a warm place or greenhouse in midwinter. Remove the lower buds, then heel in to a soil bed. Graft in spring, when semi-ripe shoots of the rose you want to propagate are available. Prepare the rootstock by cutting it down to 15 cm (6 inches).

2 Make a single, shallow, upward-slanting cut 4 cm (1½ inches) long at the top of the rootstock, thus exposing the plant tissue responsible for healing (the cambium), which allows the stock and scion to heal together.

Make an upward-slanting cut

3 Select a semi-ripe shoot about 8 cm (3¼ inches) long from the rose cultivar you want. Remove all of the leaves apart from the uppermost one, to form the scion.

4 Make a single downward-slanting cut approximately 4 cm (1½ inches) long on the bottom section of the scion, just behind a bud. This cut will expose the cambium.

5 Gently place the two sections of plant together, so that the cut surfaces match. When they are correctly positioned, carefully bind the graft with an elastic band. This will hold the graft firmly until the two sections join.

Bind the graft with an elastic band

6 Place the graft into a pot of growing mix. Water it well, cover with a plastic bag, and place it on a warm windowsill until the graft has taken.

GOOD PLANTS FOR GRAFTING

The following plants all take well to grafting: apple, camellia, cherry, grevillea, hibiscus, plum, pear and rose.

Maintenance

You get out of a garden what you put into it. Unfortunately, unless you have the most amazingly low-maintenance garden, you are going to have to get out there on a daily or weekly basis, and take care of the garden and all its living inhabitants to keep it looking its best. A little, done often, is the best prescription.

Garden tools

No gardener can function without workable and appropriate tools. The selection of gardening aids available is immense, and so careful consideration is needed to make sure you spend your money wisely.

Essential tools

Every gardener needs a spade, fork, trowel, hose and pair of secateurs. Never buy hand tools too large or heavy for the user. Some firms make 'lady's weight' items, which are lighter and smaller, and some tools are made for left-handers.

SPADE Buy a spade, not a shovel. A spade has a straight blade and is used upright. It should have a sharp cutting edge and a handle of smooth, good-quality wood. Spades are used for digging over soil and excavating planting holes. Buy one with a flange on top of the blade to save the instep.

FORK A fork normally has four prongs (tines), each 25–30 cm (10–12 inches) long and almost straight. They should be thick and strong or they will soon become bent and useless. Use a fork to turn dug-over soil or compost heaps.

TROWEL A trowel is slightly scooped with a blade 15–25 cm (6–10 inches) long. Ensure that the neck of the tool, where the blade meets the handle, is strong. Trowels are used for planting out seedlings and hand-weeding.

HOSE Hoses come in varying lengths in a variety of quality grades. The best are kink- and split-resistant and very supple, even in cold weather.

SECATEURS Secateurs should have a removable blade that can be sharpened or replaced and well-shaped handles that feel comfortable. Secateurs do a lot of hard work and it's worth spending a little more for top-quality tools. Use them for cutting flowers and for pruning twigs and small branches. Don't use secateurs to cut thicker branches or you will damage them – use long-handled loppers or a pruning saw instead.

Other useful tools

Although not essential, the following tools will make gardening easier for you:

RAKE Buy a flexible plastic or bamboo rake for gathering up fallen leaves or raking up lawn clippings. A steel-tined rake is very useful for preparing the surface of your vegetable or flower beds.

HOSE HINTS

Most quality garden hoses have ultraviolet stabilizers or protectors added to the plastic. Unfortunately, it still means that, unless you take extra care, your garden hose is only going to last a year or two if it is left in the hot summer sun. The following tips will extend its life by at least several years:

■ It is sensible to put the hose away in the shade when it's not in use.

■ Get the hose off the driveway. The weight of the car fractures the inner tubing, weakening the hose.

■ Store your hose by rolling it up. This will remove kinks and bends, which will cause extra wear. To roll up a hose easily and correctly for storage, run the hose out to its full length in a straight line. Then, starting at the tap end, pull the hose up into a circle or simply wind it onto a portable hose reel. Keeping it rolled up also makes it easy to roll out the hose, kink-free, next time you use it.

HOE Two types of hoe are used to break the soil surface and remove weeds. One is used with a chopping motion while walking forwards, the other, the Dutch hoe, is used with a spade-like action, while walking backwards. Some hoes have interchangeable heads, others have dual heads with a straight blade on one side and prongs, or tines, on the other. A hoe is one of the most useful tools for gardeners who grow vegetables or annual flowers in beds.

HAND FORK A hand fork is a small implement to loosen soil around seedlings and lift smaller plants. Use it while kneeling.

DIBBER A dibber (or dibble), which is a single prong split into two at one end, is used to lift single seedlings from a mass or for drilling a narrow hole when planting them out. Most varieties have a curved protrusion beneath the blade so that they can be used to weed the lawn, the bump acting as a fulcrum.

SHEARS Shears are used for cutting long grass or for trimming untidy looking hedges. They resemble scissors, and the blades can be easily replaced or sharpened. Edging shears have long handles so that you can use them to clip lawn edges without having to bend down.

WHEELBARROW Wheelbarrows are useful for carrying bulk mulch or topsoil, or for lugging heavy items around the garden. However, don't buy one unless you are sure you will need it.

WATERING CAN A watering can is handy for spot-watering your potted plants or for applying liquid or soluble fertilizers to your garden. Plastic watering cans are lightweight but remember not to leave them in the sun.

PORTABLE SPRAYER A portable sprayer is used to apply garden chemicals. Some are pressurized for continuous spraying, others must be pumped. One or the other will be essential if you have fruit trees or other plants that need regular spraying. Smaller, hand-held models are for individual spraying chores.

SAW A pruning saw has a curved blade with coarse teeth; a bow saw is like a big hacksaw. Both are useful when pruning trees or large shrubs.

SPRINKLER A sprinkler distributes water over a wide area of your garden with a rain-like spray. The simplest types of sprinklers emit a fountain-like, circular spray while more sophisticated models can water in various patterns that you can select to suit the shape of the area to be watered.

SHARPENING AND CLEANING SECATEURS

1 First, loosen the bolt with a spanner.

2 Remove the spring and take the secateurs apart.

3 Spray the parts with lubricant.

4 Sharpen the cutting or bevelled side of the blade on an oilstone. Make sure you hold the blade away from you.

5 Clean the cutting blade with an old rag.

6 Soak the spring and the nut and bolt in a bowl of turpentine. Rub the spring with an abrasive pad and reassemble.

STORE HAND TOOLS IN OIL AND SAND

In a small bucket, add oil to dry sand. Thoroughly mix the sand and oil together. Use the bucket for storing your hand tools.

THE GARDEN SHED

All too often the garden shed or garage becomes a dumping ground where all the nasty stuff you don't want to keep in the house gets stored: solvents, paints, weed killers, insecticides and sharp, heavy tools. The chemicals are potentially hazardous when inhaled or ingested, or when they come into contact with the skin; they are also a major cause of accidental poisoning, particularly among young children. A tidy shed is not only more efficient – it is obviously much safer as well.

Commonsense storage

■ If you have children, you should have a good lock on the shed door.

■ Never store flammables near heating devices or open flames.

■ Take care that pressurized containers are not punctured or subjected to undue pressure (don't put a heavy tool box on top of them).

■ Never store petrol in plastic containers.

■ Never store dangerous chemicals in empty soft drink bottles or food containers. Keep poisonous substances in their original containers.

■ Contact your local poisons information service about the safe disposal of chemicals you no longer require. Under no circumstances should you put them down the drain.

Terrific tools

■ Keeping your tools clean and sharp means that they are safer to use and it means that their life will be extended.

■ Clean tools by wiping them with a damp cloth or, if necessary, washing them in a detergent solution. Dry them with a clean, dry rag and hang them up if possible.

■ Disinfect pruning saws and secateurs after each use to prevent the spread of fungal diseases.

■ Keep a can of rough grease or oil with a rag in it and rub it over the metal parts of tools to prevent rusting.

■ Wipe over the wooden handles of your tools with linseed oil at least once every few months.

■ Sharpen the backs of cutting edges by rubbing them on a sandstone or an oilstone every year.

▣ RESTORING TOOL HANDLES

First, assemble the materials that you'll need for the job of restoring your tool handles. You will need the following: steel wool, a rag, a mixture of linseed oil and turpentine in an old jar, a sanding block, a fine- and a medium-grade abrasive paper and the handle that needs restoring.

1 Sand back the spade handle using the medium-grade abrasive paper and then clean the handle thoroughly.

2 Dip the rag into the linseed oil and turpentine mix. Rub the handle with the soaked rag, then leave it to dry overnight.

3 Lightly sand the handle again, this time with fine-grade abrasive paper. Repeat the whole process again if necessary.

4 Finish by rubbing the handle with some steel wool.

Watering systems

The correct type of hose, sprinkler or other system is vital if the garden is to be kept well maintained. The type depends on whether the garden is new or established. Some plants prefer overhead sprinklers (they aid pollination when the plant is in flower), others need a dribble or soaker system that keeps soil moist but flowers and foliage dry (so that fungal diseases are discouraged).

An in-ground sprinkler system will cut down your watering time considerably, but water restrictions apply in some areas. You need enough good-quality hose to reach all parts of the garden, a variety of interchangeable sprinklers ('click' fittings are excellent) and a fixed or mobile hose reel.

Lawn equipment

A motor mower is now a must for most gardens with lawn. Choose one that has the correct horsepower and a big enough catcher for your lawn. Hand-held trimmers, motorized or manual, make quick, light work of neatening rough areas along paths, around trees or next to fences.

Special-purpose tools

The following tools and garden accessories are only some of the many that have been developed to make gardening easier and more pleasurable. Some will be suitable for your needs:

- Cut-and-hold tools are useful for those with physical difficulties. They incorporate a device for holding the pruning, flower, fruit or weed after removal – secateurs and a type of weeder are available. Some manufacturers have developed tools that will hold the flower once cut as well as remove rose thorns.

- A dibber (dibble) will make planting large numbers of seedlings or bulbs easier and quicker.

- Edgers allow you to cut grass edges in difficult spots. They are designed to rotate into three different cutting positions: diagonally for tricky spots, horizontally for around trees and vertically for edges and paths. Some brands offer an easy-to-use cordless grass cutter that is powered by batteries.

- A greenhouse is ideal for people in cooler areas who want to grow plants that love warmth and humidity and don't thrive out of doors. They are great for getting vegetables and flowering potted plants started early.

- Hedge trimmers are a real boon in those gardens that have large, formal hedges that require trimming a few times a year. Some manufacturers have developed excellent, motor-driven hedge trimmers with good safety features such as a safety cutter bar, a starting lock, an enclosed handle and a shield to protect the operator's hands.

- A hose director enables you to use the hose as a sprinkler by directing water to any part of your garden. They are good where space is limited.

- A kneeler is a lightweight, padded waterproof cushion with a handle either side to make kneeling and rising afterwards much easier and more comfortable.

- Knee pads keep knees warm and dry during winter. They are comfortable and let you kneel directly on hard and stony ground.

- Long-handled tools give greater leverage and increased reach, placing less strain on your back. Long-handled loppers give greater reach, long-handled vertical shears are designed to trim grass without stooping, long-handled spades provide greater leverage, and long-handled hedge shears give a wider cutting sweep.

GARDEN TOOL DOS AND DON'TS

Do

- Store tools under cover.
- Keep tools clean (hose off, dry and give a quick rub over with an oily rag to prevent rust).
- Have a spare spade handle ready to replace one that suddenly breaks while you are using it in the garden.
- Be careful with sharp, inflammable or poisonous materials (store them out of reach of children and pets).

Don't

- Poke an incinerator fire with a hoe handle.
- Leave the wheelbarrow outside with garbage in it (it will rust).
- Cut wire with secateurs (use wire cutters).
- Store a lawnmower with grass clippings in the catcher (empty them onto your compost heap).

MAKE A KNEE PAD

1 On top of a piece of scrap timber (such as timber laminate) fold some cotton wadding several times until you achieve a thick pad the same size as the timber piece.

2 Place the cotton wadding and the timber on top of a piece of waterproof material, leaving about 10 cm (4 inches) extra on each side. You could use oilskin but that is rather expensive. The plastic just needs to be thick enough to be stapled without tearing.

3 Holding the plastic down firmly, staple one side. Staple the opposite side before doing the remaining pair. Tuck the corners in as you go. Your custom-made knee pad should last for years.

Composting

By far the largest proportion of household garbage consists of kitchen scraps, which are highly biodegradable and can be composted or processed by a worm farm. Worm farms take up very little space, so even someone living in an apartment can use one. Composting takes a little more room, but as well as diverting garbage away from landfill or the tip, composting provides you with valuable fertilizer for your garden. Alternatively, your local authority may know of community gardens that would welcome composting materials.

What to compost

Anything organic can be composted. A typical home could probably contribute:

- Grass clippings
- Fallen leaves
- Weeds
- Prunings
- Vegetable and fruit peelings
- Food scraps
- Coffee grounds
- Tea leaves
- Vacuum cleaner contents
- Faded cut flowers

TEMPERATURE TIP

If your compost is attracting cockroaches, maggots, rats or mice, add grass clippings to raise the internal temperature of the heap and keep pests at bay.

Tips for making great compost

- By puncturing the lining with a fork, you will create air channels that will encourage bacteria within the layers to multiply and break down the material quickly and evenly.

- Use either stable (or poultry) manure or blood and bone (bonemeal) to add nutrients to your compost heap.

- If you have free access to them, straw, sawdust, manure, seaweed or waste from food-processing plants, such as pea trash, rice hulls and nut shells, can also be added.

- Thick, woody prunings from trees and shrubs make good compost but make sure you remember to shred them first. If you produce enough of this waste each year, consider hiring or buying a mulcher. Thin, sappy stems can be cut up with a rotary mower before they are added to the heap.

KITCHEN TO GARDEN

Almost any biodegradable household waste can be composted.

- **Fruit and vegetable peelings** Some are particularly valuable. For instance, banana peel is high in potassium.

- **Tea and coffee** Tea leaves are rich in nitrogen. Coffee grounds contain protein as well as oils.

- **Waste paper** Cardboard and paper are useful because of their carbon content. Place cardboard at the bottom of the heap or packed around the sides. Paper works best if shredded.

- **Meat and fish** As these are organic they are suitable for composting but they tend to attract flies and sometimes vermin. Place them directly in the inside of an already composting heap and the heat will be sufficient to break down the flesh and kill maggots, while a covering of soil and grass clippings or sawdust will deter flies.

CONSTRUCTING A COMPOST HEAP

The secret to good composting is layering. Whether you create your own heap in a corner of your garden or use a special compost container from the garden centre, start with some basic layers, as follows:

- Start off with a layer of woody prunings to raise the heap off the ground and allow air to circulate.

- Next, add garden trimmings such as prunings and old plants, plus fruit and vegetable peel.

- Add a third layer of grass cuttings and leaves.

- Repeat these three layers to speed up the rotting process.

- Finally, cover the heap with a piece of old carpet or a layer of straw to prevent moisture escaping and to keep heat within the compost heap.

- As you add to the compost, intersperse alternate layers of moist and dry materials. Keep the heap damp but not wet to encourage the breakdown of material. Turn the heap regularly to improve aeration, which will in turn speed up the rotting process.

Trench composting

Trench composting can be the ideal answer for those who have larger gardens and for the more patient among us who are willing to wait for results. Trench composting is an anaerobic technique, so the compost materials will not reach the temperatures needed to kill weed seeds and pathogens.

As this is a cool process, earthworms will actively contribute to turning the organic matter through the soil. You could add commercially obtained earthworms to the trench, but populations of native worms will be attracted to the organic waste and multiply rapidly of their own accord.

Woody materials such as prunings will decay quicker if they are shredded before being buried, and a small amount of nitrogenous fertilizer may also need to be incorporated to speed up the whole process.

■ STEP-BY-STEP TRENCH COMPOSTING

1 In the late summer or early autumn, mark out the area which is to be dug over in a series of trenches and mark the lines of the parallel trenches.

2 Dig out a single trench about 30 cm (1 foot) deep, and move the soil from the trench to the very end of the proposed plot, which will be the very last section to be trenched.

3 As they become available, gradually fill the trench with plant debris, vegetable scraps and kitchen waste.

4 Dig out a second trench in a similar way to the first one. Cover each additional layer of material in the first trench with the soil dug from the second parallel trench.

5 After the first trench is full, start filling the second trench by creating a third trench. Each completed trench will gradually settle over a month or two as the plant material decomposes.

Green manures

Green manure crops are planted to improve the quality of the soil. They are usually nitrogen-fixing plants, often with strong, deep root systems that help to break up compacted soil and draw nutrients up to the surface. After a certain period they are dug into the soil.

ALFALFA/LUCERNE (*Medicago sativa*) Alfalfa is a perennial plant that prefers neutral to alkaline, well-drained soils. Plant from spring to midsummer. Alfalfa has nitrogen-fixing qualities and is exceptionally deep-rooted.

BUCKWHEAT (*Fagopyrum esculentum*) This annual is good on poor soils and will improve soil structure as well as attract pollinating bees. Plant buckwheat from spring to midsummer.

CRIMSON CLOVER (*Trifolium pratense*) This plant lasts 2–5 months and will overwinter. It prefers sandy loam soils and should be planted in spring to late summer. A nitrogen-fixing plant, it also attracts pollinating bees.

DAIKON/WHITE RADISH (*Raphanus sativus*) Daikon lasts 3–5 months and it is tolerant of most garden soil conditions. It should be planted during the spring months. Its flowers attract beneficial insects, while its huge roots break up soil to increase its water penetration.

LUPIN (*Lupinus angustifolia*) Lasting 3–5 months, lupin can be grown in acid, sandy to sandy loam soils. Plant in spring to midsummer. Lupin is an excellent nitrogen-fixing plant.

SCORPION WEED/PHACELIA (*Phacelia tanecetifolia*) Lasting 2–4 months, this plant can overwinter. It has a wide soil tolerance and will improve soil structure as well as attract beneficial insects. Plant from spring to summer.

RYE (*Elymus* sp.) This plant has a wide tolerance of soils and will overwinter. Plant in early to late autumn. Its fibrous root system improves soil structure.

Worm farms

Gardeners already know the value of the earthworm, toiling away aerating and refining the soil. In worm farms, they are also fastidious recyclers of kitchen waste and will turn your scraps into rich soil you can use in the garden or indoors for houseplants. Local councils often have information on worm farms or factories and may even provide subsidized ones.

A typical worm factory consists of a series of stacked plastic trays inhabited by a starter population of, for instance, 1000 worms on a compost-like bedding. These are compost worms, which naturally exist in the top 30 cm (1 foot) or so of soil, as opposed to earthworker worms, which burrow much deeper. Compost worms eat almost anything of plant or animal origin, converting it to castings (worm excrement) and liquid fertilizer, which is drained off through a tap at the bottom of the trays. Once they have adapted to a new food source, worms eat up to their own body weight every day. As they eat the food in one tray, they move up to the next, leaving their castings behind.

Worm-farming tips

MASHED PLEASE Worms eat more scraps if they are mashed or blended. While this may not be practical, it's worth bearing in mind that they prefer soft foods. Food for them can include: vegetable and fruit scraps and peelings, tea leaves, bags and coffee grounds, vacuum cleaner dust and hair or fur clippings, soaked and torn newspapers and cartons, and crushed egg shells.

ACIDS LATER While they will eat them, worms will leave acidic foods such as orange peel or onion skins until other, preferred food is eaten.

A LITTLE LIME Garden lime helps to counteract the effect of acidic food. A handful or so every few weeks is sufficient.

MATURE MANURE ONLY Worms can process manure from horses, cattle and dogs, but it's best to let it mature for 1–2 months as chemicals in fresh manure could kill a whole worm farm in a day.

BREEDING LIKE WORMS A worm farm takes 2–5 years to mature, at which point it may support up to 20,000 worms.

HOLIDAY HAVEN Worm farms can be left for 3–4 weeks without you having to add food as long as they already have a good supply, and are left in a cool spot under cover with the tap open.

Watering

There's a golden rule that all gardeners should follow and it is this: only water when your plants actually need it, and then water thoroughly.

How much water?

Soils vary in the way that they will accept water. Clay soils take it in only quite slowly but they dry out slowly as well; sandy soil takes it in very quickly but dries out quickly as well. Loam is the ideal – but all soils will have their water-holding capacity improved with the addition of organic matter.

You might need to do a bit of experimenting to work out how much water you need for a thorough soaking. When the soil is dry, try putting the sprinkler on, or holding the hose for a timed period of 10 minutes. Then, when any puddles have disappeared, dig down to see how far the water has gone (wet soil looks different from dry). If it's wet to, say, 10 cm (4 inches), then you'll know that you probably need to water for half an hour to get the water down to 30 or 35 cm (12 or 14 inches), which is where you want it.

WEEDS ARE WATER THIEVES

All plants consume and transpire water. In fact, far more moisture is lost from the soil by transpiration from plants than by evaporation from the soil itself. A simple way to reduce your garden's water needs is to reduce the number of unwanted plants – the weeds. It makes no sense at all to allow plants you don't want to rob water from those you do.

How often to water?

You don't want to waste water by watering more often than you need, but you do want to keep your plants happy. If they get really parched, they'll wilt, but if you watch carefully you'll learn to recognize the advance warnings: leaves and flowers look limp and lustreless; grass loses its springiness and retains footprints. It doesn't take long to develop the sixth sense that says, 'That plant looks thirsty'. Don't be deceived by the surface soil looking dry; if you're in doubt, dig down a little to check.

Of course, you'll need to water more often when the weather is hot and or dry. But do try, unless it's an emergency, not to water your garden in the heat of the day, when much of your precious water will evaporate at once. As a general rule, it's better to get the water directly to the soil, but don't apply it faster than it can be absorbed or you'll not only lose water from run-off, you'll also run the risk of compacting the surface, which will further reduce water penetration. On clay and silty soils this may mean that you can't turn the hose on full, so just be patient and keep it on for longer.

Water-wise plant selection

In dry areas, you can save a lot of water if you design a garden that will flourish on your local rainfall. Plants do not all need the same amount of water and if you've filled the garden with species that come from a much cooler and/or wetter climate than yours, you'll have to pour on the water just to keep them going. A better idea is to garden with plants that could survive in your climate without you. Those that are native to your area are a good starting point, but you don't have to be restricted to them. You'll find that there are many other places in the world that have a climate like yours and plants from those places will have a good chance of success in your garden. You can still have thirsty favourites, but don't dot them around the garden. Instead, group them all together – they can be watered more easily this way and plants that have similar watering needs tend to look best planted together.

Lawn-watering tips

It has been estimated that lawns take nearly 80 per cent of garden water, and that half of this is usually wasted in run-off or unnecessary application. Even in the hottest weather, a well-managed lawn shouldn't need more than 20 mm (3/4 inch) of water a week (including rainfall), and it only needs half that in cool climates or in winter. If the soil under your lawn is deep and fertile, apply the water in one dose. On poorer soils, give 100 mm (4 inches) twice per week. To measure the amount of water you are applying, place several straight-sided containers at various distances from the sprinkler. Turn the tap on, noting how many times you turn it, and then time the period it takes for 20 mm (3/4 inch) of water to accumulate in the containers. Next time you water you will know how long to leave the sprinkler going. If run-off occurs, slow the rate of application as every drop that runs off is a drop wasted.

You may also be wasting water if your lawn is unnecessarily large, if you have more lawn than you use. Your garden might look better and be much less thirsty if a part, or all of, the lawn is replaced with groundcovers or shrubs, or even with paving or gravel. Lawns are not essential to good garden design.

Using watering systems

A watering system with micro-jet sprays or drippers uses a lot less water than conventional sprinklers or hand-watering. That's because these systems deliver small amounts of water directly to where it is wanted. There is less wastage from run-off and evaporation, and they can be operated by timers that switch them off in case you forget to. On the downside, some systems can be quite tricky to install in already-established gardens and it is not always easy to achieve total coverage. Nevertheless, properly installed watering systems do save water and they are a very convenient way for the gardener to water.

Holding the hose can be very enjoyable and relaxing and a good way to see what's going on in the garden. But to water deeply, the way you should, you'll have to stand there for a long time and few gardeners do this. Better to put the sprinklers on for a much longer period, less often.

Water-saving tips for warm-climate gardeners

Around a third of household water is used in the garden, so any steps you take outside to reduce your usage will have a big impact on your overall household water consumption. By choosing fewer thirsty plants you can reduce the amount of watering your garden requires. You can ensure plants get the maximum drink by watering at optimum times of the day. Collecting rain water for watering the garden takes the pressure off the public water services, while using grey water – the term coined for water that's already been used in the home, for instance, for washing clothes – is an especially useful type of recycling. Here are some ways to avoid excessive use of the hose in your garden:

- Plants native to your area, whether they are shrubs or trees, tend to need less water than exotic shrubs and trees.

- Plant windbreaks to reduce the drying effect of the wind, and cover bare soil either by planting or by placing pavers and boulders. Bare soil heats up in the sun, drawing moisture from underneath to the top, where it evaporates.

- Mulching garden beds with clippings and leaves will help stop the soil from drying out and reduce your watering needs.

- Avoid using a hose in the middle of the day, when water will evaporate quickly. Fit timers to sprinklers.

- Choose sprinklers with big drops, not fine mists, which are blown away.

- Consider installing a fixed watering system with drip-feeders that deliver water directly to plant roots and eliminate wasteful run-off.

- Group plants together according to their watering needs.

- Water your plants slowly to allow the water to soak into the soil rather than run away and be wasted.

- Give your garden a good soak once a week rather than a daily drip. This effectively 'trains' your plants, encouraging bigger and deeper root systems and thus hardier plants. Frequent watering results in shallow roots, which aren't so good at seeking out water.

- Use a broom, not a hose, to clear paths and courtyards.

- Lawns tend to be thirsty and mowing them often uses polluting fuel. Consider grasses that need less water and different kinds of ground-cover altogether. If you stick with a lawn, keep the grass on the long side, say about 2 cm (3/4 inch), to shade the ground. Water no more than twice a week even when it's hot. Where possible, wash the car on the lawn and give the grass a watering at the same time.

COLLECTING RAIN WATER

At its simplest, rain water can be collected straight from the sky into bins and barrels for watering the garden or washing the car. But much more can be obtained by channelling it from the roof into a tank. If you are thinking of installing a rain water tank, check with your local authority about restrictions on size, height and location of the tank. Depending on what you intend to use the water for, you'll also need to consider the capacity of the tank. The average household uses hundreds of litres or gallons of water a day; rainfall varies considerably from place to place. Some local authorities may advise on choosing a tank.

Other considerations include what the tank is made from – usually concrete or galvanized iron (although other materials include fibreglass and recycled plastic); where the tank will be positioned (either buried or raised); and what it is lined with (linings may increase the life of the tank and enhance water quality). Whatever you choose, you need a non-porous tank interior to discourage algal growth.

With storage tanks and pumps, rain water can be used in the house, for washing clothes or flushing the toilet, for instance. If tests show it is clean and uncontaminated, it can even provide drinking water.

Mulching

Applying mulch to all garden beds regularly is the best way gardeners can save water. A recent study concluded that gardeners who kept their gardens mulched could reduce water consumption by as much as 25 per cent. A layer of mulch shades soil from the sun and shelters it from drying winds. This keeps moisture in the soil by reducing the rate of evaporation.

Mulch has other benefits as well as saving water. It improves the structure of your garden soil, which leads to better aeration and drainage, and an ability to hold more moisture for longer. Mulch also encourages beneficial soil organisms such as earthworms which, in turn, improve the fertility and aeration of the soil. Mulch also suppresses weeds by smothering seedlings as they germinate, evens out the temperature of the soil, which can lead to a longer growing season, and reduces erosion during heavy rain, which means water soaks in to where it is needed rather than running off.

What is mulch?

Mulch is a layer of material spread evenly over the soil, about 5–10 cm (2–4 inches) thick. Organic mulches are best because they benefit the soil. Inorganic mulches conserve moisture but do not condition or feed the soil.

ORGANIC MULCHES Organic mulches were once alive. They slowly rot down, releasing valuable plant foods. Typical organic mulches include compost, rotted manure, dry grass clippings, straw, hay, leaf litter, composted sawdust, peat-moss, pine bark, pine needles, wood chips and shredded prunings.

INORGANIC MULCHES Inorganic mulches were never alive and do not rot into soil-enriching humus. They are not really 'garden friendly': they add nothing to the soil structure, and once such mulches are in place, soil additives are difficult to incorporate. They tend to raise the soil temperature and some can even stop your soil from breathing, which can lead to serious problems. Stones, gravel, crushed rock or coarse sand may all be used, as can black plastic and even aluminium foil.

Ten great organic mulches

1 Compost adds humus to the soil and it also helps improve the soil's overall structure in your garden. Compost allows good soil moisture penetration.

2 Grass clippings are high in nitrogen and other nutrients. Dry them before use and mix with leaf mould or manure for easy air and water penetration. Used alone they may make a water-repellent mat.

3 Pine bark is a low-nutrient, dense, acidic mulch that may be slightly water repellent. Slow to rot, it is a good mulch for paths.

4 Leaf litter is attractive and quick to break down into a rich humus. Shred it before use and reapply annually.

5 Wood chips are attractive, natural looking and long lasting but they do not add much to the soil.

6 Cocopeat is made from waste coconut fibre. Apply it moist in a layer about 3–5 cm (1 1/4–2 inches) thick. It is a good substitute for peatmoss, which is a non-renewable product.

7 Sawdust is useful if used carefully. It must be composted before use as sawdust that is too fresh or that comes from pine wood could rob the soil of nutrients. Mix it with blood and bone (bonemeal) or old poultry manure and apply it thinly. Applied too thickly, it prevents moisture penetration. It is good for paths and between rows of vegetables.

8 Rotted cow manure is one of the best mulches. It is an excellent soil conditioner as well as being high in nutrients. Don't use it fresh as the ammonia may burn plants.

9 Seaweed is a high-nutrient mulch that rapidly enriches sandy soil. Wash it before use to remove the surface salt.

10 Mushroom compost is potentially a very good mulch but the quality does vary, with the worst being far too alkaline for good garden health. Test the pH of a sample before buying and using it.

HIGH-NITROGEN MULCH

Some mulches, such as lucerne (alfalfa), compost and sugar cane, have a high nitrogen content. These types of mulches do improve the soil fertility, but they also rot down quickly and so they need to be replaced at least once every few months.

Living mulch

Many low-growing plants make ideal living mulches. Groundcovers such as bugle flower (*Ajuga reptans*) planted into mulched soil are excellent for excluding weeds in ornamental gardens. Periwinkle (*Vinca minor*) is ideal for dry shade areas and it is easily controlled at a suitable height with a string trimmer used twice a year. Any of the prostrate-growing plants are effective in reducing weeds.

However, weeds may not always be a nuisance. They can, in fact, be helpful. A carpet of weeds can act as a protective blanket, another 'living mulch' of sorts. Many gardeners make their lives a misery worrying about weeds, but organic gardeners tend to be a bit more relaxed about invasion by 'unwanted' plants. They know that weeds are essential to the health of the soil. Bare earth is easily eroded by wind, and compacted by heavy rain or foot traffic. It is more easily leached of soluble nutrients and can also lose important gases.

If an area is to remain unplanted for a while, allowing it to become covered in weeds may not be the neatest solution, but it is sound ecologically. The weeds can be slashed just before they begin to flower and left on top of the soil as a green mulch, or dug through to add valuable organic matter.

AVOID PEATMOSS
Never use peatmoss as a mulch as it repels water once it is dry; rather, blend it into the soil and use it as a soil conditioner.

Fertilizing

Fertilizers can make the difference between success and failure in the garden but how much fertilizer you need to apply, and how often you need to apply it, depends on whether you use nature's own, free, miracle food – compost.

Why plants need fertilizing

Plants exist by converting water and minerals from the soil into stems, leaves and flowers. In the wild, those minerals would be constantly replaced: leaves, twigs, fruit and bark fall to the ground and every animal deposits plant food in its droppings. Nature is in perfect equilibrium – what goes up (into plants) must come down (and go back into the soil).

BEST TIME TO MULCH

Depending on the time of the year at which you mulch, you can influence your garden's soil temperatures. For example, if you mulch at the end of autumn, you will keep the soil warmer for longer, while mulching during the early spring months will keep the soil cooler and prevent heat being trapped in summer.

In gardens, however, things are different. The plants are not an eco-system but an unrelated mixture of species from a wide variety of habitats and soils. Each may have different nutrient needs. More importantly, there is no build-up of fallen vegetation and few animals to enrich the soil. Gardeners sweep up fallen leaves, and dead plants are removed before they can rot. The result of all this tidiness is a gradual but steady impoverishment of the soil.

The answer is not to stop sweeping and clearing up, but it is helpful if the sweepings are composted and returned to the soil. Compost has virtually all the nutrients plants need and it also does the soil good by creating humus – a vital natural ingredient, present in all fertile soils.

Unfortunately, the average suburban garden does not produce nearly enough compostable matter to supply all the garden's compost needs, but if you

CREATIVE MULCHING

Mulches are usually in position for a long time, if not indefinitely, so think about how the materials will affect the look of your garden. Inorganic materials can have a dramatic impact on the colour scheme and feel. Look for unusual shapes and textures, such as sea shells, slate or attractive pebbles, and choose colours to enhance your planting: slate-greys and blues can look marvellous against bright green foliage, for example. You can also incorporate elements that have special relevance to you – such as stone from your local area. The key is to achieve a look with which you are happy, and always remember not to despair that your garden needs to be covered over. Let your creative side loose and your mulched beds can look beautiful.

compost what you can and distribute the product around, you will not need to buy anything like the fertilizer that an uncomposted garden would require.

Major plant foods

The elements nitrogen, phosphorus and potassium (usually abbreviated to their chemical symbols NPK) are considered to be the major plant foods and are the main ingredients of all complete plant foods.

NITROGEN All the above three elements are essential, although nitrogen (N) stands out as the single most important. It is responsible for the growth of healthy leaves and is also present in chlorophyll and many other plant parts. If plants lack nitrogen, leaves gradually turn yellow, and new growth is stunted.

PHOSPHORUS Without any phosphorus (P), photosynthesis is not possible and there would be no new roots, shoots and flower buds. Insufficient phosphorus in your soil causes stunting, spindly growth and blue-green leaves. However, an excess of phosphorus can also be harmful, even toxic, to many plants, especially Australian and South African natives.

POTASSIUM Potassium (K) regulates and aids the chemical reactions within plants and it promotes stem growth. Shortage of this element causes leaves to turn a lustreless grey-green, perhaps also developing yellow spots. Affected leaves often brown at the edges, die and fall.

Packaged complete plant foods usually include percentages of calcium and sulphur as well as the three main elements. Magnesium, the sixth important element for plant growth, is normally present in sufficient quantities in the soil. A garden fed with complete plant food should not lack any major nutrients. The minor plant foods are a completely different story.

Minor plant foods

Trace elements are vital to all plants and they are usually present in well-composted soils. In other soils, deficiencies can occur because plants use up the supply or because other plant foods are applied too generously. For example, iron is abundant in most soils, yet plants can suffer deficiencies in iron if too much lime has been applied to the garden. But there are other causes of discolouration and poor growth, such as too much or too little water, attacks by pests and diseases, salty soils, misuse of poisons, too much or too little shade or an inappropriate pH reading in the soil.

If none of these applies to an affected plant, then suspect a trace element deficiency. However, they are not called 'trace elements' for nothing. Only a tiny amount is needed and it is vital that they be applied strictly as directed, as overdoses are fatal. Balanced mixtures of all the trace elements can be bought at nurseries and may be needed in gardens not regularly mulched with rotted organic matter. Apply trace elements annually or as directed on the pack.

Types of fertilizer

COMPLETE PLANT FOODS Plants have evolved on all types of soils, from extremely fertile to almost barren soil, and so they do not all need the same nutrients. 'Complete' plant foods cannot, therefore, suit all plants. They are too rich for some plants and too mild for others, but they are just right for many. Moreover, although complete plant foods all contain nitrogen, phosphorus and potassium, not all contain calcium, magnesium and sulphur or the trace elements which they would need to be truly complete. Other types of fertilizers have been developed to fill these gaps.

SLOW-RELEASE FERTILIZERS Many chemical fertilizers quickly release all their nutrients into the soil. This gives plants a sudden boost but rain or frequent watering will probably soon wash the nutrients out of the soil and into rivers and other waterways, and another dose of fertilizer will be needed. To counter

HANDY FEEDING HINTS

- Always fertilize when the soil is moist and water thoroughly after you have completed the application.

- If in doubt, apply fertilizer at half-strength, twice as often.

- Plants don't use much food in winter, so don't bother feeding then. Spring, summer and autumn feeds are generally better value.

- Nitrogen is responsible for leaf growth, but too much nitrogen can cause floppy growth and poor flowers.

- Phosphorus is vital for strong roots and stems.

- Potassium maintains the rigidity of plants and is important in promoting flowering.

Elements in organic fertilizers by percentage

MATERIAL	NITROGEN	PHOSPHORUS	POTASSIUM
Blood and bone (bonemeal)	4	21	0
Fishmeal	4	3	4
Leaf mould	7–8	0.6	0
Fresh seaweed	1.7	0.8	3
Cocoa shells	13–14	2.5	2
Lucerne (alfalfa)	0.0	1.5	0.6
Straw	0.4	0.2	0.8
Mushroom compost	0.8	0.6	0.7
Wood ash	1.5	0.5	1
Soot	5–11	1.1	0.4
Farmyard manure (dried)	2	1.8	2.2
Horse manure	0.7	0.3	0.6
Chicken manure	1.5	1.2	0.6

this, slow-release fertilizers have been developed. These react with water and temperature to exude a continuous supply of nutrients for up to a year. They are expensive but they do provide a constant food source. Dig in if possible.

SUPERPHOSPHATE 'Super' provides plants with an instantly usable source of phosphorus and a hefty dose of calcium and sulphur as well. It is good for peas (including sweet peas), beans, lupins and all other legumes, and most annual and perennial flowers. A little is good, a lot can be toxic.

BLOOD AND BONE (BONEMEAL) A natural slow-release fertilizer, blood and bone is mild enough to use on all plants. It contains nitrogen and phosphorus, sometimes calcium and a very small amount of potassium.

SULPHATE OF AMMONIA High in nitrogen, sulphate of ammonia is soluble and rapidly produces lush, new growth in lawns, shrubs, palms and flowers. Water in and use very sparingly as it is harmful to earthworms.

ANIMAL MANURE Animal manure is organic matter. All types contain plant nutrients but some are richer than others. Horse manure is fairly mild, cow manure is a little stronger, and pig and chicken manure are both extremely strong. All fresh manures should be piled up and allowed to rot for at least a month before use or you may kill the plants around which they are applied.

Leaf mould

Leaf mould makes an excellent soil conditioner, but it also has low levels of nutrients (0.4 per cent nitrogen, 0.2 per cent phosphate and 0.3 per cent potassium) and it is usually slightly acidic.

In nature, leaf mould is a material that slowly forms beneath trees over many years – so making your own at home is a long-term project. The leaves can take up to 2 years to decay into a dark, compost-like material.

MAKING LEAF MOULD

1 Rake up the fallen leaves into heaps. Alternatively, run a lawnmower over the leaves with the grass-collecting box on. This will not only gather up most of the leaves, but it will also chop them up, accelerating their decay. The best time to gather the leaves is just after it has rained when the leaves are moist; but they can also be collected dry and dampened later. Make sure you remove any foreign material, such as plastic wrappers.

2 Collect the leaves and place them in either plastic bags or heavy-duty black garbage bags. The latter are better as they block out most of the

BLACKJACK

Blackjack is an excellent, nutritious plant 'pick-me-up', which is very useful during the plant's flowering or fruiting periods. The first thing you will need is a quantity of animal manure – and make sure that it has been well rotted down. Add some soot (which provides nitrogen) and wood ash (good for potassium) to the manure. Put the mixture into a plastic-net bag. Seal the bag carefully, suspend it in a barrel of rain water and leave it in position for several weeks. Once the solution is ready, decant it as required into a watering can, diluting it until it is the colour of weak tea, and apply it to your plants.

light and encourage fungal activity. To every 30-cm (1-foot) layer of leaves add a small amount of organic fertilizer, such as dried, pelleted chicken manure or a measure of organic nitrogenous fertilizer such as sulphate of ammonia (which contains 16–21 per cent nitrogen).

3   When the bag is almost full, place it in the position where you are going to leave it while its contents decompose, and water it thoroughly so that the contents are soaking wet.

4   Over a period of about 2 years, the leaves will decompose and settle in the bag. These leaves will be pressed tightly together, with some remaining almost whole and others disintegrating completely. When the leaves are ready for use, the bag can be split open and the leaves used as a garden mulch or as a soil conditioner.

SEAWEED FERTILIZER
Visit your nearest beach and fill a sack with seaweed that has been washed up onto the shore. Tie the sack and immerse it in a large container of water. Leave it there for 7–14 days. This makes an invaluable, although very strong-smelling, liquid garden feed which can be sprayed or poured onto your plants.

Pruning

Pruning is the removal of part of a plant so as to encourage it to grow the way you want it to. Although pruning can call for some artistry, it is really not very hard to master, and when you see the improvement it brings to your plants you may even look forward to this seasonal maintenance task.

How plants respond to pruning

Whether the stem in question is a trunk, a branch or a twig, it is essentially a tube conveying sap, and if you cut it off, you divert the sap to some other stem, which will then grow more strongly.

A stem can be cut back to another, preferred stem or it can be cut back to a bud, from which a new stem will arise. On most plants buds can be seen as small nubs, either at the end of a stem (the terminal bud) or along the sides (the lateral buds). Lateral buds almost always grow in the axil ('armpit') of a leaf.

WHEN TO PRUNE IN FROST-PRONE AREAS

The right time to prune is governed by your climate. Pruning stimulates regrowth but frost will destroy the soft, new shoots. In frosty areas don't prune until frosts are past, which will be just before the new spring growth appears. If you live in a frost-free area, prune in the second or third month of winter.

Once a stem on a plant matures, the buds may lie dormant beneath the bark until pruning or some type of injury removes the growth above them and provokes them into growth.

When you cut a stem back, you remove the terminal bud, forcing the lateral buds to make side shoots. This usually makes the plant bushier. Conversely, you might choose to pinch back some side shoots, diverting the plant's energy into the terminal bud to make the branch grow longer. And by cutting back hard into old wood, you may also force dormant buds into growth. Beware, not all plants will tolerate being cut back to old wood and some may die as a result.

The way you prune a plant depends on the sort of growth that will come from each bud. If you are training a climbing rose, for instance, you might remove the ends of the long shoots to force the side shoots that will bear the flowers; if you are training a young tree to grow tall, you might well shorten the side shoots back to encourage the main shoot (the leader) to grow up faster.

The four basic pruning techniques

If you decide to prune, there are four basic techniques you can use, depending on what you want to achieve and the way the particular plant grows. These techniques – pinching, shearing, heading (or cutting back) and thinning – all start the same way, with the removal of any dead and obviously weak and sickly branches or shoots. Sometimes that is all that is needed. Take a critical look at your plant before going any further with pruning.

The three basic pruning groups

Plants are pruned according to their pruning group:

GROUP 1 Plants in group 1 are deciduous shrubs that require very little pruning by the time they reach maturity. Plants in this group do not require any regular pruning, other than to remove dead, diseased or dying wood as and when it appears on the plants, and to lightly tip the old flowering shoots.

GROUP 2 Plants in group 2 are deciduous shrubs that flower on the previous season's growth and are pruned after flowering. These plants require pruning to remove old flower-bearing wood straight after flowering has finished, giving as much time as possible for next year's flowers to grow.

GROUP 3 Plants in group 3 bear flowers on the current season's growth and are pruned hard during early spring. Prune back to a framework of older wood from which new shoots will eventually emerge.

Group 1   Group 2   Group 3

When to prune

A lot of minor pruning – pinching, removing dead wood, shortening that wayward branch – can be done any time you notice the need. But all major pruning of trees and shrubs is best done when the plant is dormant or least actively growing. For most plants, including many evergreens, this means in the winter, but there is a large class of plants that flower in early spring on stems that were produced during the previous summer. This is often referred to as 'old wood'. If you prune these in winter you will be cutting away the flower buds and will get nothing but leaf growth in that year. Instead, prune them immediately after the flowers have finished but before the new season's growth is properly under way. If you like, you can combine pruning with cutting long branches of flowers for the house, taking the branches that you plan to prune out, and finishing off the job as soon as the rest of the flowers have finished for the year.

Summer- and late spring-flowering shrubs mostly bloom on the current season's growth – stems produced after winter, called 'new wood' – and can be pruned at any time from the end of autumn until the signs of growth in spring. Whatever you do, you won't kill a plant by pruning it at the wrong time of year. The worst that can happen is the loss of that year's flowers or fruits.

SHARP TOOLS ARE A MUST

To make a good pruning cut that is clean and smooth, not ragged, your pruning tools must be kept clean and sharp.

GOOD PRUNING CUTS

A plant is a living thing and pruning is a kind of surgery from which it has to heal itself. Properly made cuts will heal quickly and bad ones will heal only slowly, if at all, and the open wounds will invite infection and decay. When you are pruning plants with alternate buds, to encourage the new shoot to grow away from the centre of the plant, prune just above an outward-facing bud.

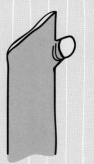

| A good cut, at 45 degrees, cut with secateurs just above the bud. | A poor pruning cut, with ragged edges, cut too far away from the bud. |

PRUNING AN EVERGREEN SHRUB

Generally speaking, evergreen shrubs need very little pruning when compared to deciduous shrubs. However, as with all types of shrubs, young plants benefit from some encouragement to form a good branching structure and evenly spaced lateral stems. In the first year after planting, prune the leading shoot to encourage a stronger system of side shoots to form. Thereafter, you need only remove weak or damaged shoots, or clip the bush lightly all over.

Pinching

Pinching is the removal of the tip of a shoot, which causes the lateral buds of the plant to begin growing. Repeated pinching will make many new shoots and give a compact, bushy plant. It can be used on annual flowers such as petunias and marigolds and also on bushy shrubs such as lavender. Usually you only need to pinch a plant twice, and you shouldn't pinch once the plant begins to show signs of wanting to flower and is large enough to do so (otherwise you will be pinching off the flowers).

Shearing

Shearing is like pinching but on an even more drastic scale. To shear, you clip the outer parts of the plant to an even surface, using a pair of hedge shears. Repeated shearing will destroy the plant's natural form, but that could be exactly what you want to achieve. Shearing a hedge is the most obvious example of this, but you might also want to shear back a groundcover to make it grow lower, stronger and more evenly, or to remove a multitude of dead flowers. Shearing is not suitable for plants that have large leaves, such as camellias – you will end up cutting a lot of the leaves in half, which can create an unpleasant sight. It is much better to trim these large-leaved plants by cutting back each shoot individually with secateurs.

Heading back

Heading back shortens a branch without removing it entirely and thus forces growth from one or more lateral buds. You might head back to reduce the size of the plant, to encourage growth from lower down where it will be stronger or more productive of flowers or fruit, or to remove a part of a branch that has been damaged. Always head back to a point from which growth will come – to another branch or to a bud – and consider whether that growth is likely to go in the direction you want (it will grow the way the bud is pointing). Don't leave the stubs to rot, and remember to go easy when heading back. You can always cut off more, but you can't stick branches back on.

GENERAL PRUNING HINTS

- Removing up to a third of the growth is generally quite safe, but some plants can take considerably harsher treatment. The golden rule is to prune after the flowers have finished, but there are exceptions – as with some deciduous shrubs, or shrubs that are grown for fruit as well as for flowers.

- Use cleaned and sharpened tools. Make sure the cut is a clean one because tearing or bruising the stems can result in an infection, and it slows down the callusing process.

- To protect your plants against the spread of diseases, wipe the blades with a cloth that has been moistened in bleach or soaked in disinfectant before pruning the next plant.

- If you are going to use a wound dressing, make sure you apply it to the plant immediately after cutting. Also, use a good-quality product rather than a tar concoction or a homemade brew.

- With shrubs, prune just above a healthy bud or buds if the shoots are opposite. Alternate shoots should be cut on an angle, while opposite buds should be cut straight, above the shoot.

- If you are trying to encourage bushy growth, you should tip-prune, which means trimming back by 10 cm (4 inches) or so, just enough to remove old flower heads and encourage branching.

- To rejuvenate an entire plant which has grown woody, you can cut it back hard (as in the case of hibiscus and photinia), or prune back sections (as for temperamental semi-hardwood perennials such as lavender and daisies) or prune back in stages, taking one third each year. This encourages growth lower down but without cutting into old wood that is less likely to reshoot.

Thinning

Thinning is the removal of whole stems, cutting them right back to their point of origin, with the aim of reducing the plant's bulk and bushiness but not making it any smaller. You might do this to let in more light and air, to reveal the lines of the branches or to channel the plant's energies into younger and more productive branches by removing old and unproductive stems. Often you will combine thinning and heading back, as in the pruning of bush roses where you cut out old branches and head back the rest.

Choosing a pruning technique

Every plant is different, and how you apply the basic techniques will vary from plant to plant, but here are a few generalizations to guide you:

TREES Some trees may need pruning when they are young to encourage them to develop into shapely adults. But training a young tree is never a hasty business and it is best to take several years over the initial pruning. An already-established tree usually needs only the removal of dead wood but it can sometimes be desirable to thin out the branches to allow more light through to reach the garden beneath. Thinning is almost always better than trying to reduce the size of a tree by cutting it back all over. Always go easy when pruning trees. Ideally, the results should not be immediately obvious. First, cut out weaker branches and then any that are growing immediately above or below others. Now stand back and take a look before cutting any more. If a tree is branching too low, you can cut out the lowest branches so as to raise the crown but it is much better to do this over a few years than all at once.

GROUNDCOVERS Groundcovers are a very mixed group. Some, such as ivy, are climbers that trail along the ground for want of something to climb up; some, such as hypericum and vinca, are spreading herbaceous perennials; while others are prostrate, spreading shrubs. An occasional shearing or general heading back will keep all these types of groundcovers dense and low.

SHRUBS Shrubs fall into two main groups: those that have several permanent branches growing from a single, short trunk and those that form clumps or thickets of more or less evenly sized stems growing straight from the ground. Shrubs with a trunk, such as daphne and most grevilleas, are usually headed back, although you might want to thin out the occasional weak or badly placed branch to keep them from becoming too bushy. On the other hand, thicket shrubs such as philadelphus, abelia and may bush are generally thinned by cutting a few of the oldest branches right to the ground. Large shrubs such as camellia and the bigger bottlebrushes can be trained as small, multi-stemmed trees by removing the lowest branches. Not all will take being severely headed back into bare wood and in most cases it is usually better to begin pruning when the shrubs are still quite young and flexible.

CONIFERS Conifers range from creeping groundcovers to the world's tallest timber trees. With few exceptions, they are evergreen and their leaves are needles: either long as in pines and cedars or short as in cypresses and junipers. They fall into two broad classes: those such as pines, cedars and firs that bear their branches in whorls, radiating out from the trunk or limbs like the spokes of a wheel, and those such as sequoias, cypresses and junipers that branch at random along the stem. This is not a commonly used distinction, but it is important when pruning because, while the random branches have

PRUNING TOOLS

Most gardeners can get by with a pair of secateurs and a pruning saw. You might also add long-handled loppers, which are secateurs with long handles. Use them for higher stems and those branches that are too big for secateurs but not quite big enough for a saw.

The most useful type of saw has a tapering, curved blade, which can get into those hard-to-get tight corners. Bigger hand saws are useful for large limbs, and you can buy pruning saws with coarse teeth on one side and fine teeth on the other. You can also buy the ordinary curved saw with a long handle to extend your reach. If you are faced with limbs large enough to call for a chain saw, get professional help: chain saws are dangerous in inexperienced hands.

Hedge shears are really just enormous scissors. There isn't much to choose in the various models, but lightness is always an advantage.

A ladder is very useful when you are pruning as it is very difficult to cut precisely if you are reaching up on your tiptoes. Be extremely careful with a stepladder – remember that it needs firm footing to be stable. Always have another person hold the ladder steady.

dormant buds all along their shoots, so that you can cut anywhere and expect growth, the whorl branches have buds only at the points where the whorls arise – at the tips or the bases of new shoots. The danger is that, if you cut between them, there will be no growth and the cut branch will eventually die right back: cut only to a lateral or, if you can see it clearly, to the cluster of buds that mark the base of a year's growth.

Most conifers are naturally shapely trees, and if you choose a conifer to suit your situation, you should not need to do any pruning. In any case, even if you do need to prune, never cut into bare wood – the dormant buds lose their viability when the leaves finally fall and so it won't regrow. The plum pines (*Podocarpus* spp.) and the English yew (*Taxus* sp.) are notable exceptions. (This is one reason why yew is so valued for hedging and topiary.)

Special pruning techniques

Some plants are trained into shapes and screens using pruning techniques such as bonsai, coppicing, espalier, topiary, pleaching and pollarding.

BONSAI This is the art of dwarfing plants by regular pruning and cramping root growth. Theoretically, any type of plant can be treated this way.

COPPICING This technique was developed to give a constant and renewable supply of wood for cane work and firewood. Basically, plants are cut back regularly to near ground level, which encourages a mass of new growth. This new growth is often more striking than older wood, and so it has ornamental value. Typical candidates for this sort of pruning are cornus and willow.

ESPALIER Sometimes called fan-training, espalier is simply pruning plants flat against a frame or wall. Camellia, cotoneaster, fruit trees, pyracantha and roses are commonly used for espalier.

PLEACHING A popular device used in garden design during the sixteenth and the seventeenth centuries, pleaching is the art of creating a hedge on stilts. European limes (*Tilia* sp.) are often used for this type of pruning, although any tree with a bushy habit would be just as suitable.

POLLARDING This technique is similar to coppicing, except that growth is cut back to a permanent framework. Plants that could be used include crepe myrtle, cornus, plane tree and willow.

TOPIARY Pruning plants into shapes such as balls, cones, spirals and animals is a popular pruning technique. Suitable species include box, conifers and shrub honeysuckle. Standardizing is a particularly popular form of topiary. Climbers as well as shrubs can be gown up on a single stem, then shaped on top into a ball, or series of balls, or a weeping plant.

Supporting plants

A number of plants need support of one form or another, either to keep them upright and protect them against strong winds and rain while they are young and not yet established, or simply to display their flowers to best advantage.

The plants most in need of support are soft-stemmed perennials and climbing plants. You may also need to support plants that have particularly heavy flower heads. Young plants will often benefit from some sort of additional support. The type of support needed is determined by the habit of the plant.

Supporting young plants

Young plants may need some kind of support to help them get established. Young trees should be staked when they are planted in windy areas to ensure that wind-rock does not disturb the roots and slow down plant growth. Staking also ensures that a strong vertical stem develops.

Climbers are best started with a small fan trellis to spread out the principal leading shoots and establish the eventual direction.

TYPES OF STAKE

■ **Stout timber stakes** These are mostly used for trees and have a pointed end for driving into the soil. They can be bought in sizes to suit the size of the tree. They must be driven well into the ground to provide a suitable anchor and positioned close to the plant.

■ **Bamboo canes** These are suitable for perennials and small shrubs. Buy small stoppers to put on the cane ends to prevent eye injuries.

■ **Link stakes** These are metal stakes that can be fitted together to form a circle. They are suitable for staking clumps of perennials.

Ornamentals

Ornamentals are the pivotal feature in just about every garden. Whether you want quick and easy colour from annuals, fancy an old-fashioned perennial border, or are looking for a low-maintenance shrub and grass garden, this chapter is packed with information to help you get the best from your favourite garden plants.

Easy annuals

Annuals grow to full size, flower, set seed and die within 1 year or a season. No other plants will give your garden the amount of seasonal colour and interest that annuals do. They're easy to grow, quick to bloom and some will keep on going for months on end. You'll enjoy growing annuals because they're fun and you see the results within weeks.

Tips for easy annuals

- Annuals prefer well-drained soil.
- Annuals can be grown from seeds or seedlings. Starting from seeds is definitely much cheaper, but starting from seedlings is a great deal easier and it puts you several weeks ahead.
- Dig into your soil a good amount of manure, water-storing crystals and a wetting agent before planting annuals.
- Buy annual seedlings in divided cell punnets, which protect their roots and result in quicker establishment and fewer failures. Because each seedling has its own cell, there is no chance of damaging the roots of other seedlings when you remove one from the punnet.
- Pinch back young plants and prevent them from flowering until they have grown for a month or so. This will let your plants develop into larger specimens that will ultimately last longer and flower better.
- All annuals need frequent watering until they are established, but once they are, reduce watering to a good soak once or twice a week.
- Remove dead flowers from the plant to prolong the flower display.
- Water with liquid fertilizer about once a fortnight.
- Most annuals need a lot of sun, so turn potted annuals regularly to give them an even supply all round.
- After each flush of flowers feed with a complete plant fertilizer.

Designing with annuals

When separate beds are set aside for growing annuals the plants are usually set out in rows. If you have a large bed, try planting very tall flowers in a group in the centre. You can then grade the sizes down until you reach the small

SAVING SEEDS

If you want to save seeds for the following year, allow the flowers to die naturally on the plant. Allow the seed-bearing organ (the capsule, or the pod) that remains after the petals have dried and fallen, to ripen and dry on the plant or the seeds will not be viable.

Remember that the flowers grown from the saved seeds may not be identical to the crop from which they are grown. Many annuals today are what are known as F1 hybrids. To produce their seeds, a plant breeder has to select two specific strains of the plant. To get identical results a second time the same genetic crosses must take place naturally, and this is not likely. However, the display of flowers from saved seeds is always interesting and you may find some exciting and unexpected variations appear in your garden.

edging plants. Alternatively, for a really informal garden, don't plant in rows at all – let the groups of plants intermingle and flow into one another to give a planting with a more natural appearance.

AN EASY BAMBOO TRELLIS FOR SWEET PEAS

If you don't have a sunny wall, you can create your own support for sweet peas by making a light bamboo trellis. Pinch sweet peas as they reach 15 cm (6 inches) high to create three or four laterals which can be trained upwards.

1 First, assemble the materials you'll need: ten x 1.5-m (5-foot) bamboo stakes, lime, twine, potting mix (potting compost), two terracotta pots, secateurs and sweet pea seedlings.

2 Choose a sunny spot in the garden. The more sun sweet peas get, the more they flower, so all-day full sun is best. Insert the first bamboo stake at an angle of about 60 degrees to the left, making sure that the stake is firmly embedded in the ground.

3 Insert four more stakes alongside the first one, and at the same angle, keeping them about 20 cm (8 inches) apart.

4 Push in the other five stakes, this time working at the same angle but in the opposite direction. This should form a diamond-shaped lattice.

5 Secure each junction neatly with some twine. Make sure you cut off any loose ends to give a professional-looking finish.

6 Place two pots, each filled with potting mix and a handful of lime, in front of the trellis. Make sure they're evenly spaced, then plant out the sweet pea seedlings.

7 As the seedlings grow, feed them weekly with diluted liquid fertilizer. Pick as many flowers as you like once they start to bloom – the more flowers you pick, the more the plant will produce.

Place the two pots of sweet peas in front of the completed trellis

Perfect perennials

Unlike annuals, which are relatively short lived, perennials are flowers that will live from year to year. Choose those that are suited to your climate and these easy-care flowers will return for a bigger and better display, year after year.

Types of perennial

There are two types of perennial flowers: herbaceous and evergreen.

HERBACEOUS PERENNIALS These perennials will die back to the ground for a period each year, reshooting a few months later to grow and bloom again. Most herbaceous perennials come from climates with very cold winters and, in order to survive, they close down their above-ground parts in autumn but the

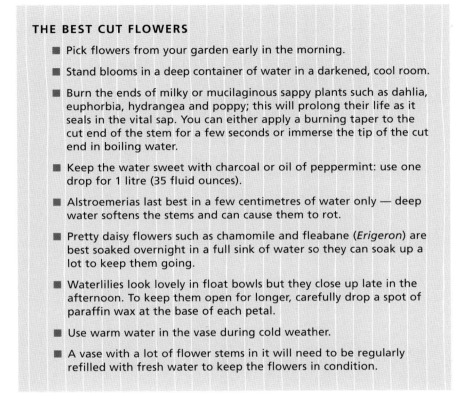

THE BEST CUT FLOWERS

- Pick flowers from your garden early in the morning.

- Stand blooms in a deep container of water in a darkened, cool room.

- Burn the ends of milky or mucilaginous sappy plants such as dahlia, euphorbia, hydrangea and poppy; this will prolong their life as it seals in the vital sap. You can either apply a burning taper to the cut end of the stem for a few seconds or immerse the tip of the cut end in boiling water.

- Keep the water sweet with charcoal or oil of peppermint: use one drop for 1 litre (35 fluid ounces).

- Alstroemerias last best in a few centimetres of water only — deep water softens the stems and can cause them to rot.

- Pretty daisy flowers such as chamomile and fleabane (*Erigeron*) are best soaked overnight in a full sink of water so they can soak up a lot to keep them going.

- Waterlilies look lovely in float bowls but they close up late in the afternoon. To keep them open for longer, carefully drop a spot of paraffin wax at the base of each petal.

- Use warm water in the vase during cold weather.

- A vase with a lot of flower stems in it will need to be regularly refilled with fresh water to keep the flowers in condition.

roots remain alive. In spring, herbaceous perennials reshoot. If you grow these winter-dormant perennials where winters are mild, they won't go completely dormant and soon die, exhausted from continuous growth.

EVERGREEN PERENNIALS If you live in warmer areas (frost-free or nearly so) you'll have more success with evergreen perennials, which come from a climate like yours. They may slow their growth in winter but they keep all their leaves. Of course, you can still grow herbaceous perennials in frost-free climates, but those from the coldest places will probably behave more like annuals, and the warmer your climate, the more this will be so.

Growing tips for perennials

- Perennials need full sun and plenty of shelter from strong winds.

- The garden bed can be any size but the smaller it is the fewer types of perennials you should try to grow. Remember, many perennials will become big and will not be suitable for narrow spaces.

- Because perennials are relatively long lived, good soil preparation is essential. Start by clearing the area of weeds and nuisance grasses.

- Always water deeply but infrequently. In hot weather on sandy soils this may need to be twice weekly but generally once a week is ample.

- Perennials should not need a lot of fertilizing. Apply a complete plant food just as their growth begin. If the soil has been well prepared, this should be enough for the whole growing season. A mulch of decayed manure or compost placed around the plants will also improve growing conditions.

- Keep the area weeded until the plants cover the ground. Or grow annuals as in-fill plants around them.

- Once your perennial plants are in bloom, deadhead them regularly to prolong the display.

- In autumn, when herbaceous perennials begin to die back, they can be cut to ground level. Evergreens are not cut back.

- Divide and replant perennials whenever the clump becomes overcrowded and congested, usually after 3 or 4 years' growth. Evergreens are divided after flowering, while herbaceous perennials are divided when they are dormant. Division rejuvenates them.

Perennial borders

Perennials can be planted among shrubs, as a complement to a display of bulbs or annuals, or in separate beds – the perennial border. A border is a planted area designed to be seen mostly from one side. You can also grow shrubs or annuals there if you like (a mixed border). Most perennials need full sun, although there are some that will take shade.

The great attraction of a perennial border or bed is the wonderful massed display of colour that they produce. Of course, you have to choose the colours and their placement within the border and that is where your artistry comes in. Your job is to know when each species flowers and in what colour, and to place those that bloom at the same time in pleasing colour combinations. It is a good idea to do this on paper in the first instance. Draw the bed to scale on graph paper and allot a space to each type of perennial you want to grow. They don't all have to flower at the same time, but those that do should look good together. By choosing species that bloom at different times you can have a succession of flowers in a succession of colour schemes.

Supporting perennials, bulbs and annuals

Soft-stemmed herbaceous plants will need help to ensure that the wind does not cause delicate stems to snap, particularly when they are in flower. There are various staking options, and much depends on the setting for the plants. In a border where the plants are quite closely packed, the supports will not show and you can use types that have little aesthetic appeal. Link stakes, which slot into each other to form a ring around the plant, are useful for this kind of job.

For plants grown in containers, which are normally on show, more attractive forms of staking are useful. You can use branching twigs, inserted around the edge of the pot, as these look much more attractive than either link stakes or bamboo canes held together with string. Alternatively, you can make your own supporting cage from supple stems such as bamboo or willow. Insert about eight stems around the edge of the pot and tie them at the top with raffia to make a feature of the support. This also works well with heavy flowers that tend to flop, such as hyacinths.

DIVIDING PERENNIALS

To divide plants, lift (dig up) the whole clump, shake off the excess soil and pull the clump apart or cut it into sections. With very large, heavy clumps, you may have to use an axe, a cleaver or a sharp spade. Replant the divided sections straight away, trimming off any very long roots. Remember the outermost growths are the youngest and the most vigorous. In some cases, the centre of the plant may have died out and so it can be discarded. If you are unable to replant at once or if you have pieces to give away, wrap them in damp newspaper or hessian (burlap) and keep in a shaded, sheltered spot.

ORCHID GROWING TIPS

- Orchids don't grow in ordinary soil. They prefer a specially formulated orchid mix that caters for their particular needs.

- When an orchid has filled its pot to the brim, take the clump out and chop it up into smaller pieces that can be repotted.

- Discard any dead- or dry-looking bits and replant your smaller pieces, each still with its leaves and roots, into fresh orchid mix.

- Don't bury the bulb, which should be sitting above the surface. You can repot at any time, but spring and early summer are best.

- There are plenty of orchid foods available on the market. Try selecting one that comes as a two-part preparation: one for flowering time, the other for foliage growth.

- Water plants regularly during the hot months, but allow your orchids to virtually dry out between waterings in cooler weather.

Glorious bulbs

Few plants offer as much pleasure for so little effort as do bulbs. Even people without gardens can enjoy them in pots and, while most people think of bulbs as spring flowers, there are also bulbs that bloom in all other seasons.

Bulb growing tips

- Daffodils are probably the most popular bulbs, available today in pink, white and cream as well as yellow. As with all bulbs, they look their best when they're planted in informal clumps or drifts.

- Some bulbs have a wonderful perfume. Freesias, hyacinths and jonquils are particularly noted for their heady scents.

- Ranunculus grow from tiny tubers. One tiny ranunculus tuber can produce up to thirty blooms, ideal for cutting. Make sure you don't over-water as they are susceptible to rotting in wet soils.

- Are your daffodils no longer flowering? Remember to divide them every 3 years or so by removing the offsets and replanting them separately into freshly dug-over, improved soil.

▧ If lifting your bulbs and replanting them sounds like too much of a drag, then try selecting old-fashioned favourites that pretty much look after themselves. Plant them in bold drifts with cool-season grasses that don't need mowing as regularly. This technique is called naturalizing. Try autumn crocus, baby gladiolus, babiana, bluebell, freesia, ixia, sparaxis, triteleia and watsonia.

▧ While most bulbs like a full-sun position, some are able to tolerate more shade. If you have a shadier garden, plant bluebell, freesia, grape hyacinth, snowdrop and triteleia.

▧ Because bulbs have evolved to withstand cold winter temperatures, it is important to wait until the heat of the summer is completely over before planting them. Early autumn is probably the best time to plant most bulbs, although tulips should be planted in late autumn once the soil temperature has dropped.

▧ If you are growing them as cut flowers, place potted bulbs in the shade for a while – this will lengthen the flower stems, which is ideal for cutting. Gradually bring them out into full sun, then plant some seedling annuals between the new shoots.

▧ Use a premium potting mix (potting compost) when you are growing bulbs in containers. Free-draining, enriched composts with added peatmoss are vital.

SHADE-LOVING BULBS

Achimenes hybrids

Calla lily (*Zantedeschia aethiopica*)

Clivia (*Clivia miniata*)

Cobra lily or Jack-in-the-pulpit (*Arisaema sikokianum*)

Cyclamen (*Cyclamen persicum*)

Dog-tooth violet, trout lily (*Erythronium dens-canis*)

Fritillary, crown imperial (*Fritillaria imperialis*)

Liliums (some only)

Spanish bluebell (*Hyacinthoides hispanica*)

Squills (*Scilla* sp.)

Tuberous begonia

Wood anemone (*Anemone blanda*)

▦ PLANTING BULBS

1 Dig a hole for each bulb, allowing the appropriate depth for each. For example, daffodils need a depth of about 10 cm (4 inches). For small groupings, use a trowel, but for larger plantings, use a bulb planter, which will make the job much easier.

2 Position each bulb with the pointed end facing up – this is vital for the successful emergence of the plant.

3 Plant the bulb firmly in the soil, avoiding any air pockets. Backfill the hole with garden soil and then apply a layer of mulch to help conserve moisture, protect the soil from temperature fluctuations and reduce weed growth. Water the plant thoroughly.

Chilling bulbs

Spring-flowering bulbs normally require a period of cold temperatures below 9°C (48°F) in order to start the flowering process off. A biochemical reaction occurs within the bulb when the optimum temperature is reached. This is followed by a response in the plant to increasing day length and warmer temperatures. Indoor forcing is a way of inducing that reaction artificially. In cool zones, you only need to plant bulbs out in autumn and wait for the shoots to appear in spring because the cold winter ground provides sufficient chilling for them to flower.

In warm areas, where the soil does not get cold enough in winter for the bulbs to successfully flower, they will respond to an artificially induced chilling period. To do this, buy bulbs as soon as they first go on sale and place them in your refrigerator crisper until mid- to late autumn. Be prepared to keep them here for a while – it could mean a period of up to 4 months in 'the chiller' before the garden soil is cool enough for planting.

Terrific trees

Treeless houses can look just as bare and unfinished as roofless houses. By simply planting trees around your home, you will not only improve its appearance, you will also make it a more comfortable and pleasant place in which to live – and add considerably to its value. Remember, however, that in time the trees you plant will grow to dominate your block, so it's vital to position them carefully with their ultimate height and spread in mind.

A few dos and don'ts

- Do find out how big your tree will grow and make sure it will fit your garden without the need for constant pruning.

- Do feed your tree appropriately to encourage vigorous new growth and make sure you stake it for the first year only.

- Do water your tree diligently for the first 6 weeks to give it a chance to establish itself properly.

- Don't plant your tree closer than 5 m (16 feet) to your house. Its roots could damage your foundations and block drains.

- Don't pave close to your tree. Allow space for the trunk to develop and for air and water to penetrate down to the roots.

DANGER SPOTS FOR PLANTING TREES

- You should never plant a tree under electric wires. If the trees grow to touch the wires it can be very dangerous and you will be charged with the cost of clearing them.

- It is also unwise to plant trees near sewer lines because, if they ever leak, fine roots will enter and cause plumbing problems. This is due to the fact that as tree roots grow, they thicken considerably, widening the crack in the pipe and allowing in more roots. Eventually they block the pipe. Roots can't enter good pipes, and modern, plastic pipes laid in long lengths are less likely to be penetrated than old terracotta pipes with their many leaky joins.

- Surface roots of trees can crack and lift paths and paving if planted closer than about 5 m (16 feet). Roots have also been blamed for cracking houses. The problem is worst on clay soils. In dry spells, as the tree takes up water, the clay shrinks and houses crack as they settle. When it rains, the clay expands, causing further movement cracks. This doesn't happen on sandy soils as they hardly shrink or expand at all. Generally, the bigger the tree will become, the further from the house it should be planted, especially in clay soil.

- Don't prune your tree at the wrong time. Autumn is the best time for pruning because the sap flow slows down at this time of year.
- Don't expect grass to grow beneath your tree once it's mature.

When and how to plant trees

- Avoid planting trees during the extreme temperatures of summer and winter. In the first year, water deeply to help the tree to grow strong, deep roots.
- To plant, first water the tree in its pot. Dig a hole twice as wide as the pot, drop in a small amount of fertilizer and cover it with garden soil. Don't add compost or manure at this stage or the tree may keep its roots in the 'pot' of good soil you have created.
- Carefully take the tree out of its pot, untangle the roots and cleanly remove any roots that are too long. Place the plant in the hole, making sure that the soil level will be the same as it was in the pot. Backfill, pressing the soil into any air pockets, and water well. Top this up with more soil if there is any settlement.

PLANTING A BARE-ROOTED TREE

1 Dig a hole.
2 Take the rootball out of its protective covering.
3 Check that the roots are healthy.
4 Position the tree in the hole.
5 Backfill the soil around the tree.
6 Create a 'doughnut' ring around the plant to hold water. Water it in. (The 'doughnut' will help to retain the water and stops any run-off.)

SHOULD YOU STAKE TREES?

Sooner or later trees must cope with wind. Help them make strong roots by not staking them. If the wind bends the trees, then let them bend, that is how trees cope with wind. Only if young trees are in danger of blowing over should you stake, but aim to remove the stakes as soon as the trees are firmly rooted.

DON'T OVERPLANT

Saplings look small but they will soon be a hundred times bigger. Trees that are planted too closely together may force each other to adopt unnatural, unappealing shapes. Also think about your neighbours. Consider the shade your tree will cast on their property, the amount of their precious garden space its branches will invade and the litter it will drop.

SUPPORT FOR YOUNG TREES

It is sometimes necessary to provide young trees with support for a short time to prevent them from being rocked around during windy weather. Three stakes are usually used and the tree is secured to them with ties in figure-eight loops.

1 Position the stakes around the stem, bending towards the tree at an angle of 45 degrees at a point about 30 cm (12 inches) above ground.

2 Tie the tree to the stakes, making sure there is a spacer between plant and stakes to prevent rubbing.

3 Ensure the ties are 4 cm (1$^{1}/_{2}$ inches) below the top of the stakes to prevent the stem from hitting them.

TRANSPLANTING A TREE

1 Before you lift your tree, dig a large hole in the new spot and improve the removed soil by adding well-rotted manure and compost. Then add just a sprinkle of water crystals and use this improved soil for backfilling.

2 Using a sharp spade, cut through the roots in a circle at least 40 cm (16 inches) away from the tree trunk (or ten times the width of the trunk). Now you will need to widen this trench sufficiently to allow you to comfortably get under the roots.

3 Slide the spade under the roots and lift the tree onto some hessian (burlap) or an old sheet, trying to keep as much soil on the roots as you can.

4 Wrap the rootball in the hessian or old sheet so no soil escapes. This method is called 'ball and burlap'.

5 Use the wrap to slide or lift the plant into its new position.

ABOUT PALMS

Never too big for even the smallest yard, palms add a tropical, summery ambience and are ideal for shelter and privacy. They are widely used indoors and many can be grown in pots for years.

■ Most young palms like a shaded or semi-shaded aspect. Most adult palms have at least their heads in the sun and many grow well in quite open positions, but it is always best to provide shade for seedlings and very young plants.

■ Most palms prefer a well-drained soil that contains plenty of organic matter and, generally, the better the soil, the better the results. Sandy soils should be improved by the addition of decayed manure or compost several weeks before planting and the planted palms should always be well mulched.

■ Potted palms can be planted out at almost any time of the year but in cooler areas avoid planting in winter because there will be little or no root growth until the soil warms and the days lengthen. Dig a wide hole, about three times as wide as the top of the pot. Water the palm in its pot an hour or two before planting. If you have improved the soil with organic matter ahead of time you can simply remove the plant from its pot and position it in the hole. Backfill the hole and firm the soil around the plant so that the finished level is the same as it was in the pot. Give the area a good watering and then mulch around the base. Add slow-release fertilizer or blood and bone (bonemeal) before planting, covering it with soil so that the roots do not come into contact with the fertilizer.

■ Once they are established, many palms are very drought tolerant. However, all palms will do and look better if they are given regular, deep soakings during dry periods in the warmer months. Keeping the root zone well mulched will retain soil moisture and improve growing conditions around the roots.

■ Palms like to be fertilized during the warm months when they are actively growing. Make sure the soil is well watered before applying fertilizer. Use any complete plant food, blood and bone (bonemeal), rotted manure, slow-release or soluble or liquid fertilizer.

■ Palms cannot be reduced by pruning. They die if the top is removed and often recover only slowly if green leaves are cut from them.

6 Place the plant in the prepared hole, backfill with the improved soil, then water in well using a watering can with a little soluble seaweed solution added to the water. Prune off any unnecessary growth, and cover it with an old sheet or shade cloth to protect it from the sun. Keep the soil evenly moist, especially if the weather turns warm or windy. It will take up to 6 weeks for the plant to re-establish itself in its new home.

7 Insert a stake if your transplant seems top-heavy, but be careful not to damage the rootball. Use three stakes if necessary and attach them with flexible ties — such as budding tape or pantihose — in a figure-eight. This allows the trunk to bend with the breeze and still remain stable.

FALLING LEAVES
Never put fallen leaves in the garbage or burn them, as decayed leaves enrich soil. Pile them in a hidden corner, let them to decompose and then spread them on the garden.

Ornamental grasses

Ornamental grasses are grass-like plants with long, strappy leaves, produced in dense clumps. They can be anything from small mounds 15–20 cm (6–8 inches) tall, to fountains of foliage reaching 2 m (6½ feet) and more and with long flower spikes towering above that.

Using ornamental grasses

Smaller growers can be massed as a groundcover, used as edging along paths or flower beds, or grown in pots. Larger species can be grown in a mixed flower border or different types of grasses can be clumped together in a display. If you have the space, massing the bigger growers will create a prairie effect. Almost all types of grasses look and grow well beside water.

Growing tips for ornamental grasses

PLANTING Late winter or spring is the best time to plant although grasses that are purchased in pots may be planted any time. Grasses grow quite quickly and so they must be spaced according to the ultimate size of the plant or you'll have to replant them too soon. Dig a wide planting hole and make a mound in the centre. Spread the roots over the mound, backfill and water in. These plants will need regular watering through the first spring and summer.

CARE In late autumn or winter, cut the foliage mass to the ground, especially with herbaceous types, or the dead top-growth will make the new spring growth look somewhat untidy. Evergreen species don't have to be cut back but weather-worn or old foliage can be sheared off at ground level during the late winter months. New shoots appear in early spring and, at that stage, you can mulch around the plants with rotted cow manure or compost, or simply give them a ration of complete plant food and water it in thoroughly.

PROPAGATION You can divide your grasses in late autumn or early spring. This takes some amount of brute force and a very sharp saw or knife. After dividing and replanting, cut the foliage back by one-third to reduce moisture loss.

GARDENING FOR THE SENSES
An added feature of grasses is their sound. They rustle and sigh in the breeze and so are a joy to both the eyes and ears.

Cacti and succulents

Cacti are specific types of plants, almost always without leaves and with spines in clusters. 'Succulent' describes any plant with fleshy leaves or stems that store water. All cacti come from the Americas but succulents are found in many dry places. They both have a stark beauty and add drama and contrast, and you won't see more spectacular flowers than those of many cacti.

Where to plant cacti and succulents

There are thousands of different types of cacti and succulents ranging in size from little 'buttons' to trees, but they all have one thing in common: drought tolerance. In gardens, they are useful for hot, sunny areas and look best and most believable if grouped together in a dry landscape.

Individual plants, especially the tree- or shrub-sized ones, often make striking specimen plants that look stark against the sky and contrast well with softer, more pendulous plants. In pots, cacti and succulents are in a class of their own. They thrive in places where more traditional flowers would quickly wither.

Maintenance tips

- Cacti and succulents aren't all from desert climes. Many are from seasonally dry climates such as the monsoonal tropics or from places with a Mediterranean climate.

- Almost all types need sun and very well-drained soil but there are some that will tolerate partial shade and you should check on the needs of unfamiliar types before placing them.

- Where most people live, rain falls more regularly than in the places where most cacti and succulents originate. These are, therefore, truly plants that can live on rain. Even wrong-season rain need not hurt them if the soil drains freely. You don't even need to feed them; the soil you have is almost certainly rich enough.

- In pots, they will need more frequent watering because of the restricted root room and you should keep them lightly moist during their growing season. Unlike other plants, they won't die if you forget – they'll just do better if you remember.

CACTUS TREES

If you don't want to devote a large area of the garden to cacti and succulents, consider using one of the larger types as a specimen tree. There are several big cacti – like the types you have probably seen in American westerns. Some euphorbias will develop tree-like dimensions over time but don't plant water-loving species around them.

Superb shrubs

A lovely garden can be created almost entirely from shrubs. These are the plants that give the garden form and definition and much of its colour and texture. With careful planning you can have shrubs in flower every month of the year.

When you are planning your garden, select shrubs to suit the position. Will the shrub thrive in full sun or does it prefer shade? Consider how high and wide it will grow. Don't buy a large-growing shrub for a small space thinking you will keep it pruned. You will get tired of pruning and end up removing it.

CHOOSING A SHRUB AT THE GARDEN CENTRE

When buying shrubs, biggest is not always best. Look for well-shaped plants that have a good cover of healthy leaves. Avoid ones that have woody roots protruding from the drainage holes, those that are too tall for the pot size and those that have knobbly, thickened bases to their stems. All these signal that it is pot bound, which means its roots will be so tightly packed they may never spread out after planting.

Shrub-planting checklist

- Container-grown shrubs can be planted out almost any time of the year except in areas that have heavy frost in winter.

- Check that the position you have chosen for your shrub suits its requirements in terms of sun or shade, shelter, drainage and the area available for healthy growth.

- Dig a hole that is at least twice as wide as the potted plant and about the same depth. Loosen the soil in the bottom of the hole but do not dig down into a clay layer or you may create a well in which the plant roots may drown.

- Do not put compost or manure in the planting hole. Blood and bone (bonemeal) or slow-release fertilizer may be sprinkled in the bottom of the hole but it must be covered by 3–5 cm (1¼–2 inches) of soil so that the roots do not come into contact with it.

- Thoroughly water the plant in its pot, loosen by tapping the base and sides of the pot, and then slide the plant out gently.

- Place the plant in the hole so that the soil level is the same as it was in the container. Backfill the hole with the soil you have dug out and firm the soil in well – but don't compact the soil and crush the roots by stamping around too much.

- Water the planted shrub thoroughly again to eliminate air pockets and to settle the soil around the plant's roots.

- Mulch the area around the shrub but remember to always keep the mulch well clear of the stem.

ABOUT FERNS

■ Ferns like bright light but they don't like direct sun. They need humidity and shelter from strong wind, although some species will grow quite well in fairly exposed places.

■ The ideal soil for ferns is a well-drained loam with a high organic-matter content. Although ferns do like moist soil conditions they will not tolerate heavy, waterlogged clays and any effort you put into soil improvement will always pay off. Simple things like mulching around ferns with old manure, compost or decaying leaf litter effectively improves growing conditions.

■ When growing ferns in pots, use a top-quality potting mix (potting compost) that has good moisture-retentive properties. Suitable potting mixes should be available from garden centres and nurseries. If you want you can use a standard-grade mix and then add about one-third by volume of peat or a peat substitute, or even sieved cow manure.

■ Ferns will always need watering during prolonged periods of dry weather, and a thorough soaking of the area is better than frequent light sprinklings. On hot, windy days, when the humidity is low, it may also be necessary to spray ferns frequently to cool and humidify the atmosphere. In winter, when days are short and cold, watering should be less frequent. Potted ferns should always be kept just moist but never allow water to remain in the saucer permanently. Twenty minutes or so after watering, empty any excess water from the plant saucer. Don't keep potted ferns in heated rooms as the atmosphere will be much too dry for them.

■ Ferns like to be fertilized during their growing season, which is from spring through to early autumn. A little, but often, is always better than applying large, strong doses all at the one time. Ferns thrive on regular but weak doses of organic fertilizers such as seaweed extract, fish emulsion or liquid blood and bone (bonemeal). Slow-release granules are also convenient to use and they are available in blends that are suitable for ferns.

■ Ferns generally need little or no pruning other than the removal of dead or dying fronds. If a fern with creeping stems exceeds its allotted space it is a simple matter to sever that stem (rhizome) and then discard it – or pot it up to regrow.

Pruning shrubs

Pruning is not done as a matter of course with shrubs and many of them will never need pruning unless to rejuvenate a very old plant or to remove the odd wayward stem and generally tidy up its appearance. However, if you do want or need to prune, remember to try and do so immediately after the plant has flowered. The only exception to this rule is if you have plants that you are growing for their berries, which form after the flowers, but these types of shrubs rarely need pruning.

Growing roses

Roses are undeniably the best-loved of all flowers. These glorious plants are generally quite adaptable, but they do grow and flower best in cool to mild climates – those that do not suffer from extremes of cold or excessive heat and humidity.

What roses need

FULL SUN Roses are definitely not shade lovers – they must have a position where they receive at least 5 hours of direct sun every day, more if possible. Where summers are very hot, give them the sun in the morning and early afternoon as late shade helps preserve the flowers.

AIR MOVEMENT The more humid your climate, the more open, sunny and breezy the rose-growing site should be. Humidity and a sheltered, still position are an open invitation to fungal diseases. The perfect place for growing roses is a breezy position, but without constant wind.

RICH, WELL-DRAINED SOIL Roses are at their best in very fertile soil that is moisture retentive but never sodden for long periods of time. They will grow well in both clay-based, fairly heavy loams and in lighter, more sandy soils. If you grow them in clay soils, make sure the soil drains freely, and make sure sandy soils contain plenty of rotted organic matter.

FEEDING Roses have big appetites but you can satisfy them by mulching at least once a year with rotted manure and a ration of rose food.

WATER Keep roses moist at all times but never allow the roots to sit in water.

PRUNING Prune back heavily once a year in winter.

ONCE-FLOWERING OR REPEAT-BLOOMING

Some roses, usually the older varieties or natural species, flower only once in spring. From beginning to end the show lasts 4–6 weeks and can be truly spectacular. Today's popular hybrid tea roses and many others have a repeat-blooming or 'remontant' habit, that is, flowers come in flushes throughout spring, summer and autumn. Often there is an abundant display in spring and a secondary show in autumn, with a succession of individual blooms in between.

Repeat-blooming may seem the better deal, but don't automatically choose a remontant variety over a once-bloomer. In hot climates, the summer flowers are often burned and not very attractive, and in rainy or humid climates they can be destroyed by the weather and diseases.

PLANTING CONTAINERIZED ROSES

Roses bought in pots don't really need any special attention and they can be planted out like any other containerized plant.

1 Dig a hole that is two or three times wider than the pot but about the same depth. Loosen the soil in the bottom of the hole.

2 Crumble some of the excavated soil back into the hole so that it forms a high mound in the middle.

3 Take the rose from its pot and carefully untangle and tease out the roots. Place the plant into the hole, making sure you place the roots over the mound and spread them downwards and outwards.

4 Refill the hole with the crumbled excavated soil, ensuring that the rose is planted no deeper in the ground than it was in the pot. Tamp down the plant gently to firm the soil around the roots and water in the rose thoroughly. Top up with more soil if there is subsidence.

5 Mulch around the plant with compost or some other rotted organic matter and again water thoroughly.

6 After a few weeks, new growth will begin and you can sprinkle a ration of complete plant food or slow-release fertilizer around the rose.

■ PLANTING BARE-ROOTED ROSES

In winter, dormant roses are sold with their roots wrapped but with very little soil around them – this form of plant is called 'bare-rooted'. When you get them home, unwrap and immediately soak the roots in a bucket of water while you prepare the planting hole. If you are not able to plant your bare-rooted roses immediately, then simply open the packaging to allow ventilation of the stems and to keep the plants cold but not frozen or exposed to frost. Don't allow the roots to dry out but don't sit them in water either. Plant them as soon as possible.

1 Make the holes wide and about 30 cm (1 foot) deep, and make a mound as described on page 123 for containerized roses.

2 Spread the roots downwards and outwards over the mound and refill the hole with the excavated soil. If any of the roots are damaged or too long, trim them back with very sharp, disinfected secateurs – the roots can be shortened to about 20 cm (8 inches) without harming the plant.

3 Make sure you don't bury the rose too deeply as the graft union (the bend or lump on the stem between the roots and branches) must be above soil level when planting is complete.

4 Don't add fertilizer at this stage but you can mulch around the plant after you have watered it in. Use well-rotted cow or poultry manure, compost, straw or any combination of these materials.

5 Water once a week if necessary (feel the soil under the mulch first and if it is moist, don't water).

6 When you see new growth, sprinkle a ration of complete plant food, rose food or slow-release fertilizer around the plant and water it in.

DON'T ENRICH THE PLANTING HOLE
It is not a good idea to enrich the soil in the rose-planting hole with compost or rotted manure. By doing so, you will create a well of fertility which will encourage the roots to stay within that area and not to spread into the surrounding soil as they must do if the rose bush is to flourish.

Pruning roses

Just about all kinds of roses will send up vigorous new shoots from the base of the plant each year. After about 3 years, each of these shoots will have grown old, and will have become less productive and vulnerable. Fewer and fewer flowers will be produced and the decrepit stems will become easy targets for various pests and diseases. By remembering to prune out the oldest branches each year, right at the base, and cutting the younger ones back to a healthy bud, you will make room for and encourage the fresh new stems that will carry masses of flowers.

Climbing roses produce many long canes from their bases and these should always be tied to their support horizontally. The flower stems will then arise all along the tied-down cane. In autumn, prune off 25–30 cm (10 inches to 1 foot) from each cane and, in winter, remove any old woody canes (note that there won't be any to remove on newly planted climbing roses). Shorten all new canes that have not yet grown long enough to be tied down. Also during winter, shorten all the lateral branches from the tied-down canes that have flowered back to the third set of leaves from their bases. Those lateral branches that have not flowered should be tied down horizontally but not shortened.

ROSE POTPOURRI

Ingredients
4 cups dried roses
4 cups dried geranium leaves
1 cinnamon stick
12 whole cloves
1 heaped teaspoon orrisroot chips
5 drops rose geranium oil
10 drops rose oil

Method
Combine all the above ingredients, then place them straight into an airtight container. Leave this mixture for a few weeks so that all the different scents have a chance to blend into a lovely rose potpourri.

DISBUD ROSES FOR BIGGER BLOOMS

For larger, prize-winning blooms, you should 'disbud' the rose bush by removing all the side buds while they are still quite small. This will allow the plant to concentrate its energy to the top bud. The end result is fewer, but larger blooms.

Hints for cutting roses

- Avoid picking flowers in the first year of growth.
- When pruning, never take more than one-third of the flower stem; this helps to keep the rose bush productive and in shape.
- Use a sharp blade and always cut to an outward-facing bud.
- Cut roses early in the morning when the plant's moisture and sugar levels are at their highest.
- Remove thorns and leaves that will be below water-level in the vase.
- After cutting, immerse the stems in warm water and cut them once more, this time under water. Add a floral preservative to help prolong the life of the blooms.

Climbers

Climbing plants can be used to cover fences or sheds, to decorate blank walls, to screen out unsightly views or cast shade from a pergola. They can also be a feature in themselves if they are grown over an ornamental arch.

Types of climbers

Climbers can be divided into three groups: clingers, twiners and scramblers.

CLINGERS Clingers, such as ivy, attach themselves with aerial roots or sucker pads, and require no further support.

TWINERS Twiners, such as clematis, for example, will twist their long, flexible stems around the support provided.

SCRAMBLING PLANTS Scrambling plants climb by using hooked thorns along their stems – rambling roses fall into this category.

Growing climbers

ASPECT Almost all climbers flower best in the sun. If you want to grow a flowering climber over a pergola, you should choose one with pendulous blossoms, such as wisteria, otherwise all the colour will be on top. If you are growing the climber on a trellis panel or a steel mesh fence, the vast bulk of the flowers will be on the sunny side. However, there are some climbers that tolerate degrees of shade. Climbers such as clematis, which are described as needing a cool root run, like cool, shaded conditions at ground level but want their heads in the sun. Heavy mulching around the root area is one way of keeping the roots cool, but this can also be achieved by growing small groundcovering plants around the base of the vine. Some climbers, including hoyas and ivy, will grow wholly in bright shade but this is not usual in the world of climbers.

SOIL Many climbers are long-lived plants but even those that are not will respond well to some good soil preparation before planting. Always check that the soil is adequately drained so that the climber's roots will not be sitting in a waterlogged hole. See pages 40–43 for more information on soil improvement and drainage.

WATER NEEDS All newly planted climbers, like any other plants, need regular watering until they are established. Check new plantings daily during summer, and water if the ground feels dry. Until the roots have made their way out into the surrounding soil, the plants are very vulnerable to water stress. Once established, they usually need a deep weekly watering during the warm months, but check the needs of individual climbers as some are more drought tolerant than others. If you mulch the soil in which climbers are growing you will both improve its fertility and conserve soil moisture.

PRUNING A GRAPEVINE
Unless the grape you have is a fruiting one, its growth can be kept in check by pruning during summer. To do this, remove any wayward, long tendrils all the way back to the secondary growth or the older wood. In this way you will keep only the healthy shoots required.

PRUNING Most climbers need pruning to keep them to their allotted spaces. Prune deciduous climbers in winter and evergreens straight after they bloom unless they flower in autumn, in which case prune in spring.

PRUNING WISTERIA

These vigorous climbers need severe cutting back. Young lateral shoots not needed for the framework of the plant are cut back annually in midwinter.

1 Start by untwining any tangled shoots and stems. These may need to be cut out in sections to prevent other shoots from being damaged.

2 Space the remaining shoots to give an even covering over as much of the support as possible. Tie into position the shoots that are to be used as part of the plant's framework.

3 Cut back long lateral growths which are not to be used as part of the framework to just above a bud, 15–20 cm (6–8 inches) from where they emerge from the stem.

CLIMBERS IN POTS

While most climbers are planted directly into the ground, they can also be grown in containers. A large container, filled with good-quality potting mix (potting compost), can be ideal, for example, when a climber is needed to cover a pergola over a paved area and it is impossible to plant into the ground. However, do consider the area you want the climber to cover in relation to the size of the pot, for the pot holds all the water and nutrients available. Will it be big enough to keep all those stems and leaves full of water? To provide cover for a pergola, you will need a very large container, and possibly several with a climber in each. All will need frequent watering and fertilizing.

The less vigorous climbers such as hoya and waxflower (*Stephanotis floribunda*) are best for pots. Such climbers are too small to cover big areas but look lovely on wall-mounted trellises or twining up a pole. In tubs, very vigorous growers, such as wisteria, are best trained as standards or free-standing shrubs rather than as climbers. A very sturdy support is needed until they become self supporting.

4 Tie as many shoots as possible into a horizontal position, to help cover the frame and to encourage flowering. Fix the ties into a figure-eight around the stem and and around the supports.

FIXING VINE EYES

Wires need to be held on a support with 10–15-cm (4–6-inch) hooks which are screwed into the boundary and are called 'vine eyes'. These hold the climber about 5 cm (2 inches) away from the support and allow air to circulate behind, helping to prevent fungal diseases, such as mildew. Always choose plastic-coated wire and tighten it in place using 'bolt tensioners' at the end of each horizontal wire. Or you can use vine eyes on their own to pin individual stems in place, tying the branches to each vine eye with soft twine.

PLANTING CLEMATIS

Before planting clematis, it is important to make sure that the potting mix (potting compost) that it is growing in is well-watered. The best way to do this is to plunge the pot into a bucket of water and let it soak.

1 Lift the pot from the water and allow any surplus water to drain away before removing the plant from its pot.

2 Dig a hole that is at least twice the size of the plant's rootball in order to encourage the new roots to grow out into the surrounding soil after planting and to flourish on its own.

3 Refill the hole, firming the soil around the new plant as the hole is filled.

4 After planting, spread out the shoots to give them as much room as possible. For long straggling shoots, position one tie about every 30 cm (1 foot) along the stem to hold the plant close to the wire so that the new growth can take hold.

5 Where possible, push the new growths into the space between the wires and the support structure – as the plant grows out towards the light it will cling to the wires. After planting and tying are complete, water the plant with at least 9 litres (2 gallons) of water to settle the soil.

Edibles

Growing your own herbs, fruit or vegetables must surely be one of the most rewarding of activities, and it's not as difficult as you might think. As long as you choose the right crops for your climate, keep the edible garden a manageable size for you, and give your plants some ongoing care, you can bite into fresh, delicious home-grown produce.

The herb garden

No garden is complete without herbs. They're invaluable in the kitchen and can also be used in cosmetics, craft arrangements and natural remedies. Even if you never use them, most make delightful garden plants, some even repelling insects.

Choosing herbs to grow

The herbs to grow are the ones you like best, those that feature in your favourite recipes or the craft activities you most like to do. You will probably need several plants of these herbs to avoid harvesting them to death. However, don't let unfamiliarity stop you from trying out a plant or two of a herb with looks or fragrance that appeal to you. If you never use them, so what?

Herb-growing tips

- Herbs grow naturally in many different soils and climates. Some thrive in extremely dry areas, others in tropical rainforests and temperate forests, so if you choose the appropriate herbs for the prevailing conditions you cannot go wrong.

- Most herbs prefer full sun and free-draining soil.

- Don't pick more than one-third of a young plant or more than half of a mature specimen at the one time. The more often you pick, the bushier and healthier herbs become.

- Don't over-fertilize – this will cause too much soft, leafy growth at the expense of essential oils.

- Many herbs grow better when planted next to other herbs, but some will struggle in the wrong combinations. For example, mint hates growing near parsley. If your herbs aren't doing well, and they are growing in the right conditions, maybe they are in with the wrong crowd.

- Snails and insects like herbs too. Be vigilant and pick off grubs by hand, and trap snails with small saucers of beer (see page 239).

- To develop full flavour, most herbs should have at least 5 hours of sunlight a day or 16 hours under fluorescent lights (placed at 5–10 cm/2–4 inches above plants).

- Always gather herbs just as they are coming into flower: this is when the flavour is the strongest.

TOP TEN HERBS

1 **Parsley** The mostly widely grown herb, growing to 45 cm (1½ feet) from a thick taproot. Rich in iron and vitamins A, B and C, it is great in salads, soups, stuffings and garnishes. Legend has it that you have to be wicked to be able to grow parsley successfully. Replace regularly as parsley has a habit of disappearing from the garden just when you think it is established for good.

2 **Chives** A perennial herb with fine, hollow leaves, it adds an onion flavour to food and can be used as a companion plant for roses.

3 **Rosemary** A woody shrub that loves full sun and dry conditions. It is the perfect herb to use with lamb.

4 **Thyme** A symbol of courage and vitality. Thyme is used in egg and cheese dishes. Grow it as an aromatic groundcover in a sunny spot.

5 **Dill** This herb is great for using in pickling, with fish and in soups. It has attractive, fine foliage and needs to be forced with lots of nitrogen-rich fertilizers.

6 **Mint** A herb that grows well in cool, moist areas, even shade, although it can become a pest if it likes the conditions too much. It can also be used in drinks and salads and for flavouring the traditional favourite, roast lamb.

7 **and 8 Marjoram** and **oregano** These closely related, strongly flavoured herbs are excellent for flavouring soups and pasta. They also make great groundcovers in a sunny spot.

9 **Sage** A close relative of ornamental salvia, with grey leaves, useful for stuffing, and for flavouring soups, veal and poultry.

10 **Basil** An extremely popular cooking herb for use in soups, tomato dishes and pasta. This herb is a summer-growing annual and needs replanting each spring. It is also an effective companion plant for tomatoes, as it repels whitefly and other pests.

HERBS FOR POTS
Some herbs are more suited to pots than others. Try basil, bay, bergamot (bee balm), chives, feverfew, lemon thyme and mint.

ORNAMENTAL HERBS WITH ATTRACTIVE FOLIAGE

Silver foliage Artichoke, cotton lavender, curry plant, *Echium*, *Euphorbia marginata*, horehound, lavender, mugwort, rue, sage, southernwood, *Thymus* 'Silver Posy' and 'Lemon Queen', wormwood

Gold foliage Ginger mint, golden box, golden lemon balm, golden marjoram, golden sage *Thymus* 'Doone Valley'

Variegated leaves *Ajuga* 'Glacier', *Salvia* 'Tricolor', variegated apple mint, variegated oregano, variegated scented geraniums

Purple leaves *Ajuga* 'Purpurea', bronze fennel, Japanese perilla, opal basil, purple sage

PLANTING A CONTROLLED MINT GARDEN

Mints have long been grown for their oil-rich leaves. However, mint is a vigorous plant and can easily take over if you don't take steps to control it.

1 Place the mint in a pot and add potting mix (potting compost).

2 Dig a hole in the garden bed and insert the pot – the lip of the pot should protrude so that the runners won't easily spread into the surrounding soil.

3 You can do the same thing with most varieties of mint, such as spearmint. Remember to mulch the pot and water well.

Herbs in pots

Most varieties grow very well in pots, which means that even if all the garden you have is an apartment balcony you can still have the pleasure of growing fresh herbs. You might even like to keep them on the kitchen windowsill so you can just reach out and harvest them as you need them – but only if the window gets the sun. It is preferable for the pots to be outside in the fresh air.

HERB OR SPICE?
Have you ever wondered what the difference is between a herb and a spice? Herbs are the leaves of plants, while spices are produced from the other parts, such as flowers, seeds and roots.

Cooking hints for herbs

- When you crush, chop or heat the leaves of a herb, an oil is released, and it is this oil that imparts flavour.

- Chop herbs with scissors, a flat knife or a mezzaluna. Chop large bunches of more robust herbs like parsley in the food processor.

- Fine herbs, such as tarragon and chives, can be left in large pieces, shredded or snipped.

- Coarse herbs such as rosemary and parsley will sometimes benefit from some fine chopping.

- Add an exotic flavour to your vinaigrette or your mayonnaise by finely chopping or pounding the herbs in a mortar and pestle, then add them to the rest of the ingredients.

- Herbs such as basil, coriander (cilantro), mint and sage will discolour if they are chopped too early before use.

- Whole leaves of mint or basil can be steeped in water to make 'tea'. Crush them gently in your hand first to release the aromatic oils.

FREEZING HERBS

1 Some herbs that are suitable for freezing are basil, borage, chives and parsley.

2 Collect tender young shoots and keep them out of direct sunlight so they stay cool and fresh before freezing.

3 Wash the herbs thoroughly in cold water before cutting them into small sections using a sharp knife or scissors. Place the chopped herbs into the compartments of an ice cube tray and fill each compartment with water, or bundle them into plastic bags. Place the herbs directly into the freezer.

Preserving herbs

AIR DRYING When air drying, remove all of the lower leaves and wipe off any moisture on the stems with paper towel. Gather together bunches of five to ten stems, and secure them with an elastic band (if you use string, the stems may fall through the loop as they dry and shrink). Hang the bunches upside down in a dark, well-ventilated place at a temperature of about 20°C (68°F)

LAVENDER ICE CREAM

In a saucepan put 8 washed and dried flower stems of English lavender with 2 cups of thick cream and one small piece of lemon rind. Heat until almost boiling, then stir in 1/2 cup sugar until dissolved. Strain through a fine sieve, then gradually pour onto 4 egg yolks, lightly whisked in a bowl. Return to the pan and stir over a low heat until the mixture is thick enough to coat the back of a spoon – do not boil. Pour into a chilled metal tray to cool. Freeze until frozen around the edge, but not in the centre. In a food processor or bowl, beat until smooth. Freeze again and repeat this process twice more. Cover with grease-proof paper and freeze. Serves 6–8.

until they are dry. The drying time will vary from days to weeks, depending on the thickness of the stems. Store them in a dark and airtight, labelled glass jar.

OVEN DRYING You can dry herbs in a slow conventional oven at 100°C (200°F/Gas 1/2), for several hours until they are dry. You can also use a microwave oven. Wrap chopped herbs loosely in paper towel and cook them for a minute at a time on High. Always have a cup of water in the microwave because herbs do not contain much moisture and the oven could be damaged.

MAKING HERB VINEGAR

Freshly picked herbs make a wonderful addition to a good white wine vinegar or cider vinegar. Use herb vinegars infused with herbs such as basil, chives, dill, fennel, mint and tarragon to add flavour to salad dressings, marinades and sauces.

1 Pick the herbs, wash them and pat them dry.

2 Loosely fill a clean jar with them, pour on enough vinegar to fill the jar, then replace the cap.

3 Store in a warm place for about 3 weeks or until the vinegar is full of flavour. For a stronger flavour, strain the vinegar and add fresh herbs.

4 When the vinegar is ready, strain it and pour into clean, attractive bottles.

5 Finally, clearly label each bottle with a non-removable label or marker.

Fresh and healthy vegetables

Nothing beats garden-fresh vegetables – and you don't need much space to grow them. Any sunny spot, even a pot, can produce a few favourites and with an area of just 4 x 4 m (13 x 13 feet) you can grow an amazing range of the freshest food there is.

Keep the garden beds accessible for planting, weeding and harvesting. Many fruits, vegetables and herbs are highly decorative, so even if you don't have room to devote a whole patch to them, you can grow them in borders with your ornamental garden plants.

Good soil is essential

Fertile, free-draining soil is essential for good crops and you'll certainly have to improve what you have. Start by removing whatever is growing on the site and then dig the soil over, breaking up clods as you go. Work in plenty of well-rotted manure and compost and a small handful of complete plant food per square metre (yard). The dug-over soil should end up dark, fine and crumbly.

If your soil is sticky, heavy clay, don't dig. Instead, build a 25-cm (10-inch) high retaining wall around the site and fill with brought-in, good-quality soil.

If your soil is very sandy it will drain well and be very easy to dig but you'll need to add lots and lots of organic matter to give it fertility and some body. In any type of soil, adding organic matter will increase its bulk, but don't worry about that. The raised soil level helps ensure good drainage. Rake over to make it level and then water the area deeply.

Choosing the right crops

Select only varieties that you do or will eat. As vegetables planted at the same time will mature at the same time, it's a good idea to plant small batches 2 or 3 weeks apart which should each yield no more than you can eat in 2 or 3 weeks. That way you will have a continuous supply without any wasteful and discouraging gluts. Few vegetables can be grown all year round, so be sure to choose varieties that are right for the season.

Growing vegetables

Vegetables can be started from either seeds or seedlings. Seeds are far cheaper and there's a much wider range of varieties available in seed packets than is

SUCCESSIVE SOWING

Successive sowing means you plant the same vegetable, successively, at several different locations, at 10–14 day intervals for a continuous harvest.

VEGETABLES FOR EVERY PURPOSE

Easy-to-grow vegetables

Bean, green	Lettuce
Beetroot (beets)	Onion
Capsicum (pepper)	Pea
Carrot	Radish
Cucumber	Squash
Garlic	Tomato

Vegetables that tolerate some shade

Cabbage	Radish
Chicory (endive)	Spinach
Lettuce	Silverbeet (Swiss chard)
Pea	

Vegetables that tolerate acid soil

Chicory (endive)	Shallot
Fennel	Sweet potato
Potato	

Vegetables you can grow in containers

Bean (bush varieties)	Pea (with a trellis)
Capsicum (pepper)	Radish
Carrot (short-rooted varieties)	Silverbeet (Swiss chard)
Cucumber (bush varieties)	Summer squash (bush varieties)
Eggplant (aubergine)	Sweet potato
Kale	Tomato
Lettuce	Watercress
Onion	

available as seedlings. You can plant a few seeds now and save the rest for later sowings and most can be sown directly where they are to grow. Do pay attention to the directions on the pack, especially the sowing depth, and you must never allow the soil to dry out while the seeds are germinating (which may take 2 weeks). When the seedlings do appear the excess seedlings have to be thinned so that the spacing between each one is correct.

Bought seedlings, being already several weeks old, are ready to eat much sooner and they can be spaced correctly from the outset. On the downside, seedlings have to be planted all at once and you may not want a dozen of that variety maturing and ready to eat all together.

Vegetables are usually grown in rows. Single rows are the traditional choice but some garden experts are now recommending wide rows, that is, three to five rows closely spaced to form one wide row. This increases the yield per square metre or yard, but be careful not to produce gluts.

PLANTING SEED POTATOES
Keep some seed potatoes until they sprout. This is called 'chitting' potato tubers and will give your plants a head start.

1 Using a spade or hoe, double dig a trench.

2 Create a flat-bottomed or V-shaped trench 15 cm (6 inch) wide.

3 Cut the seed potatoes into pieces so that each piece contains an eye.

4 Plant the pieces of potato in the trench with the eye facing upwards.

5 Backfill the trench and water in thoroughly.

Routine maintenance
All vegetables should be grown quickly, and so don't neglect to water them often – daily or even twice daily when it's hot and rainless. Frequent watering

SUCCESSION PLANTING
Succession planting means planting a second crop after you've harvested a first, in the same position, so you get two crops from the same space in just one season.

CROP ROTATION

Crop rotation is the natural way to keep your garden soil and plants healthy. Long before fungicides and pesticides came onto the scene, farmers discouraged pests and diseases by not planting the same crop or related crops in the same patch of soil 2 years in succession. Instead, they rotated their crops into different beds over a 3- or 4-year cycle. That way, those pests that fed on particular plants died when their food source was not replanted. Below is a 3-year crop rotation plan based on a vegetable garden divided into three beds.

Bed one Grow all or some of these: any bean, lettuce, peanut, any peas, silverbeet (Swiss chard), spinach, sweet corn.

Bed two Grow all or some of these: broccoli, Brussels sprouts, cabbage, cauliflower, kohlrabi, radish, turnip.

Bed three Grow all or some of these: beetroot, carrot, celery, cucumber, garlic, leek, onion, potato, tomato, zucchini (courgette).

The next year grow the contents of bed one in bed two; of bed two in bed three and of bed three in bed one. Repeat after every harvest.

will wash the nutrients out of the soil and so you should also feed the vegetables at fortnightly intervals (monthly in winter). You can use liquid or soluble fertilizer or sprinkle complete plant food alongside each row. If you have a good supply of rotted manure, using it to mulch the vegetables will eliminate the need for fertilizer and help conserve soil moisture.

Rich soil and plenty of water are magnets for weeds and these mustn't be allowed to remain. Pull or hoe them out very regularly – well before they flower and set seed. If you turn the weeds upside down and don't water for a day or two, you can leave them to rot back into the ground.

EDIBLE THINNINGS
Thinnings of many vegetables are delicious in salads, or used lightly wilted. Try beetroot, chicory (endive), radish, silverbeet (Swiss chard) and turnip.

FEED LETTUCES

Lettuces will 'bolt' into flower if they are not fed enough or if the weather is too hot. Giving the plants light side-dressings of nitrogen fertilizer or liquid feeds every 10–14 days helps.

▓ MUSHROOM KIT

Mushrooms can be grown and harvested from kits all year round.

1 To make the mushroom kit you'll need peat, lime, mushroom spore and a suitable container, such as an old wooden box, lined with plastic.

2 Moisten the peat with a little water until it feels damp all over and releases some water when you squeeze it.

3 Thoroughly blend the peat and lime together.

4 Spread the peat and lime to about 15 cm (6 inches) over the mushroom spore. The fruiting bodies, or mushrooms, will appear in about 4 weeks.

RED HOT CHILLI PEPPERS

Chillies are so versatile and there are many different types to choose from. Some varieties add pep to savoury food, some can be used in desserts and some are simply ornamental. Spring is the season for sowing chilli peppers.

Ornamental chilli This is a non-edible variety with much smaller fruits that change with maturity from green or purple to yellow, orange and scarlet. The fruits, or berries as they are often called, are extremely hot, so take care to keep pets and young children away from them.

Edible chillies Either cherry-like, conical or the typical long-pointed shape, hot chillies are eaten either green or red, and can be used fresh, pickled or dried. Dried, ground chillies can be made into cayenne pepper and paprika, while fresh chillies can be kept in oil and, after a few months, added to sauces like tabasco.

Capsicum The large-fruited, non-hot varieties are also known as bell peppers, sweet peppers and pimentos. These can be eaten unripe (green) or ripe (yellow or red), raw in salads, cooked in sauces – and they are delicious char-grilled for antipasto.

Storing commonly grown vegetables

VEGETABLE	STORAGE METHOD
Bean, broad (fava)	Freshly harvested pods will keep in the refrigerator for up to 2 weeks. Shelled beans can be dried, or preserved by bottling.
Bean, French climbing, dwarf	Do not wash the vegetable after it is harvested. Freshly picked beans will keep in the refrigerator for up to a week. Alternatively, they can be successfully bottled or pickled when mature.
Beetroot (beets)	Swollen roots of the beetroot will keep for up to 3 weeks in the refrigerator and the leaves for up to a week if stored in an airtight plastic bag. Roots can be pickled or bottled.
Broccoli	Heads will keep in the refrigerator for up to a week, after which broccoli gradually turns yellow and becomes tasteless.
Brussels sprouts	Early winter sprouts left on the stem and hung in a cool, dry place will keep for up to a month. Singly harvested, they will keep for 7–10 days in the refrigerator. In both cases, first remove all the loose and discoloured leaves from the heads and only wash the vegetables just before you are ready to use them.
Cabbage	Cabbage will keep for several weeks in the crisper compartment of the refrigerator. Pickled as sauerkraut, cabbage makes a delicious preserve.
Capsicum (pepper)	Capsicums will keep for up to a week in the refrigerator. They can also be grilled (broiled) or baked and, with the skins and seeds removed, preserved in spicy vinegars. Hot peppers can be dried successfully.
Carrot	Like potatoes, carrots can be stored in the ground in cool-winter areas. The soils must be kept well drained and not waterlogged. Leave the leafy tops attached. Once cropped, the top can be removed and the carrots stored in containers packed with dry sand. Keep stored in a cool position. Carrots will also keep crisp in the refrigerator for 4 weeks or so if protected in plastic bags. They are delicious if pickled or bottled.
Cauliflower	Heads will keep up to a week in the refrigerator.
Celery	Celery stalks will keep crisp for up to 10 days in the refrigerator. Leaves can be dried and chopped and used as a dried herb for flavouring purposes. Seeds are also dried and used in soups and pickles.
Chilli	Keep in a cool, dark place for up to a week or in a sealed container in the refrigerator for 3 weeks. Chillies are also excellent when dried.

VEGETABLE	STORAGE METHOD
Corn	Sweet corn means there is plenty of sugar in the vegetable when it is harvested. The sugar soon turns to starch and the vegetable loses a great deal of its flavour, so freshly picked corn should be eaten as soon as possible. Storing in the refrigerator for a couple of days will slow down the sugar loss. Alternatively, kernels can be stripped from the cob and then snap frozen.
Cucumber	Will keep in refrigerator for 7–10 days but at very cold temperatures the flesh will turn soft and translucent, rendering the cucumber inedible. Cucumbers are ideal for pickling, especially if the fruit is picked when young, at the 'gherkin' stage and 5–7 cm (2–2³/₄ inches) in length.
Eggplant (aubergine)	Recently cropped fruit will keep for up to 7–10 days in a cool spot. This vegetable is ideal for pickling.
Garlic	Leaves are left attached to the bulb then left to dry in clumps in full sun for a few days. On no account let bulbs get wet. Move inside if rain threatens. Hang in an open mesh bag in a dry, airy position.
Kohlrabi	Bulbs can be stored in the refrigerator for 7–10 days.
Leek	Will keep for 7–10 days in the refrigerator.
Lettuce	Will keep for 7–10 days in the crisper section of the refrigerator.
Marrow	Handle carefully and do not wash or brush skin of the fruit before usage to prevent skin damage. Marrow will keep for up to a week in the refrigerator.
Mushroom	Mushrooms can be stored in the refrigerator in paper bags (not in plastic bags or they will sweat) for around 5–7 days. They can also be dried or pickled and stored in bottles ready for use.
Onion	Store bulbs in a cool, dry place in an open-weave mesh basket to allow free air circulation around them. Do not store close to other vegetables.
Parsnip	Parsnips can be kept in the ground 2–3 months after reaching maturity in cool to cold climates, but see that beds are kept reasonably dry during this storage period. Low temperatures convert starches to sugars, giving a sweet root. Freshly cropped vegetables will keep in refrigerator for 2–3 weeks, slightly less in cool, dry cupboards where they tend to lose their firmness.
Pea	Pods keep for a short time in the refrigerator. The seeds will lose a great deal of their sugar content within a few days, converting it to starch.

Storing commonly grown vegetables

VEGETABLE	STORAGE METHOD
Potato	Keep the harvested crop in a cool, dark, airy place and exclude sunlight to prevent the skin becoming tinged with green. Young or 'new' potatoes will not store for long periods.
Pumpkin	Handle these vegetables carefully and do not wash or brush the skin of the fruit before storing. It will keep for several months in a cool, airy place or packed in boxes. Check occasionally for rotting or damage to the skin and flesh by vermin.
Radish	Radishes will keep for a week to 10 days in the crisper section of your refrigerator. Put them in a bowl of cold water to freshen them up.
Silverbeet (Swiss chard)	Silverbeet will keep for up to 2 weeks in the crisper drawer of the refrigerator but it is best eaten when freshly picked, before the leaves become limp and unattractive.
Snow pea (mangetout)	Pods keep for a short time in the refrigerator.
Spinach	Spinach leaves keep in the refrigerator for up to a week but taste much better if they are eaten immediately.
Squash (summer)	Handle carefully and do not wash or brush skin of fruit before usage to prevent skin damage. They will keep for up to a week in the refrigerator.
Sugar snap pea	Pods keep for a short time in the refrigerator. The seeds will lose a great deal of their sugar content within a few days, converting it to starch.
Sweet potato	Very easy vegetable to store but do not wash before putting away. Will keep for at least 4 months in this condition. Do not store in refrigerated conditions below 10°C (50°F).
Tomato	Tomatoes will keep between 2–4 weeks in the refrigerator although they tend to lose their flavour over long periods. They can be pulped then bottled or processed into soups and sauces and frozen. Tomatoes are best left at room temperature.
Turnip	Turnips can be kept in or out of the refrigerator.
Zucchini (courgette)	Handle carefully and do not wash or brush the skin of fruit before usage. They will keep for up to a week in the refrigerator.

DROUGHT-TOLERANT VEGETABLES

Artichoke	Chilli	Okra
Capsicum (pepper)	Corn	Tomato
Cardoon	Eggplant (aubergine)	Zucchini (courgette)

Support and protection for vegetables

Plants that have weak stems or a climbing habit will require some support. Among these are beans, cucumbers, peas and tomatoes (tall varieties). The form of support will be determined by the plant's habit. Beans, which are vigorous growers, will need 1.8-m (6-foot) canes, tied together in a teepee shape or in a row. The canes must be anchored firmly, as the weight with the full crop is considerable. Tomatoes are best supported with a single, stout bamboo cane. Tie the stem on as it grows. Cucumbers can be trained flat against a trellis panel. With any fast-growing climbing vegetables, you will need to pinch out the growing point once enough fruiting trusses have formed, and you may have to remove some of the leaves from the side shoots so that the fruit can ripen.

HARVESTING LEAFY VEGETABLES

1 Start in the morning while the weather is still cool and, with a sharp knife, cut through the stem just above ground level and trim off any damaged or dirty leaves.

2 Wash the vegetables in cold water, and leave them in there for about 30 minutes after they have been harvested. This will lower their temperature dramatically and prolong their keeping qualities.

3 Remove from the water, and allow to drain.

4 Store the vegetables in clear, open plastic bags and leave them in a cool, damp place until required.

INTERPLANTING

Interplanting means to plant more than one type of plant in the same place, in among each other. Ideally, mix early- and late-maturing types, such as carrots with cucumber.

EARTHING UP

Some vegetables will need to be earthed up in order to grow properly. Those that are grown for their blanched stems, such as celery and leeks, need to be earthed up for this purpose (although this is not the case with self-branching celery). Others that grow from side shoots below the surface of the soil, such as potatoes, must be earthed up to prevent the tubers turning green (if they do, they are toxic and must not be eaten).

BRAISED GREEN BEANS

In a large frying pan, fry 1 chopped onion with 1 crushed garlic clove in 3 tablespoons olive oil, until soft. Add 500 g (1 pound) green beans and fry. Add 400 g (13 ounces) tinned, chopped tomatoes and simmer until the beans are tender. Season well. Serves 4.

Home-grown fruit

There's nothing sweeter than home-grown fruit. However, fruiting species are generally not easy-care plants. Most need spraying, many need pruning and there are other periodic jobs that need to be done. If you know you won't get around to these chores, it's a good idea to stick to flowers and shrubs.

The biggest problem with growing your own fruit is getting the quality of produce you've come to expect from your fruit shop. You wouldn't buy small, spotted or deformed fruit but that's precisely what you'll get if you don't take the same care of your trees as commercial growers do. That means a regular program of spraying, feeding, watering and pruning. If you don't like the idea of spraying, you must be prepared to accept damaged produce. Moreover, if you don't spray, your trees could become so infested that the fruit won't be worth harvesting and the neglected trees and rotting fruit will be unsightly as well as being a source of infestation for other fruit trees in the district.

Which fruit?

Your climate will dictate which fruit you can grow. Many of the most popular fruits, such as apples, cherries, peaches, pears and raspberries need to be

SHORT OF SPACE?

In small gardens, fruit trees can be trained against sunny house walls and fences. If you grow them this way you need to pay a little more attention to pruning in order to maximize the yield. Patterns include:

- Cordon, where a single stem is grown at an angle.
- Fan, where several branches fan out from one point on the trunk.
- Espalier, where the branches are trained horizontally from the trunk.

grown in (or do best in) places with frosty or cool winters, while citrus, mangoes, papaya and others like winters that are frost-free or warmer. If you try to grow fruit well outside its preferred climate, the number and quality of the fruit you pick will be low and the plant, stressed by the conditions, will be more likely to suffer attacks from pests.

Some fruit trees grow quite big and it is always a good idea to check the ultimate height and spread of any that you buy. If space is restricted, consider planting dwarf varieties only, or perhaps espalier a plant or two against a sunny wall. Even if you have plenty of space, smaller plants can be a good idea as the yield is smaller and less likely to create a sudden glut.

Fruit-growing tips

- All fruit needs full sunshine. In shade or semi-shade your tree will not yield well. It will lack vigour and be susceptible to disease and insect attack. Protect it from strong winds and it will grow better.

- Gardeners in temperate climates are able to grow a large range of fruit trees – from apples, berries, citrus, pears and stone fruit to tropical delicacies and even nut trees.

RIPE FIGS

Figs must be allowed to ripen on the tree. They are ready for picking when the flesh yields to gentle pressure from being squeezed between your finger and thumb.

- Position is everything when it comes to fruit. Avoid planting in low-lying patches which will encourage root rot and collar rot, and improve drainage either by adding manure and gypsum to your soil or by mounding the soil to elevate the bed.

- Regular water supply is important for ensuring good cropping. Water crystals, deep weekly watering during summer and a layer of compost as a mulch will all help to conserve moisture.

- In warmer areas, select low-chill varieties which don't need cold night-time temperatures to set fruit. For example, try tropical nectarines, not cherries.

- For the home garden, select plants that are self-fertile (that is, plants that don't need another variety with which to cross-pollinate).

- Peaches and nectarines must be pruned regularly by 50 per cent of the previous year's wood in winter. This stimulates new fruiting wood.

- Apple trees and pear trees should be thinned in the centre to form an open vase shape. This lets in the sun and promotes heavy cropping.

- If growing a fruit tree on grass, leave a 1-m (3-foot) diameter circle of bare soil round the trunk. Dig a hole only slightly larger than the plant container before planting. Do not add any organic material.

Ongoing care

To consistently produce good-quality fruit, plants need plenty of water, regular feeding, and removal of pests and competing weeds. Some plants will also need pruning, usually annually but sometimes less often. Pruning not only helps to produce the best-quality fruit, it also controls the plant's size, making harvesting and spraying easier.

WATERING Watering is most important during spring, summer and early autumn and is best done weekly or fortnightly (depending on temperature and windiness). Water slowly (to avoid run-off) and water deeply. Light sprinklings are not helpful at all.

FEEDING Feed fruiting plants two or three times a year. Use complete plant food and spread it beneath and beyond the foliage canopy but away from the trunk (there are no feeding roots there). You'll need at least 2 kg (4½ pounds) per mature tree, less for youngsters, but this will depend on the tree. Or, you can feed with composted manure as this acts as a soil-improving mulch, but as it is relatively weak you will need 6–10 kg (14–22 pounds) per mature tree. Timing of feeding is given in the individual entries.

PROBLEMS Weeds compete with the fruiting plant for water, food and space, and they can harbour pests and diseases. Remove them promptly, and don't grow grass or other plants under fruit trees – keep the area clear and well mulched instead. Pests are most prevalent during the warmer months and will soon build up into a plague if left unchecked. Inspect plants often and take prompt action when insects are seen. Identify them (some may be harmless or beneficial), but if they are pests, dispose of those you can see by hand. If the numbers are too great, use an appropriate chemical spray (see page 246).

BERRY CARE TIPS

All berries should be picked when they become well coloured. They store in the refrigerator for up to 3 weeks, or you can freeze them for later. Well-grown berries will fruit for up to 20 years and produce 5 kg (11 pounds) of berries each year.

- In general, fruit is produced on year-old wood, so carefully prune and remove older, unproductive stems to ensure cropping from one year to the next, and a plant that can be harvested with ease.

- Prepare the soil before planting by adding organic matter and humus. Generous amounts of well-made compost will provide the plants with excellent nutrition. Do not add lime.

- It's best to plant out young trees during the winter months when the bushes are dormant.

- When well established, mulch generously with leaves, woodchips or sawdust to a depth of 10 cm (4 inches) to provide protection and moisture for the surface roots. Thick mulch will also suppress weeds.

- Berries should appear in the second or third year. Fertilize each tree in spring with compost or rotted manure, and foliar spray with seaweed fertilizer during the flowering period to assist with fruit set and to supply necessary trace elements.

CHILLING Some plants need a period of low temperatures or they won't fruit. This is known as their chilling requirement and is expressed in the number of hours they must be exposed to temperatures below 10°C (50°F). The figure is cumulative and does not have to be in one stretch – days can be warmer than 10°C (50°F) as long as nights are cooler.

Extending the season

If you extend the warm season you can grow plants that would not normally survive at lower temperatures. To do this, you need to insulate the plants from cold while affording them plenty of light. Cold frames and cloches are the easiest means of doing this. A greenhouse is essential for larger plants.

Cold frames

These days most cold frames are made of aluminium, being both light and inexpensive. You can usually buy these frames in flatpacks to assemble at home. They let in more light than the traditional wooden or brick cold frame, but can blow over in high winds unless firmly anchored.

Choose a size that is appropriate: if you are growing taller plants in pots, you may need to raise the sides of the cold frame on bricks. Remember that cold frames are not frost-proof, although they provide some protection. In severe weather, and depending on how frost-tender the crops are, you should provide added insulation – either bubble plastic, inserted in the frame against the sides, or hessian (burlap) sacking tied around the frame.

CITRUS CARE TIPS

- Citrus trees need regular feeding and watering. Feed them in winter with citrus fertilizer. Water first – never apply powdered fertilizer to dry soil as it can burn the roots.

- Limes and cumquats grow well in pots. The best way to feed pots is with controlled-release fertilizer as it releases as it's needed.

- Watch for citrus leaf miner, a tiny insect that causes deformity and hinders growth. Spray affected trees with white oil.

When temperatures rise, cold frames can overheat. They should have ventilation but simply propping open the lid or leaving it slightly ajar will do.

For a permanent cold frame, you need to choose an appropriate site. This should make the most of winter light, so a sunny spot is required. Lightweight aluminium frames can be moved around the garden to take advantage of the best light. This also ensures you make the best use of the soil.

Cloches

These come in various different forms, but there are two basic types. These are tent-shaped (with a pitched roof) and tunnel-shaped (with a rounded roof), plus various permutations of these two. The material used can be glass or plastic. If your cloche is tunnel-shaped or you have a row of tent cloches, remember that end pieces are necessary to prevent the wind from funnelling through the tunnel and killing off your precious plants.

You can buy cloches from garden supply stores or, if you prefer, you can make your own. Small individual cloches can be made simply from empty plastic bottles with the base cut out. These provide useful protection for small, tender plants and create an effective barrier against slugs and snails. Remember that in many instances cloches can enable you to get two crops a year out of the same plot, but you must ensure that the soil is fertilized adequately to support such a high yield.

Greenhouse tips

Greenhouses are available in various different styles and materials, each with its own advantages and drawbacks.

- Softwood frames need regular painting, western red cedar needs occasional treatment with preservative.
- Aluminium is maintenance-free.
- A traditional span roof is ideal for vegetables at ground level.
- Half-boarded or those on a low wall are more economical to heat.
- Lean-tos retain heat well.
- A conservatory is similar to a lean-to but generally more sturdy.
- A plastic walk-in tunnel is inexpensive but not a good insulator, although it is ideal for vegetables in summer.

Lawns

A healthy, lush green lawn is truly a thing of beauty. However, in order to create and maintain a good-looking lawn, you'll have to put in the necessary time and effort, as well as a bit of forward planning. If you prefer a more low-maintenance solution, the answer is to grow groundcovers instead, or even a delightful fragrant herb lawn.

Planning a lawn

A lovely lawn sets off most gardens. The amount of time and care you give a lawn depends on the type of grass you choose and the degree to which you allow it to become an obsession. There is no plant that grows as relentlessly as grass, and the time spent behind a lawnmower can be torture for some, while it is relaxing therapy for others.

A lawn means different things to different people. It may be the garden's showpiece, a foil for shrubs and flowers, a playground, a picnic spot or just groundcover. Whatever your lawn means to you, however, you will need to spend time maintaining it. When planning a lawn, consider the following:

- Don't rush into establishing your lawn: taking time to think about it and to plan it carefully will pay off in the long run.

- Before you plant, ensure the soil is well prepared and remember to consider the climate in which it will be grown, the amount of direct sun the area receives and the primary use the lawn will have.

- There are grasses that withstand heavy wear and grasses that cope with shade, but none do both, and no turf withstands constant rough wear without looking the worse for it.

- Plan your lawn area so that it will be easy to mow and maintain. Avoid sharp corners and wiggly edges, and don't have lots of small garden beds – they not only make mowing hard but spoil the effect of a sweeping lawn. Concrete mower strips make edging easier but should not be put in until after the turf has been established. If they are installed before the turf and the soil subsides even slightly, they will be more of a hindrance than a help.

DROUGHT-TOLERANT GRASSES

As summers are getting hotter in many areas, we need to look for drought-tolerant lawns that are less dependent on watering. Hybrid couches and fescues are the hardiest, while bluegrass and buffalo grasses are reasonably tolerant. The grasses to avoid include ryegrass and bent.

TIME AND MONEY
All lawns are a long-term investment in terms of both time
and money. Even if you are content to have your lawn grow
reasonably well and not be too overrun with weeds, you will
need to spend some time on maintenance. To achieve the
perfection of a velvety smooth, immaculate lawn you will
need to spend a great deal of time on it.

Choosing your grass

Lawn grasses fall into two main categories to choose from: warm-season
grasses and cool-season grasses:

WARM-SEASON GRASSES These are perennial, running grasses best suited
to frost-free areas. Many lose colour in winter but they do not die off unless
winters are severe (in which case they are inappropriate). Buffalo, couch,
Durban and kikuyu grasses are all examples of warm-season grasses.

COOL-SEASON GRASSES These grasses are mostly tufty and tussock-forming,
although there are a few that will run. They grow well in cool climates and
during the cooler months in a warm climate but they are very difficult to
maintain during hot, humid summers when they are highly prone to attack
by fungal diseases. Bent grass, fescue, Kentucky bluegrass and ryegrass are
all examples of cool-season grasses.

Preparing the ground for a new lawn

Friable, sandy loam is the best soil on which to establish turf. The soil needs
to be loose and workable to a depth of 15–25 cm (6–10 inches). The
incorporation of large quantities of organic matter into the soil well ahead of
turf laying or seed sowing will improve aeration and drainage and in sandy
soils will aid moisture retention.

If you have a clay subsoil you may need to bring in soil and cover the area to
be turfed to a depth of at least 10 cm (4 inches). Try to get a guarantee from
the soil supplier that the soil is weed-free and check that it is not full of silty
clay that will set like concrete after watering. Added soil must be well mixed
with the existing soil so that water, air and roots can penetrate easily. Heavy

clay soils are best treated with an application of gypsum at a rate of about 300 g per square metre (10^1/$_2$ oz per square yard), or if the soil is known to be very acidic, garden or agricultural lime can be applied at a rate of 100 g per square metre (3^1/$_2$ oz per square yard). Clay soils should never be cultivated when they are very wet or very dry – they need to be just moist.

Levelling the ground

There are various ways to level the ground, and the method you end up using will depend on the size of the area you wish to level. For large areas, the simplest solution is to knock wooden pegs (on which height markers have been indicated with black pen) into the ground, each to the same depth. You can then run string between the pegs at the desired height, and adjust the soil surface so that it is level with the string. If you decide to lay turf on the area rather than sow seeds, remember to allow 5 cm (2 inches) on top of the desired height to account for the thickness of the turf.

Removing weeds

The area to be turfed should be free of stones, roots and any other debris. Be sure to remove all weeds, paying particular attention to those with bulbs, as they are very hard to control once grass is established.

TOP LAWN TIPS

- Always water well before feeding.

- Mowing close to ground level increases the risk of weed invasion.

- Mow frequently, not severely – to cut down on the severity of the mowing try raising the height of the mower blades.

- Areas of lawn that experience heavy use, such as gateways and the track to the clothes line, should be aerated each year.

- Top-dressing can introduce unwanted weeds into your lawn and is best done only if your lawn is uneven.

- If your lawn has been incorrectly fed over the years the soil may have become quite acidic. A pH test (kits are available from your local nursery or garden centre) could help you diagnose this, and the problem can be rectified by an application of lime.

THE BEST TIME TO SOW LAWN SEEDS
Always make sure that you sow your lawn seeds in mild
weather on a day that isn't rainy or windy.

Adding fertilizer

The surface should be raked level and be fine and crumbly. Apply lawn starter
fertilizer or blood and bone (bonemeal) and lightly rake or water it in. Water
the area lightly for a few days before sowing seeds or laying turf so as to firm
the soil and provide a moist layer on which grass can establish.

Checking drainage

Check the drainage of the area where the lawn is to go. Dig a hole, fill it with
water and see how long it takes to drain away. If water remains in the hole for
more than 24 hours, you will have to consider laying subsoil drains or creating
a slight slope on the area. A slope of 1 in 70 will prevent wet spots.

Establishing a lawn

Lawns can be established by laying turf, which will give you an instant lawn,
or sowing seeds. The latter option is much less expensive but you will need to
keep the sown area free of any traffic for several weeks.

Turf

Turf grass is living grass that is available in machine-cut rolls. It has been
severed from most of its root system so it needs to be laid as soon as possible
after cutting. Try to ensure that the turf is delivered only when you are ready to
lay it. If there is any delay in laying, keep the rolls in a shaded place and keep
them damp. Covering them with wet hessian (burlap) helps. To lay the rolls,
place them on the prepared ground with their edges pushed firmly together. If
the ground slopes, lay the rolls across the slope, not down it, and stagger the
joins to prevent erosion.

Roll the newly laid turf to ensure good contact with the soil. Thoroughly water
the turf and keep it moist for the first 10–14 days. This may mean watering
more than once a day in hot or windy weather. After this, cut back watering to
every second day. In 3 weeks the grass should be established and watering can
be reduced to a heavy soaking once a week. Mow lightly after about 3 weeks.

■ LAYING TURF

Turf provides an almost instant effect, although it may be several weeks before it is fully stable. Ideally, turf should be laid in autumn. However, if the soil is too wet to work on in autumn, the turf can be laid in spring.

1 Starting from one corner, lay the first row of turf along a plank or garden line to get a neat, straight edge.

2 From the same corner, lay the second row at right angles to the first. Set each piece like bricks in a wall, so the joins are staggered.

3 Work from a flat board to avoid damaging the turf by walking on it, and to firm it into place. Push the joins together tightly.

4 Spread over a top-dressing of sandy loam and brush or rake it into any gaps to stop the edges from drying out and shrinking.

Seeds

For even coverage, mix lawn seeds with some dry sand or dry sawdust. Divide the area to be sown into sections, and divide the seeds into the same number of lots so that sowing can be fairly uniform. After sowing, lightly rake the seeds into the surface soil and water gently, being careful not to allow pools to form that may wash the seeds into patches. You may need to water several times a day if the weather is windy or hot. The surface must be kept just moist at all times after seeding or results will be poor.

Germination time varies with grass types and may be anywhere from 5 days to 3 weeks. Warm-season grasses are usually sown in spring or early autumn. Cool-season grasses may be sown in mid-spring or late summer. Don't mow until the grass has reached 4–5 cm (1 1/2–2 inches) high.

■ SOWING LAWN SEEDS

Seeds take a lot longer than turf to establish as a lawn, but if they are sown during the spring or autumn months they will produce a good-quality result. Also, you can select a grass seed mixture to suit your own purpose, while specialist turf has to be ordered well in advance.

1 Rake the prepared soil to form a seed bed with a fine tilth, removing any stones and using the rake to gently break up any clods of soil in the bed.

2 Mark out the area into equal squares. Weigh out the seeds for each square, then sow them evenly, half in each direction. Lightly rake.

3 Apply the seed by sowing it evenly with your hand at about knee level, to allow it to disperse evenly as it travels outwards.

Mowing the lawn

As a general rule all lawns should be high cut rather than shaved. Cutting a lawn too short weakens the grass, which gradually becomes thinner. Weeds soon take over, worn patches develop, and the ground becomes compacted before hardening in the heat of summer. When grass is left longer it will grow vigorously to form a thick, healthy turf. This in turn will allow the grass to grow much stronger as the roots will penetrate deeper into the soil.

A handy hint is never to remove more than one-third of the leaf blade at any one cutting. If grass has been allowed to grow very long it is better to reduce the height gradually rather than to cut it low with one mowing and risk scorching what is left. As winter approaches, raise the mower height to help maintain the grass through the colder months. Grass growing under trees should be cut very high, to 8–10 cm (3¼–4 inches), if it is not to die out.

PLANTING BULBS IN LAWN

The easiest way to plant bulbs in grass is by using a bulb planter. Do not plant the bulbs in regimented rows, but scatter them to achieve a natural 'wild' effect.

1 Scatter a handful of the bulbs to achieve a natural look. Plant them where they land. Twist the bulb planter into the ground to the desired depth and, still twisting, pull it out again.

2 Gently place the bulb in the hole in an upright position and do not press it down too firmly.

3 Place some of the plug around the bulb until level with the top. Add the remainder and press into place.

Bulbs for planting in grass: *Colchicum, Crocus, Ixia, Leucojum, Muscari, Narcissus, Ornithogalum, Scilla, Sparaxis* and *Triteleia*.

About lawnmowers

- The lawnmower that is most commonly used is the rotary mower. Rotary mowers have horizontal cutting blades that revolve at a high speed. The cutting height is adjustable and these types of mowers are fairly easy to maintain. If the blades are kept well set and are sharpened you get a most satisfactory cut.

- Mechanical cylinder mowers have the blades on a turning cylinder that moves against a fixed base plate. There is also a roller behind the cutting cylinder. Cutting height is adjustable but they are more complex than rotary mowers and require more regular sharpening and maintenance. These mowers do, however, give a finer and much better finish to the lawn.

- The hand cylinder mowers of today are lightweight and can be pushed with only a little effort. These types of mowers are ideal for small, flattish lawn areas and are very simple to maintain. If the blades are kept sharpened they give a good finish to the lawn and they can be used by almost anyone.

- Ride-on mowers are used only on very large expanses of grass. They come in a range of sizes to suit everything from the large private lawn to huge parks. They are, of course, expensive but are the only practical answer to very extensive lawn areas.

COMPOST CLIPPINGS

When you mow it is best to dispose of most of the clippings into your compost heap, leaving just a small amount for use as mulch. Piles of dead grass can create fungal problems.

Edging the lawn

If you have a mower strip or neat and well-spaded edges on your garden beds, edging will not prove to be too much of a chore. Well-trimmed edges can be counted upon to create a general appearance of neatness and if you have them you can sometimes get away with mowing less often. Grass tends to grow faster on the edges as there is generally no foot traffic there, and edges

MOWING IN HOT-SUMMER AREAS

Most gardeners yield to the inevitable temptation to lower the mower's blades for a 'close shave', hoping to extend the time between cuts. This is the worst thing you can do. Lift the mower blades in early summer because short grass is stressed grass, more likely to turn into a browned-off dust bowl than a bowling green. Be prepared to let your lawn grow a little taller than normal, as this helps stressed grass cope with wear and tear. Cut just a little, more frequently, and you'll be rewarded with lush growth. Make sure you keep your mower blades sharp, as torn grass edges brown quickly in the summer heat.

often get more water than the rest of the lawn from overspray when watering garden beds. After trimming your lawn edges, rake or sweep up the lawn clippings and add them to your compost heap.

Edging tools

There are several different kinds of edging tools available. String trimmers, or 'whipper snippers', do a quick job but they should never be used to trim the grass around your trees. There are many sad tales of dead or dying trees that have been accidentally ring-barked with one of these tools – and it is too late, after the event, to do anything about it. If you are using this kind of tool, make sure you are wearing strong boots and safety goggles to protect yourself and don't allow children to play in the area until the job is complete.

On a firm surface beside a path a mechanical, long-handled edging tool does a very neat job and it is easy to use. There are two types that can be operated by hand, giving you a choice of cutting head. One has a sharpened disc that rotates as it is pushed along, while the other has sharp-angled blades. A more expensive type has a petrol-driven motor. If the cutting edges of these tools are kept sharp, they are not difficult to use.

There are also some very satisfactory hand tools. Long-handled clippers are made with blades set at the vertical or horizontal. Vertically set blades are easiest to use along spaded edges of garden beds while horizontally set blades may be easier to use against a mower strip or other firm edge. Both can be used from a standing position, an advantage for anyone who finds bending or

TIDY UP
If friends are coming around and you're embarrassed about your lawn, get out the edger and mower – you'll be amazed by what a fresh haircut can do. Also, a blast with hose-on fertilizer and weedicide will smarten up your grass by midsummer.

kneeling difficult. For smaller lawns or for gardeners who are happy to work on their hands and knees there are cordless electric hand shears and the simple but very effective sheep shears.

Whichever tools you choose, make sure that you keep them clean and well sharpened. They will last twice as long, be easier to use and do the job well.

Maintaining the lawn

Once you have established a beautiful swathe of lush, green lawn, ideally you will want to keep it that way. Following are the main tasks you will need to consider in order to maintain your lawn as you like it.

Top-dressing
Top-dressing has no intrinsic benefits for the lawn and is only necessary to fill in hollows and to maintain levels. It is best done in spring or early autumn. If there is a large hollow, apply only 1–2 cm ($^1/2$–$^3/4$ inch) of top-dressing at a time and wait until the grass grows through it before applying more. Washed river sand or good-quality sandy loam is best for top-dressing.

Fertilizing
Hungry, impoverished lawns will very quickly become infested with annoying and unwanted weeds. It is good to feed your lawn at least four times a year, at the beginning of each season. However, very high-quality lawns should ideally be fertilized every 4–6 weeks during the growing season.

The trick to successful fertilizing is to use a specially formulated, slow-acting lawn food that will sink down past the shallow roots of the grass, inducing the roots to grow downwards towards the food. Use a complete lawn food, pulverized poultry manure or blood and bone (bonemeal). Don't use sulphate of ammonia as it makes the soil acidic and kills valuable earthworms.

If you have big trees growing in your lawn, the grass will need more fertilizer, as the tree will be constantly robbing nutrients from the ground around. Never apply fertilizer to dry soil as this can severely burn the grass. Feed your lawn immediately after rain or a good watering.

HOSING ON FERTILIZER

Revive a dull lawn with some hose-on seaweed fertilizer:

1 Pour seaweed concentrate into a bottle that clips onto a hose fitting.

2 Following the manufacturer's instructions on appropriate application rates, hose the fertilizer onto your lawn.

Watering

It is better to water lawns heavily and less often. Heavy, infrequent watering encourages deep rooting so that the grass is better able to withstand drought. Grass watered heavily every week or 10 days is much stronger and healthier than grass given a daily sprinkle.

Lawn sprinklers range from sophisticated underground systems with pop-up heads to simple, fixed, single-head sprinklers. There are sprinklers with rotating heads – those that have a wide wave action – and travelling sprinklers with a tractor action. Your choice will be determined by the size of the lawn and the size of your wallet. When you are using a sprinkler, keep checking that the water is soaking into the grass and not overspraying onto paths and drives or simply running off and going to waste. You should also check the level of water penetration by digging into the soil half an hour or so after you have

LAWN TIP FOR HOT AREAS

In hot areas it is wise to sprinkle your lawn with a soil-wetting agent once at the beginning of summer to help moisture penetrate. It works wonders on any type of soil and is possibly the best thing you can do for your lawn. If a lawn is watered too frequently there is no need for the grass to make good long roots – this means that shallow roots will be cooked in very hot weather and the turf will further deteriorate.

turned off the sprinkler to see how far it has soaked into the ground. Garden centres and large hardware stores keep a wide range of sprinklers so that you can select the one that suits you best.

Rolling

Many people think that regular rolling will help to produce the perfect lawn, but this is not necessarily so. When fresh turf is laid it is a good idea to roll it, especially if the area is large. Rolling newly laid turf ensures that there are no air pockets between the turf sod and the soil. It also provides good contact so that growing roots may penetrate well into the ground.

As a general maintenance procedure, however, rolling your lawn can be counter-productive. The only turf that can be rolled regularly without some damage is turf growing on a well-formed, deep sand bed. Bowling greens and golf greens have this type of base but very few home lawns are grown on a base prepared to this standard. Rolling lawns grown on average garden soils, and especially on clay-based soils, results in soil compaction and greatly reduced aeration of the soil. This is turn leads to poor root growth and it may impede water penetration as well.

Dealing with lawn problems

Despite the best of intentions and many hours of hard work, there are some common problems suffered by every lawn owner. Some of these worries can be ignored by the less fastidious gardener, but for more troublesome issues there are many techniques that can help.

Aerating compacted lawns

In compacted or poorly aerated soils, root growth, and therefore grass growth, is poor. To improve conditions, you need to get air and water into the soil. Do this by using a coring machine, but only if you have sandy soil. In clay, it is better to use a garden fork pushed into the ground and worked back and forth in rows about 10 cm (4 inches) apart. Then apply sand mixed with lime or dolomite and brush it into the holes. The lime, used at the rate of about 100 g per square metre (3^1/$_2$ oz per 3 square feet), opens the clay and improves aeration. Clay soils are best worked when slightly damp. If the soil is too wet you will create more problems and if it is too dry it will be too hard to work.

RESHAPING YOUR LAWN

Occasionally your garden beds and lawn will need reshaping because there are areas where grass is no longer thriving, or perhaps shrubs have outgrown their bed and need more room. If you need to reshape your lawn, do it in autumn so it grows back before winter.

Experiment with new shapes with a hose or length of rope, a sprinkle of lime, or turf spray paint. Once you have settled on a new shape, create a well-defined edge with a sharp spade. If you need to remove large areas of turf, consider hiring a turf cutter.

A word of warning, however: although replacing or installing edging is a suitable garden job for the cooler weather, be careful not to do this after long periods of rain, because the ground may have become soggy and the edging may shift as it dries out. In addition, turf will not tolerate wear and tear well when it is waterlogged.

SPIKING OR SCARIFYING A LAWN

For lawns growing on poorly drained or compacted soil, you need to allow more air to penetrate around the roots to let them breathe. The easiest way to do this is to make a series of puncture holes.

1 Press the tines of a hollow-tined spiker into the lawn to about 15 cm (6 inches). The next time the tines are inserted, fresh soil will displace the soil already there and leave it on the grass.

2 After an area of lawn has been spiked, the soil 'cores' can be removed and small heaps of fine topsoil can be brushed or raked into the holes left by the hollow-tined spiker.

3 As an alternative, if you have a small garden you can use a simple garden fork to make the holes over the lawn area.

Thatch

If the lawn feels soft and spongy to walk on, it is usually due to a layer of dead grass clippings or 'thatch' which has formed on the soil surface. If allowed to remain, this layer may harbour pests and diseases, as well as weed seeds, and can inhibit the penetration of water, air and fertilizer.

Bent, buffalo and kikuyu grasses are especially prone to thatching. Bent and kikuyu may need to be dethatched each year with a scarifier or vertical mower. After dethatching, rake off the excess grass, then water and fertilize the lawn.

Buffalo lawn cannot be dethatched or scalped to get rid of the thatch – you will probably kill it. To get rid of the sponginess in buffalo, sweep or hose top-dressing mixed with poultry manure, or blood and bone (bonemeal) and hydrated or slaked lime into the thatched areas of the lawn.

EARTHWORMS

Earthworms do a great job of aerating the soil, leaving little mounds on the surface. They are harmless, beneficial creatures but if you are a lawn perfectionist and want to eradicate them, fertilize the area with sulphate of ammonia.

DETHATCHING A LAWN

Once a year, usually in late winter, it is a good idea to thoroughly rake the entire lawn to remove dead grass (a process known as dethatching).

1 Use a rake to remove the thatch from your lawn. A spring-tined rake is ideal for dragging out the layers of dead material.

2 The raking must be vigorous enough to 'comb' the soil surface, so that the roots of the grass plants are broken and 'pruned' sufficiently to encourage new root growth.

3 Remove all the waste and dispose of it away from the lawn. This prevents any pests, diseases or weeds that may be in the waste infecting your lawn.

Help for sparse lawns

Lawns can become thin and sparse for a number of reasons:

- The grass has been mown too low. Constant low mowing weakens lawns severely. Warm-season grasses such as couch should be mown at 2–3 cm (3/4–1 1/4 inches), while buffalo and kikuyu grasses should not be cut at less than 4 cm (1 1/2 inches). Cool-season grasses are generally cut at 4–5 cm (1 1/2–2 inches), except for bent grass which can be cut quite a lot lower.

The wrong grass has been chosen for the site or the site conditions have changed. You may have started off with an open, sunny lawn, but with tree growth it has become too shady. Areas under trees can be dry and there is a lot of root competition as well. Soil dryness and root competition may also lead to poor water penetration. Use a commercial wetting agent on this area to ensure deep moisture penetration. If that doesn't work, put down another kind of grass in the problem area or grow groundcovers instead.

The area has been subjected to very heavy wear and tear so that the soil has become hard and compacted. To remedy this see 'Aerating compacted lawns' on page 164.

The lawn has been killed with kindness. Lawns are sometimes made sparse by over-enthusiastic watering. A well-established home lawn should not need watering more often than once a week if it is done deeply. In very hot, windy weather it may be necessary to water twice.

Grass growth may also become poor and thin if soils become too acidic. This is most often caused by regular use of sulphate of ammonia and some other high-nitrogen fertilizers. Switch to organic fertilizers and give the lawn a dressing of lime or dolomite during winter.

Mosses and fungi

Cool weather encourages moss to grow in grass, lichens to cover flagging and fungi to emerge from rotting timbers. There are two ways of dealing with this: either celebrate it as a seasonal treasure or combat it with chemicals.

CREATING A PATH

If your lawn is the main route from one part of the garden to another, such as the vegetable plot, it may be worth thinking in advance about creating a pathway through it. The best form of path to choose for lawn is one of stepping stones that are sunk slightly below the level of the grass (about 2.5 cm/1 inch below the surface). This will not only prevent the grass from wearing unattractively on your chosen route through it, but ensures that the lawn mowing is seamless, because you can simply run the mower over the stones.

Providing the drainage is adequate, the warmer weather will kill off most mosses in your lawn so you can afford to relax and take the time to look closely at these treasures and appreciate their beauty.

Many people have come to like moss so much that they will go to any lengths to get it to grow on pots and statuary. To speed up the softening effect of mosses and lichen on stonework or terracotta, smear on natural (plain) yoghurt or paint over with sour milk. You'll soon have a lovely culture of moss and mould. Use this method to make composite concrete look like stone.

If you are despairing over paths slippery with moss, apply a bit of bleach with a stiff-bristled brush; this method will remove the moss without giving your paving the 'brand new' look you'll get with water blasting.

Some fungi and toadstools can be colourful in their own right. Other fungi work in a symbiotic relationship with plant roots, and can improve plant growth. Many lawn seeds now come with fungal spore added to the seed and starter fertilizer, as it aids germination rates and significantly affects the success of the turf.

FAIRY RINGS

After rain you might find fairy rings popping up in your lawn. These are small to large circular areas of dead grass, often with 'mushrooms' appearing in a mysterious ring pattern.

The soil under the dead grass is frequently packed with white thread-like fungal growth that causes the grass to die by depriving it of water and nutrients. The fungus start growing at one point, but gradually spread out into a circle so that the rings expand each year. Often the grass in the centre of the ring is green, as it is only where the fungus is actively growing that it does any damage.

The fungi causing fairy rings are common in pastures and turfed areas, and can grow for many years unless treated. They are spread via the mushroom-like fruiting bodies, especially in warm and moist conditions.

The main treatment is to ensure adequate water penetration into the areas where the fungus is actively growing. Hollow-tine forking or coring (see page 165) the affected areas as deeply as possible will assist water penetration, as will wetting agents.

Lawn weeds

Most serious weed problems result from low mowing or occur in grass that has never established well because of shade or a poor choice of grass type. Weeds are best dealt with in spring before they set seed over summer. So, to have a lush green lawn underfoot that not only looks and feels great but also sets off the appearance of your house and garden, get out the gear and start work in spring. Keeping weeds out of your grass used to mean hours of backbreaking hand-weeding, but modern treatments have made the 'bowling-green' effect attainable for the weekend gardener.

- The first step is to feed. Hungry grass is slow to repair damage caused by pets, insect attack and active children. Liquid 'weed and feed' hose-on products will give your lawn an instant pick-me-up and help to control the majority of lawn weeds.

- Remove individual weeds by hand as soon as you can see them. You can use a small-pronged weeder to remove them and, if that sounds too hard, cheat a little and use some 'lawn sand', which is simply one part dry sand mixed with one part of sulphate of ammonia. Scatter this mixture over the weed-infested areas and within days weeds will bolt out into growth, then turn black and die.

- For heavy weed infestation, selective herbicides can be used, but before you buy one make sure you read the label to check that it is suitable for your grass and your weeds.

- After weeding and fertilizing your lawn, use a slow-release lawn food to continue giving a safe, sustained supply of nutrients over the rest of the growing season.

Lawn pests

CATERPILLARS Grass-eating caterpillars feed on the leaves and may defoliate the lawn. In late summer and autumn they appear, feeding mostly at night and then hiding during the day. Control these pests by spraying them with a proprietary caterpillar killer or a lawn grub killer.

LEATHERJACKET OR CURL GRUBS These fat, creamy white grubs are most destructive during summer and autumn. Lawns growing under stress and lawns that are mown too often and too severely are most affected. Birds feeding on a lawn can indicate the presence of the grubs. Other telltale signs are yellow patches on the lawn which are caused by the grubs eating the grass roots. Spray the lawn with a lawn grub killer as directed on the pack.

ANTS Ants make nests in dry areas. If the lawn is badly disrupted by ant nests, treat it with a commercial wetting agent, followed by a deep watering. Ants are not a threat to turf, just their nests.

FUNGAL LEAF SPOT
This mostly occurs in areas with warm, humid summers. Whole areas of turf may appear yellowish, but close examination of the leaf blades shows brownish or reddish spots. Spray with a lawn fungicide and don't water for 48 hours afterwards.

Bare patches

Nothing disfigures a lawn more than bare patches, especially at gateways and other entranceways. To fix this problem you can use either a hollow-tined roller or a strong fork to work lots of holes deep into the soil to allow air and water to penetrate. You might also find aerating shoes at your local hardware store or garden centre (see 'Aerating compacted lawns' on page 164). Areas of lawn that experience heavy use should be aerated several times a year. Whichever method you use, be sure to scatter coarse, dry sand over the surface before watering – this will flow into the holes to provide long-lasting drainage plugs.

REPAIRING A LAWN

Damaged lawns can be repaired by simply replacing a section of turf, or by lifting and turning the damaged turf, or by re-sowing the problem area.

1   Using a spade, remove the damaged section of lawn. Cut an area the same size as the new piece of turf.

2   Lay the new section of turf down by hand, being very careful to butt it flush with the adjacent edges.

3   Tamp down the new turf well, and water it in thoroughly. Avoid walking on the area for a few days.

A SPRING MAKEOVER FOR YOUR LAWN

With the arrival of warm weather, your grass has a surge of energy and makes new growth. Spring is therefore an ideal time to smother weeds and repair bare patches. Lightly fork over worn areas and mossy patches in the lawn, then give the whole area a vigorous raking over. An application of a 'weed and feed' product that clicks onto your hose will work wonders. Finally, sow some lawn seed or plant runners in any bare areas – and the job is done.

Groundcovers

Are your weekends spent slaving away maintaining the lawn and weeding garden beds? If you don't need a putting green, why not replant your lawn with an easier alternative? Give away this backbreaking work forever – once the warm spring weather arrives, plant groundcovers, the plants that lie low and let you lie in.

Groundcovers are living carpets. They squeeze out the weeds, cover bare soil so that weed seeds can't find space to germinate and are less demanding than lawn in terms of water, fertilizer and labour requirements. They provide the seasonal interest, flowers and coloured foliage that turf lacks. If you plant in spring these carpet-like plants will be well established by summer so that your garden will need very little attention next year. This garden is so much more restful than one that requires a great deal of labour for its upkeep.

In nature there is always something growing on the ground under trees and shrubs, except where there is very deep leaf litter or the light levels are very low (as on the floors of rainforests, which are clear of growth). In the garden, groundcovers can perform this function too as there are many that will tolerate some shade, while even in the sun groundcovers can be much more attractive than grass. They're especially useful on sloping ground where mowing would be difficult or even dangerous, or where erosion is likely.

Choosing groundcovers

As with any other type of plant, it is important to choose the right groundcover for the aspect, climate, soil and space available in your garden.

Some groundcovers can grow very vigorously, and can even become invasive, especially in moist, shady spots, while other mat-forming plants are more sedate and much easier to keep confined.

Groundcovers come in a number of different forms, including running, trailing or mat-forming plants, or those with simple horizontal growth. Some climbing plants not usually thought of as groundcovers, such as ivy, can be used as such and, in fact, any low plant can serve this purpose.

Before selecting a groundcover, mentally divide your garden into low-, mild- and high-traffic zones. Low-traffic areas, such as garden beds where weed seeds rather than trampling feet are likely to be a problem, can look great with the addition of rock cress (*Arabis*), bergenia, bugle flower (*Ajuga reptans*), campanula, catmint, dianthus, Japanese windflower, lamb's ear, snow-in-summer and verbena. All will thrive depending on the position.

GROUNDCOVERS FOR SHADE

Ajuga reptans (bugle flower)

Arabis caucasica 'Variegata' (rock cress)

Asarum europaeum (wild ginger)

Astilbe chinensis 'Pumila'

Campanula poscharskyana

Convallaria majalis (lily of the valley)

Epimedium (barrenwort)

Hedera helix (ivy)

Lamium maculatum (dead nettle)

Nepeta hederaceae 'Variegata' (catmint)

Vinca minor (periwinkle)

GROUNDCOVERS FOR SUN

Cerastium tomentosum (snow in summer)

Erigeron (fleabane, babies' tears)

Gazania sp. (African daisy)

Grevillea 'Sunkissed Waters'

Hypericum calycinum (rose of Sharon)

Juniperus horizontalis (creeping juniper)

Mentha sp. (mint)

Stachys byzantina (lamb's ear)

Thymus sp. (thyme)

Trachelospermum jasminoides 'Tricolour' (star jasmine)

LAWN SUBSTITUTES

For a green lawn look try these great alternatives to grass:

- Hot, dry areas: *Coprosma* x *kirkii*, creeping boobialla (*Myoporum parvifolium*), gazania, lippia (*Phyla nodiflora*)

- Under trees: bugle flower (*Ajuga reptans*), catmint (*Nepeta hederacea*), clivea, common yarrow (*Achillea millefolium*), mondo grass, spider plant (*Chlorophytum*), turf lily (*Liriope*)

- Sunny spot groundcovers: aurora daisy (*Arctotis* sp.), Canberra grass (*Scleranthus biflorus*), *Grevillea poorinda* 'Royal Mantle', veldt

- Shady spot groundcovers: isotoma, ivy, kidney weed (*Dichondra repens*), pratia, periwinkle (*Vinca minor*)

High-traffic zones, such as those where children play, call for tough plants. In these difficult areas only the toughest plants will survive. Choose from hardy selections such as fleabane or babies' tears (*Erigeron*) or mini mondo grass.

Planting groundcovers

Most groundcovers are long-term plantings and so it is worth putting some effort into good soil preparation and weeding. As there may be root competition for the new plantings it is a good idea to dig in some well-decayed manure or compost a few weeks before planting, but be careful not to build up the soil level under the canopies of existing trees more than a few centimetres or inches and don't pile soil or mulch up around their trunks. Raising the soil level under trees can suffocate the surface roots and lead to the eventual death of the tree.

DEALING WITH DOGS!

If your dog urinates on the lawn, the grass can die in that spot and nasty brown patches appear. The best idea is to saturate the affected patch with water for 5–10 minutes after the dog has urinated. If you're not quick enough and the grass dies, you might just have to replace a patch of lawn with a plug, or overseed it (see 'Repairing a lawn' on page 170).

Weed eradication is most important as it is very frustrating to find weeds coming up through the groundcover. Most weeds will not be entirely eliminated in one go. Dig out or spot-spray with glyphosate the weeds you can see. Once they are dead, fork over the soil again, water it and wait for the next crop of weeds to emerge. If you do this two or three times before you plant the groundcover you have a good chance of reducing the bank of weed seeds lying dormant in the ground. Perennial weeds, such as onion weed and oxalis, which arise from bulbs, will need a determined effort to eradicate them.

Early care

The ultimate spread of a groundcover will depend on the type of plant, soil conditions and the degree of care received. The spacing of individual plants at planting time will depend on how fast you need the cover and how large you

PLANT AN AROMATIC CARPET

Surround yourself with fragrant flowers and aromatic foliage to give you pleasure all year round. Low-growing, matting plants release their delightful fragrance when crushed underfoot, and provide an unusual cover for many situations. Here are just some ideas:

- A path of pennyroyal (*Mentha pulegium*)
- Carpeting patches of thyme between stepping stones
- Corsican mint as a groundcover in a fernery
- A herbal carpet in an area too small for a mower
- A cover of bugle flower where lawn will not tolerate shade
- A spectacular carpet of thyme on a sunny bank (there are many sorts to choose from: creeping thyme comes in pink, crimson and white-flowered varieties, and there are also golden, orange peel-scented and variegated leaf types)
- A fragrant chamomile footrest beneath the garden seat

Choose herbs that grow with stolons or runners so that they can cover any bare patches which may develop. The mint family will grow where drainage is poor or there is dappled shade, otherwise most herbs like good drainage and plenty of sun.

expect each plant to grow. Most spreading groundcovers grow quite quickly and it is not a good idea to overplant an area simply to get an instant effect – the plants will have nowhere to grow.

It is important to mulch areas of bare soil between plants while they are growing as this helps prevent further weed growth and also helps feed the plants and condition the soil. Most groundcovering plants will need regular feeding during the growing season because of the intense root competition that exists if they are planted under mature trees and shrubs. Regular, deep watering is needed too, especially in the early stages when the roots will be concentrated at the surface and likely to dry out.

Later maintenance
Once established, most groundcovers need little maintenance beyond shearing off spent flower stems or trimming to confine them to a specific area. If they grow too tall, shear them at the start of the growing season or after blooming to reduce their height. When weeds appear through the groundcover, pull them out promptly or paint them with herbicide, being careful not to get any of the chemical on the groundcover. Don't let weeds flower and set seed.

A FRAGRANT THYME LAWN
Consider growing a lawn of thyme – what a luxury of luxuries to stretch out on a fragrant thyme lawn, with the crushed leaves releasing their subtle perfume.

GROW A CHAMOMILE LAWN
Chamomile (*Anthemis nobilis*) is best known for its herbal properties but it can be grown as a lawn substitute. The fine, feathery, fragrant leaves and its creeping habit make a soft groundcover. It is not suitable for regular foot traffic but it can be walked on occasionally or sat on. Chamomile flowers in summer (the flowers are used to make chamomile tea) and this may not suit everyone's idea of lawn. If it is mown to remove the flowers, a very high setting must be used on the mower to avoid damaging the plants. A non-flowering variety, 'Treneague', is the most suitable for lawn use but this is often hard to obtain. Chamomile is suitable for most climates, except the

USING GROUNDCOVERS IN ROCKERIES

Many groundcovers are suitable for rockeries but it's essential to choose the right plant. For a small rockery, choose plants that won't outgrow their space too soon, but in large rockeries you may have room for more spreading groundcovers. Rockery plants should not need moist soil, as the soil in rockeries tends to dry out fairly quickly.

Establishing a rockery

A rockery is best sited on sloping ground where it looks natural and rocks can be bedded into the ground. This means that drainage is rapid. Rockeries in full sun can also be hot as rocks store heat.

Choose rocks that come from the area to blend in with the site, but never remove rocks from the natural environment. In most areas rock should be available from building and swimming pool excavations. If they look too raw, mix some cow manure and water to a thin slurry and paint it over the rock – it will hasten the weathered look.

Rock gardens are high-maintenance areas, at least in their early years, so it is important to remove weeds and grasses from the area before planting. Make sure that grasses are not able to invade the area later, even if this means putting some kind of physical barrier into the soil. Roots of trees adjacent to the area may also invade once the soil has been loosened and new plants are regularly watered and fed.

Selecting plants

For a hot, dry rockery choose colourful ice plant (*Lampranthus*), creeping thyme, gazania or Moroccan glory vine (*Convolvulus sabiatus*). A rockery in semi-shade could be planted with campanula, bugle flower and mondo grass. In cool zones there is a great choice, including alpine phlox, lithospermum, maiden pinks, rock cress, snow-in-summer and thrift. In warm areas grow catmint, dampiera, ox-eye chamomile, roses and verbena. If you have a very large area to cover choose creeping boobialla, prostrate rosemary, shore juniper or trailing lantana.

Aim for harmony of colour or repeat the same plant in different parts of the rockery. For instance, if you use a grey-foliaged plant, it may look better to place two or three together in different parts of the planting. An attractive display may be made using only one type of plant, such as gazania, in many colours. An exception to this would be a rockery planted with a collection of true alpine plants, many of which are cold-climate miniature treasures. (See also pages 176 and 207.)

tropics, but in cold areas it becomes dormant in winter. It prefers a sunny position and well-drained soil and can be grown from seed sown in spring or by division of the roots of established plants.

1 Start by raking level the site for the lawn, firstly using a large rake to break down any large clods of earth, then a smaller rake with fine teeth to leave a smooth, even finish. Finally, remove any stones.

2 Mark out the area using a garden line or string. This will mark the boundaries of the lawn and act as a planting guide for the position of the outer rows of plants.

3 Start by putting the outer row of plants in first, gently firming each plant into the soil to help them to establish quickly – loose planting often leads to poor establishment due to drying out.

4 Plants that have lots of stems and form clumps can be carefully divided into two sections to increase the number of plants and help the lawn to thicken up quickly.

5 If the plants have become long and straggly, clip them over with a pair of garden shears. They will need to be trimmed anyway and it is much easier to do this while they are still in the nursery tray. Also, clipping will make them branch from the base and spread along the soil.

6 Once planting is over and all the plants are firmed into position, water the whole area with several cans of water or use a hose.

MONDO GRASS

Perhaps the most popular groundcovering grass of all is the Japanese mondo grass. The common name is actually a misnomer as it belongs to the lily family but has grassy foliage. It is fantastic en masse and can be used effectively as a turf substitute in the shade (especially the 'mini' cultivar) or as a border between beds and pathways. White, variegated, giant, dwarf and black cultivars make the long-lived mondo grass (*Ophiopogon* sp.) a very useful ornamental for foliage contrasts. Mondo lawns and long borders can be expensive to put in, however. Try and buy the smallest pots you can, as it clumps up quickly once planted.

Containers

Containers make it possible for everyone to have a garden, even people who have only a tiny suburban courtyard or a balcony. And even if you don't have these, you can always have a few indoor potted plants. Remember though that container plants will rely heavily on you to supply all the water and nutrients they require.

A container garden

Containers open up a whole world of possibilities to the gardener. Owners of small gardens – including roof-top gardens – can plant up pots that take advantage of even the tiniest space and can be moved around as required. Whatever the size of your garden, you can use containers to decorate every surface, including walls and steps.

You can grow almost anything in containers, from edible plants to water-loving ones. You can even grow trees, but obviously they will never reach the size they would in an unrestricted situation, simply because you would not be able to provide a container large enough for the full root span. While you are not obliged to opt for slow-growing trees and shrubs, it will mean less work for you if you do. Likewise, selecting drought-tolerant plants will cut down on the chore of watering in summer in warmer areas. Make sure that the potting mix (potting compost) that you choose is suitable for the plants you want to grow, and obviously choose waterproof containers for any water plants.

Container materials

PLASTIC POTS Plastic pots are cheap, durable, colourful and they are light to move around. Some look convincingly like terracotta. Being waterproof, they don't dry out as fast as porous containers and therefore they require less-frequent watering and feeding. On the downside, they don't always look very good in your yard, especially if you have a wide mix of colours and styles. If you are using a lot of plastic pots, stick to the one colour.

ROSES FOR CONTAINERS
Any rose can be grown in a pot, as long as it has adequate fertilizer, water and a rich soil, but some roses have been bred with dwarf root systems, making them ideal for containers. Look for these patio roses at your local nursery. Mini roses are easily grown in tubs and look beautiful in posies. White 'Popcorn', a soft lime called 'Green Ice', a ginger called 'Teddy Bear' and lolly pink 'China Doll' are tiny and delightful roses.

TIMBER CONTAINERS Wooden pots usually look attractive, especially in rustic or natural-style gardens. Like plastic, they are waterproof and generally look best if you stick with the one style throughout the garden. The disadvantages of wood include its weight and the fact that it will eventually rot, although that does take a long time to happen. If you choose wooden pots, raise them off the ground to minimize rotting on the bottom.

CERAMIC POTS Ceramic pots include unglazed terracotta and glazed earthenware or stoneware. Terracotta pots are the traditional containers for plants and they will look good in most settings. Glazed pots are more showy in themselves but remember to be careful in your choice because patterned pots will introduce a particular style that may or may not suit the rest of your garden. Glazed pots and unglazed stoneware containers are waterproof, but terracotta pots are porous. This means that they can dry out fast and always require more frequent watering than waterproof pots. More frequent watering means more frequent feeding because watering will wash nutrients out of the soil with every application. The disadvantages of ceramic pots include their fragility, weight and cost but they may still be right for you.

CONCRETE CONTAINERS Because of their weight, concrete pots are best placed permanently. They vary in size, some being big enough for quite large trees, and when sold with a matching pedestal can make an impressive focal point in the garden. Weight and cost (especially the cost of the bigger, more decorative pots) are the main disadvantages of concrete.

Be creative with containers

A workable planting scheme for a container garden requires a lot of forethought. The pots themselves will play a major role in the final appearance of the garden, and you need to pay attention to container shape, texture and colour to ensure that your chosen pots complement the textures, forms and colours of the plants. If you can create interesting contrasts or subtle harmonies, it will beautifully unite the display. Look for plants with exciting forms – deeply coloured, interestingly shaped foliage, for example – and match these to plain or patterned containers in good-quality materials. You can also paint or decorate your containers to provide interest, but try to keep the patterns clean and simple. In fact, simplicity is the key to success.

Containers are wonderful for changing the mood or defining the style of a specific area of your garden. You could use metallic pots to achieve a futuristic look, or traditional wooden trugs to convey a cottage-garden atmosphere. Why not use one or two really large specimens in containers to create a stunning focal point? Try architectural plants, such as agaves and phormiums, or even a cactus or succulent if your climate will allow. Use a simple flower or pot colour that coordinates with your garden furniture to enhance a seating area, or even introduce some fragrant plants to enjoy as you relax, such as fragrant nicotianas and lavenders and sweet scented-leaved pelargoniums.

Container size

■ Container size varies from huge half-barrels to tiny wall pots, and you can find both free-standing containers and those specially constructed to hang from either walls or brackets.

TREES AND SHRUBS SUITABLE FOR CONTAINERS

Virtually any plant can be potted up in a container, as long as it is treated properly. Proper care for container-grown plants will vary according to the particular type of plant it is. Some plants may require root pruning every few years (which is, in effect, 'bonsaiing'), and some may need taking cores of the rootball out each year. This can be an arduous task when heavy pots or moist potting mix (potting compost) is involved. It's better to choose dwarf or smaller-growing specimens. Some examples include:

Fruit trees: 'Ballerina' apples, cumquat, 'Honey Murcott' mandarin, 'Pictazee', 'Nectazee', flying dragon rootstock on citrus or smaller growers such as 'Lisbon' and 'Meyer' lemon.

Screening trees: dwarf lillypillies, small pittosporums ('Silver Pillar' and 'Tom Thumb'), smaller sasanqua camellias such as 'Mine-no-yuki' and 'Yuletide', yew

Flowering shrubs: dwarf apricot oleander, dwarf duranta ('Blue Boy' or 'Towards 2000'), Elfin series daisies, 'Little Lianne' and 'Petite' sasanqua camellias, Japanese barberry, *Weigela florida*

YEAR-ROUND INTEREST

Plan your container garden so you have some permanent structure (in the form of a containerized evergreen, for example) with a changing seasonal display of flowering container plants to add the high notes.

- For the more imaginative gardener, containers can be custom made or adapted from all kinds of household relics, from cast-off old metal colanders to bread bins (boxes) and even old boots.

- If you are planning to grow edible plants in containers, then the depth will be an important consideration, since plants that are eaten for their roots will need space in which to develop them.

- Some purpose-made containers can be purchased for specific plants. For example, strawberry planters make economical use of space. These consist of a series of small planting pockets in the sides of a terracotta container, which allows you to grow the maximum yield of strawberries from a container taking up relatively little floor space. Growing bags containing specially formulated potting mix (potting compost) for tomatoes and other nutrient-hungry plants are another option but, in a small garden where the container is clearly visible from the house, it might be more aesthetically pleasing to disguise these plastic bags with a wooden surround or something similar.

- Weight is an important consideration for balconies and roof terraces. You not only have the weight of the container to take into account but also that of its contents, which will be particularly heavy when wet. Before using weighty containers on a balcony or roof terrace, you should consult a structural engineer for advice on what to purchase and where to site it.

- If you have very little room to spare in your garden, you can use hanging baskets or wall pots, suspending them on heavy-duty brackets or hooks and pulleys. Remember, however, that these containers tend to dry out extremely quickly due to the large surface area that is exposed, and will require watering twice a day in very hot weather – be realistic and ask yourself if you will do this.

CONTAINER SHAPE
Deep containers are ideal for growing large bulbs, perennials, shrubs and small trees. Wide, shallow containers are useful for small-growing plants, such as alpines, annuals, slow-growing succulents and many small herbs.

Positioning pots

- Groups of pots can be used for greater impact or to conceal an unattractive feature and pots of different shapes and sizes can look better when grouped together. They're easier to water as well.

- The arrangement and placement of plants is important in achieving an overall, pleasant effect. Pots should be uniform, all terracotta or all plastic, not a mixture. Place them in some logical order, perhaps grouped around a large central pot with a feature plant.

- For quick, temporary added height, upturn an empty pot and use it as a pedestal for another.

- Raised pots look great when trailing plants are allowed to cascade from them and one beautiful, well-planted urn on its own can make a stunning focal point of your garden.

MOVING A HEAVY CONTAINER

When you have to move heavy containers around, you must plan ahead. You need a helper, and you will also require a heavy-duty board and several dowels – lengths of narrow-gauge piping are ideal. With the aid of your helper, slide the container onto the piece of board, the front end of which has been raised using a length of piping or dowelling. Then slide a second piece of piping under the front end of the board, and roll the board with the container on it forward, placing a third piece of piping under the front end. Pick up the first piece of piping as it emerges from the tail-end of the board, and insert it at the front. In this way, you can roll the board, with the heavy container on it, over level surfaces.

- With a little thought you can place pots with great effect. For a classically formal look, position a matched pair of pots either side of an entrance, a pathway or a stairway.

- Add interest and beauty to a pergola by festooning it with hanging baskets bursting with flower and foliage.

- When choosing plants, take into account the conditions in your garden. A sunny, exposed site may be perfect for a Tuscan theme with bright red geraniums in terracotta troughs.

- Window boxes or troughs are the ideal shape for those long narrow spaces in smaller gardens.

- To add height, grow potted standard bougainvilleas which flower for months and love the basking sun, as do potted gerberas.

- For a damp and shady position, try planting begonias, dwarf arum lilies, ferns and impatiens.

Avoid mishaps

Wind and weight are two important factors to consider when placing pots. Even quite heavy pots can be blown over by strong winds, especially if the plants within them are large, and you should consider what effect this would have should it happen. If the result would be dangerous, don't put the pot there – sooner or later a gale is a certainty. Hanging baskets are also severely affected by winds and they should never be placed in exposed locations.

Pots or baskets are heavy – and they are doubly so when watered. Always satisfy yourself that your deck, pergola or balcony will hold the wetted weight of the pots or baskets you have in mind.

GROUPING CONTAINERS

If you vary the size and scale of the containers, you will improve the look of the planting. Staggered planting heights allows you to appreciate the flowers of all the plants, which might otherwise be hidden behind each other. You can also purchase containers in a range of sizes, and several sizes in a single material usually look good together.

Choosing a potting mix

A good-quality potting mix (potting compost) is essential for success with container-grown plants. Modern potting mixes are clean, weed free and disease free. They are designed to be fast draining yet moisture retentive and, because they are relatively lightweight, they make it easier to move pots from place to place. There are specially formulated mixes for plants with specific needs, such as African violets, cacti and orchids, and there are mixes for specific uses, such as hanging baskets or terracotta pots. These latter types of mixes are more moisture retentive to suit their particular purposes.

▓ PREPARING POTTING MIX (POTTING COMPOST)

Container-grown plants benefit from a good, loam-based potting mix mixed with a measured amount of base fertilizer to keep the plants in good condition. It is easy to mix this up yourself.

1 Loam-based mixes consist of 7 parts sterilized loam, 3 parts medium-grade sphagnum moss peat, 2 parts grit or sharp sand, plus a base fertilizer.

2 Start by mixing the loam, peat and sand together until they form a uniform mixture. Then draw the resulting mix into a heap.

3 Sprinkle the base fertilizer over the heap and mix it in until there is no visible trace of the fertilizer – the potting mix is now ready for use.

Drainage

Good-sized drainage holes are vital in pots as even the best potting mix (potting compost) won't drain if there is nowhere for the water to go. Avoid pots with drainage holes that seem too small for the volume of soil they will contain, unless you have the tools to drill more.

Never let pots stand in saucers of water. The practice is most dangerous with small pots as these are easily waterlogged from below, but it is not good with any pot. Good drainage is so important you should raise the pot on bricks or stones or on pot feet which can be bought at nurseries. This allows excess water to run away freely, minimizes water damage to the bottom of the pot and the surface on which it is standing, and deprives critters of a place to live.

Potting a plant

You should always match the size of the pot to the size of the plants it will contain but, of course, plants grow and you should allow for this up to a point. If you are planting annuals from seedlings that are 5–6 cm (2–2½ inches) tall but will soon grow into flowers 40 cm (16 inches) tall, choose a pot suitable for the mature size, not for the seedlings. But if you are planting a slower-growing shrub or tree it is better to pot it up progressively each year or two than to plant it into a very large pot at the outset. Small plants in big pots cannot use all the food and water available.

Potting mixes (potting composts) contain little or no plant foods and you should blend some into the mix at planting time. The amount to mix in varies with the size of the pot and the type of fertilizer but in all cases it is better to be stingy rather than generous, as too much fertilizer can kill plants. Not enough fertilizer just makes them grow slowly and is easily rectified. If you are unsure about this, read the directions on the fertilizer packets before buying one. The one to choose should explain how much to use in various sized pots. Slow-release fertilizers are a good choice for containers so long as you remember when to replenish them.

Plants should be potted so that they are no deeper in the new potting mix than they were in the pot in which you bought them. To achieve this, partially fill the pot with potting mix and then sit the plant in it, adding or subtracting

ROOTBALL RATIO

Always try to choose the right pot for the plant and keep everything in proportion. The best container size for any plant is one that is roughly 5 cm (2 inches) larger than the diameter of the rootball, and roughly 10 cm (4 inches) deeper. After a year or so, depending on the speed of growth, you will need to repot the plant into a larger container. Planting a small plant in a much larger pot is not a time-saving solution, as plants do best in pots only slightly larger than their rootball. Check regularly that the roots are not growing through the base of the pot. If they are, it is time to repot.

potting mix until the level is right. Unpot the plant and check that the roots are not spiralling around the base. If they are, gently tease them out. You can trim any that are overlong using sharp, very clean secateurs. Place the plant into the new pot and fill it with potting mix to within 2 cm (3/4 inch) of the rim. Gently firm the mix around the roots but don't compact it or you will lose aeration. Water the plant in well.

■ PLANTING SWEET PEAS ON A WIGWAM IN A CONTAINER

1 Select a suitable container. If required, make some drainage holes in the base. Line the base with sheets of newspaper to stop the potting mix (potting compost) running out of the drainage holes. The paper will rot away within a couple of weeks.

2 When the potting mix is up to the required level, place the wigwam in a central position, pushing it lightly into the potting mix. Using a piece of wood as a scribe, mark a line in the potting mix around the outside of the wigwam legs.

3 Remove the wigwam frame and gently plant the sweet peas into the potting mix. Replace the wigwam frame in its original position and press firmly into place and sit back and wait for the display.

Watering

Don't water potted plants according to a schedule, say, every 3 days. Instead, water when they need it. This will be much more often in summer than in winter, in sun than in shade, in porous than in waterproof pots, in smaller than in bigger pots, in a windy than in a sheltered spot. Test whether or not water is needed by feeling down into the top 3 cm (1 1/4 inches) of soil. If it is quite moist, don't water, but if it feels just damp, it is time to water. You'll soon get to know the watering needs of your different pots and won't have to feel the soil. Generally speaking, don't allow the potting mix (potting compost) to go completely dry as it can then be quite difficult to re-wet.

Over time, potting mixes can become water repellent and no matter how much water you apply, most runs straight through to the bottom and the mix remains dry (although the surface looks wet). To test for this, water thoroughly

EMERGENCY RESUSCITATION

If you do allow a plant to dry out to the point of wilting, you can usually revive it by giving it a long, deep drink. Plunge the entire container into water, and hold it down so that the potting mix (potting compost) is beneath the water level. Keep the container submerged until any air bubbles stop rising. Remove and allow to drain. The plant should then revive.

and then, after the water has drained from the surface, scratch the soil in several places. If it is dry underneath, apply a wetting agent but do use strictly as directed as overdoses can be toxic to plants. Reapply as needed.

Fertilizing

Only apply fertilizer during the growing season for that particular plant. Most plants grow more vigorously from spring to mid-autumn and do not need fertilizer from the end of summer until early spring, but they do need water. Some plants are dormant or at their least active during the hot months of the year and grow during autumn, winter and early spring. These should be fed in autumn and in early winter.

Always apply fertilizer to moist potting mix (potting compost), never to dry, and always give it at the recommended rates – more fertilizer does not equal more growth; it makes the soil salty and toxic. Slow-release fertilizers can be very convenient but you can also use complete plant food or soluble or liquid fertilizers, and it is a good idea to alternate between types.

Remember, the more you water, the more fertilizer you will have to apply and the best way to give it is in frequent but very small doses, say, a quarter strength four times as often.

Fertilizer release rates

It is useful to know the rate your fertilizer will release into the soil. Release rates are as follows: slow-release 14–21 days; liquid feed 5–7 days; quick-act- ing 7–10 days; and foliar feed 3–4 days.

Potting on

Plants that have outgrown their containers should be potted on (or potted up) and this is best done either in early spring or in early autumn.

- Check your plant by removing it from the pot and examining the roots. If you see much more white (roots) than black (soil) then it's definitely time to pot on. Roots protruding strongly from drainage holes is another good sign that potting on has become necessary.

- To pot on, remove the plant from its existing pot. If you don't water it for a few days beforehand, then the soil will shrink and the process will be much easier.

- Tease out any compacted or spiralling roots and trim any that are overlong and not healthy looking.

- Replant into fresh potting mix (potting compost) placed in a pot that is one size bigger than the existing pot.

- Water in well and place the plant in a bright but shady and sheltered spot for a week to recover before moving it to its original location.

- If the plant in question is already in a large enough pot, then scrape away about 3 cm (1¼ inches) of potting mix from all around and replace the plant in its original container with fresh potting mix poured around the outside. This is not potting up, but is called repotting as it does not involve a bigger pot.

SUPPORTING SMALLER CONTAINER PLANTS

Supports benefit not only containerized climbers but also some weak-stemmed annuals and perennials. Perennials such as daisies and pelargoniums will benefit from some form of ring staking and the plants will eventually bush out, disguising the ring support. Other useful staking devices are twiggy bits of brushwood inserted around the perimeter of a container, or metal-linked stakes that fit together to provide a containing girdle for your plants.

CONTAINER MAINTENANCE TIPS

■ Group your containers together to reduce the impact of exposure and to make watering easier.

■ Regularly pinch back shoots to help your plants bush out.

■ Deadheading is essential for most flowering plants because this helps to maintain flowering over a long period of time.

Edible container plants

Some edibles are easier to grow in containers than others. Avoid cauliflower, celery, corn, parsnip, pea and swede (rutabaga). Among the easiest are the many beans, beetroot, carrot, cucumber, lettuce, potato, radish, spring onion (green onion), silverbeet (Swiss chard), tomato and zucchini (courgette). Capsicum (pepper), chilli and eggplant (aubergine) are not difficult but require warmer temperatures and more sun to ripen. Blueberries, raspberries and strawberries are among the easiest edibles to grow in a container. Tree fruit such as 'multigraft' apple trees that have two or three varieties on one dwarf rootstock are ideal.

Hanging baskets

Every home, no matter how big or small, has a transition zone, the space that connects the inside of the house to the outside. Whether it's a porch, a veranda or a large pergola-covered entertaining area, this area can be the most exciting and enjoyable of all.

One of the most satisfying gardening activities is to grow plants in a hanging basket in this space linking the house with the garden. Choose annuals filled with seasonal colour or a mass planting of mixed seedlings, pendulous plants and even grow a small shrub or two.

In recent years many improvements have been made to moisture-retaining products, potting mixes (potting composts) and fertilizers, making growing plants in baskets a much easier pastime. Water crystals act like a reservoir in

THE YEAR-ROUND EDIBLE CONTAINER GARDEN

Summer Beetroot (beet), capsicum (pepper), carrots, chillies, cucumber, eggplant (aubergine), French beans, lettuce, potatoes, raspberries, runner beans, silverbeet (Swiss chard) strawberries, tomatoes, zucchini (courgette)

Autumn Apples, carrots, blackberries, raspberries (autumn fruiting), runner beans

Winter Lamb's lettuce

Spring Radish, spring onion (green onion)

the soil by holding water in the basket. Potting mixes (potting composts) have improved enormously with premium-quality ingredients being used. Controlled, slow-release fertilizer means plants need only be fed once every 9 months, and generally that's sufficient for the life of the display. There is even a product that, when watered onto the soil, draws the moisture down into the mix.

Top-quality potting mixes contain all three of these products – slow-release fertilizer, water crystals and wetting agents.

There is also a new product for lining the inside of the basket. In the old days bark was removed from trees under licence and used for lining the insides of hanging baskets. New liners made from sheep wool waste are environmentally friendly and recycle an excellent product.

Baskets are very decorative in courtyards and balconies but they dry out quickly, particularly in hot, windy weather. As a rule, the bigger the basket the less often you'll have to water and the more scope there will be in plant selection, so choose something at least 30 cm (1 foot) wide or larger.

■ PLANTING A HANGING BASKET

1 Start by placing the basket upright in the top of a large empty plant pot. This will make sure the basket is held in position so that it can be filled without rolling about on the work surface. Line the lower half of the basket with a layer of sphagnum moss.

2 Press this layer of moss firmly against the wire mesh of the basket, before adding potting mix (potting compost) to the same level as the moss lining. Add water-retaining granules (follow manufacturer's instructions).

3 Insert the first layer of plants into the basket by passing the roots of the plants through the mesh around the sides of the basket, and resting the roots on the potting mix, with the tops of the plants hanging down the outside of the basket.

4 Line the top half of the basket with a layer of sphagnum moss before adding potting mix, but make sure you leave sufficient space for planting. Insert the second layer of plants into the basket.

5 Position the largest plants in the centre of the basket, but angle them slightly outwards towards the rim of the basket.

6 Add smaller plants around the edge of the basket, before topping up the potting mix so that it is almost level with the rim, but leave room for watering. Hang the basket in its desired position and water thoroughly.

Window boxes

It is a good idea to plan any window box planting to create displays that will look attractive at different times of the year. In spring, small bulbs are ideal: crocuses and dwarf narcissus, combined with early primulas; in summer, try dwarf cosmos or dwarf wallflowers with miniature lavenders and thymes; in early autumn, dwarf chrysanthemums can replace the wallflowers, and in winter replant the window box with heathers and hardy cyclamen.

Indoor plants

Air inside the home and workplace is polluted by fumes given off by electricals such as computers, TVs and microwaves, and by chemically treated surfaces, paints and plastics. Apart from producing oxygen, plants absorb poisonous gases, especially those produced by plastic furniture and synthetic carpets.

The best thing you can do for your indoor environment is to bring a little of the outdoors inside. 'Plantscaping' your home need not be boring. There are many imaginative ways to decorate with plants.

How to choose an indoor plant

First, consider what you want your plant to do. Ask yourself the following:

1 Should the plant feature flowers or foliage? Which would you prefer?

2 Should it stay small, grow tall, wide or narrow? For example, choose small plants for a kitchen windowsill and choose tall ones with striking foliage for your large living areas.

3 Should it be mobile? Sometimes smaller plants that can be spelled outdoors in the shade for half the time make ideal table-setting decorations.

Positioning indoor plants

Few plants grow in the dark so don't expect your house plants to perform miracles. Give them a little sunlight and as much daylight as possible. Avoid draughts, as nothing dries out a pot faster than a windy corridor or foyer. Finally, indoor plants often have the odd flower when you first buy them, but remember that the nursery has grown the plants in perfect conditions, so be satisfied if you have happy, healthy leaves; flowers are a bonus.

Growing conditions for indoor plants

Will your plant have to endure heating in winter, poor light or air-conditioning? Because there is no such thing as a naturally occurring indoor plant, we have to mimic outdoor conditions. Most indoor plants grow best in bright positions. However, if you have a full-sun position inside, try to keep your plants some distance from the glass. This can really heat up and will actually cause sunburn (dead, brown patches on leaves) or bleaching (whole leaf turns yellow or white). Cacti, croton, ixora, mother-in-law's tongue and succulents should be content in such a spot, provided they are given regular drinks.

Hardy plants — such as aglaonema, aspidistra, cissus, fatsia, kentia palms, madonna lilies and philodendrons — will tolerate low levels of light, provided you don't let them get too wet. If the spot you have in mind is really terrible, try rotating your plants every 2–3 weeks. Take them outside into a shady area, or let them stand in the rain occasionally.

Tips for growing indoor plants

HYGIENE To keep your plants thriving, wipe over the leaves with white oil or a moistened tissue to remove the dust and grime that clogs up the pores.

SUCCULENTS FOR POTS

In future, we will be forced to look at plants that need less water and lawns, the biggest guzzlers of water, will be too costly to maintain. Xerophytic, or drought-tolerant, plants that store water in their stems, leaves or roots will be the answer.

Water conservation has started to put succulents in the spotlight. For half a century they have been hidden in the collector's corner, or growing quietly on Grandma's porch, but now they've hit the big time.

Succulents are unquestionably tough, surviving hot summers without water and in 50°C (122°F) heat, but they can also be breathtakingly beautiful. The symmetrical, statuesque and organic shapes look like an underwater landscape, yet they can survive on a dribble of water.

Their colour range is fabulous as well: black, purple, grey, pink, red, gold, green and combinations of the lot can be found in their stunning foliage. They look like very glamorous plants and yet they are as tough as old boots, provided you give them adequate drainage. Succulents are perfect for pots, coastal landscapes, gravel gardens, as accent plants, and yes, for Grandma's front porch!

REPOTTING The best time to repot is when the plant will recover quickly. This is usually just after flowering, or at the beginning of spring. Vigorous plants will need repotting every year, while slower plants such as rhapis palms will last for 3–4 years. If the leaves on your indoor plant are getting smaller, appear to wilt soon after watering, or if roots appear on the surface, then your plant needs to be in a bigger pot. Quality potting mixes (potting composts) contain slow-release fertilizer and water crystals and will save you maintenance time. If you're using a cheaper mix, don't forget the plants are totally dependent on you for food, so give them some 9-month slow-release granular fertilizer.

FEEDING Plants need feeding if their leaves yellow, start to show chlorosis (yellowing between the veins) or have different leaf sizes. For optimum health, vigour and flowering, try a two-pronged approach to feeding. First use a slow-release fertilizer designed specifically for indoor plants. For maximum benefit throughout the warmer weather, apply this in late winter. Second, apply a diluted

LIGHT REQUIREMENTS

Plants for bright light areas

Asparagus 'fern', begonia, cacti and succulents, chenille plant (*Acalypha hispida*), cocos palm, croton (*Codiaeum variegatum*), flamingo flower (*Anthurium* sp.), flowering plants such as African violet, Cape primrose, cyclamen and gloxinia, lipstick plant (*Aeschynanthus* sp.), ponytail palm (*Beaucarnea recurvata*), pygmy date palm (*Phoenix roebelinii*), zebra plant (*Aphelandra squarrosa*)

Plants for medium light areas

Aluminium plant (*Pilea cadierei*), arrowleaf, bromeliad, devil's ivy (*Epipremnum aureum*), dumb cane (*Dieffenbachia*), dwarf umbrella tree, fiddle leaf fig (*Ficus lyrata*), happy plant (*Dracaena fragrans*), Japanese aralia (*Fatsia japonica*), Norfolk Island pine (*Araucaria heterophylla*), peacock plant (*Calathea makoyana*), prayer plant (*Maranta* sp.)

Plants for low light areas and air-conditioned rooms

Aglaonema, arrowhead (*Syngonium podophyllum* – plain green forms), aspidistra, fruit salad plant (*Monstera deliciosa*), kentia palm (*Howea forsteriana*), madonna lily, parlour palm, peace lily (*Spathiphyllum* sp.), philodendron, rhapis palm, rubber plant (*Ficus elastica*), tree ivy (x *Fatshedera lizei*)

liquid fertilizer every fortnight during the growing season. Good organic fertilizers can be applied to the soil and used as a foliage spray. Use foliar feeding at half strength, and apply it more frequently than you otherwise would.

WATERING Indoor plants need regular watering, especially during the warmer weather, or when you are applying liquid fertilizer. Although water is vitally important, don't make the mistake of sitting plants in saucers. This may rot the roots, and should only be done if absolutely necessary, such as with African violets or ferns. Sit the pots on pebbles or on stands to keep the roots free draining. It is also better to water house plants thoroughly once a week than to sprinkle them daily. They can even be taken outside for a hose down. And, most importantly, appoint someone in your house or workplace to do the watering. More indoor plants die from overwatering than from all the other causes combined. In winter, when plants are not growing, don't water until

WHILE YOU'RE AWAY

Holidays can spell disaster for your pots. Move them into a shady corner, and group them with the toughest on the perimeter. This will be easier to water and reduce the impact of wind and sun.

Use saucers, but remove them when you return. Any precious plants should be put in a moist area of the garden, and dug back up later.

Put indoor plants in the bath on an old towel, water them thoroughly, and leave the tap dripping slightly. Make sure the plug is not in place. Water will get sucked up along the towel to the rootballs, and the room will stay cool and moist, further protecting your plants. (Note that this may not be an appropriate method if you live in an area with water restrictions.)

Or you could use a wick watering system. See 'Wick watering' below.

the surface becomes dry. If hot, dry air from heaters is a problem, try misting the leaves rather than watering the soil. An atomizer can also be handy in air-conditioned rooms throughout summer. The best way to tell if your indoor plants are dry is to use your finger. If the soil is dry at the second knuckle, then you need to water. Try not to let them wilt between waterings, as this will put them under stress and make them prone to disease attack.

WICK WATERING

1 Wrap a cotton wick around the rootball so that a length of wick is left at the bottom of the plant. Feed this end through one of the drainage holes in a plastic pot and place the plant in the pot.

2 Put the plant and pot in a decorative container, then place the end of the wick in a small container of water.

Pot-plant pests

The most common indoor plant pest is mealy bug. Almost anything is a good meal for this fuzzy, cotton wool-like pest. The best method of control is to keep plant leaves clean and spray or soak the rootball in a pesticide solution.

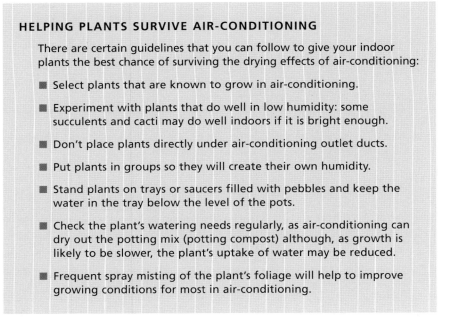

HELPING PLANTS SURVIVE AIR-CONDITIONING

There are certain guidelines that you can follow to give your indoor plants the best chance of surviving the drying effects of air-conditioning:

- Select plants that are known to grow in air-conditioning.

- Experiment with plants that do well in low humidity: some succulents and cacti may do well indoors if it is bright enough.

- Don't place plants directly under air-conditioning outlet ducts.

- Put plants in groups so they will create their own humidity.

- Stand plants on trays or saucers filled with pebbles and keep the water in the tray below the level of the pots.

- Check the plant's watering needs regularly, as air-conditioning can dry out the potting mix (potting compost) although, as growth is likely to be slower, the plant's uptake of water may be reduced.

- Frequent spray misting of the plant's foliage will help to improve growing conditions for most in air-conditioning.

The other problem is scale. This looks like small, raised lumps, and can be white or dark brown. Scale particularly affects palms, and can be treated by white oil.

Sometimes indoor plants can get spider mites, a particularly difficult pest to control. Mites thrive in dry, dusty conditions, so regular spells outside and a good hosing will help to prevent attack from these pests.

PLANTING A TERRARIUM

For planting a terrarium, choose from African violets, miniature lilies, parlour palms, small-leaved madonna lilies and plants with contrasting foliage, such as hypoestes, nerve plant and peperomia.

1 Select a suitable vessel. Anything with a sealable top can be used, although the larger the better. You can purchase terrarium glass jars from your nursery, or use your imagination — cookie jars make perfect containers. You will need peat-based mix or some African violet potting mix (potting compost), some charcoal, paper towel and sphagnum moss.

2 Place a layer of charcoal on the bottom of the jar. This helps absorb wastes and cleanses the sealed environment.

3 Fit a cloth, such as some paper towel, to stop the potting mix from working its way into the charcoal layer.

4 Add a small amount of peat-based mix or African violet potting mix.

5 Gently plant your chosen plant, firmly tamping it down around the roots.

6 Decorate the top with a layer or two of pebbles or sphagnum moss.

7 Water in gently, washing down any dirty leaves. Replace the lid.

AFRICAN VIOLETS

African violets need lots of light and year-round feeding. Stand each plant on a container of water with added drops of African violet fertilizer. Make a hole in the lid of the container and pass a cotton wick from the pot, through the drainage hole and into the water container. This way it's impossible to over-water! Alternatively, just run the wick between the plant and a small container of water.

Each year African violets need repotting. Don't be tempted to plant them in large pots as they tend to get waterlogged and die.

Propagation

African violets are easily propagated using leaf cuttings. Place the leaf stalk (petiole) into a peaty mix and keep it moist. New leaves grow from the stalk, feeding off the original leaf until they develop roots. Pot them into small pots and place them on a sunny windowsill.

Propagating African violets from leaf cuttings

1 Dampen some peatmoss.

2 Spread the peatmoss in a seedling tray.

3 Pluck some leaves from an African violet and plant the petiole (leaf stalk) in the peatmoss.

4 Keep moist till roots appear, then plant out.

Features

A well-chosen and positioned garden feature can bring your garden alive, whether it is a water feature, a rockery, an arbour, or simply a stepping stone pathway or garden seat. And, of course, most garden features have a practical function, too, from providing access from A to B, to allowing you to sit down, create shade or provide privacy.

Water features

Water has long been considered desirable in gardens, both for its appearance and the opportunity it offers to grow an exciting new class of plants – the aquatics. Water plants can bring a pond to life and include some of the loveliest flowers of all.

Planning a water feature

The allure and charm of a water feature is one of summer's underrated garden pleasures. The water reflects the light and cools the air, and moving water creates a peaceful ambience. A water feature can be as simple as a shallow bowl with duckweed or as elaborate as a naturalistic pool with cascades.

Many people would love to have a water feature, but the thought of pumps, digging huge holes, liners and the like is off-putting. Installing a pond in the garden can also be a fairly expensive business. However, there is an easier and cheaper way to do this – simply use a very large pot.

Large containers such as wine barrels, stone and glazed pots, old coppers and plastic terracotta lookalikes are all suitable candidates for a water feature in a pot. Really, you can use any large container, but you'll have to make sure the inside is waterproofed with a sealant and any drainage holes are plugged up (a cork, sealant, epoxy putty or silica gel will all do the job).

Most flowering aquatic plants like the sun, with lilies, lotus, Louisiana iris, reeds and water poppies all suited to a sunny spot. If you have a shady area, try arum lilies (either the green, white or dwarf types), dwarf papyrus, sedge, syngonium and water lettuce.

You can also use floating pond weeds, but these grow quickly, so either stock fish to keep them in check, or regularly scoop out the excess to allow the other plants the growing room they need.

Ponds take time to install but, once established, require less work than garden beds. Position is everything. Avoid placing ponds under trees, as overhanging branches will drop leaves and flowers that upset the biological balance of the water. When selecting water plants, take the position of your water feature into consideration. Arum lilies cope well with shade, are long flowering and

FISH AND WILDLIFE

Fish are useful for controlling mosquitoes. Goldfish are most popular for ponds and are readily available. If the pond is sufficiently large, it will generate food for fish, so even if you forget to feed them they won't starve. Frogs reduce insect numbers as well.

Overstocking with fish can lead to polluted water, algae and the spread of disease. For every square metre (square yard) of pond surface, allow a maximum of ten fish about 5–8 cm (2–3¼ inches) long. Unless you are willing to install filtration systems, avoid koi carp. They make a lot of mess that will need to be cleaned up.

Some larger gardens will have enough room for a wildlife pond which can be a haven for birds, tortoises, native fish, frogs and insects. It also should include a central island to act as a refuge from feral animals. Try to allow room near the pond for a planting of grasses and native plants which provide food for the wildlife the pond will attract.

evergreen. Waterlilies don't like splashing water, need lots of sun and die down over winter, making them suitable for bigger ponds and still pools. Small pots may only take a handful of floating weed.

Planting water plants

Apart from floating plants, which are simply thrown in, aquatics are usually planted in pots of good soil and then submerged. That way they are easier to lift and divide when growth becomes congested and they are easy to remove if you find they are spreading too much and taking over the pond.

If the plants are to be grown in deep water, it's always a good idea to submerge the pots in stages, gradually setting them deeper and deeper as the

PLANTING TIP

A good idea when planting aquatic plants in a pot into a water feature is to place a layer of gravel or shingle on the surface of the potting mix (potting compost). This prevents soil particles from floating to the water's surface.

SAFETY ISSUES

Water seems to have a magnetic quality for young children so safety around a pond is extremely important. There are some essential points to remember if the two are definitely going to meet.

- Choose features that can be covered with a grid and cobbles such as wall fountains, springs and cascades. If you decide to construct a raised pool then build the walls at least 60 cm (2 feet) high and overhang coping stones. If you really want an open water feature, make sure that the garden you create has a separated area with childproof locks or catches. As an extra precaution use a grid just under the water's surface, strong enough to support a child's weight.

- Make pool edges as safe as possible by using heavy marginal planting to create a physical barrier. A shallow, gravel-edged feature is safe because of the gentle gradients to the edge.

- Natural stone is prone to slime up and become slippery, whereas concrete flags have a much better grip and so are much more appropriate. You should also check that edging stones or copings are well laid and mortared to prevent tipping.

plants grow. If you lay 2–3 cm (³/4–1¹/4 inches) of gravel on top of the soil in the pots you will minimize discolouration of the water by the soil and also prevent fish from stirring up mud.

Use pots without drain holes or line them with plastic to prevent soil washing into the water. Remember, full-sized waterlilies and lotus need at least 45 cm (1¹/2 feet) of water above them, measured from the top of the pot.

PLANTING WATERLILIES

1 Fill a large pot with good soil enriched with well-rotted cow manure. Hollow out a planting hole for the roots.

2 Set the roots into the hole with the crown just above the soil level. Try to work quickly to avoid drying out the roots.

3 Hold the plant in position and bury the roots with soil. If the soil isn't fertile, add some slow-release fertilizer.

POND POSITION

Position your pond so it will get sunlight for at least half a day. This gives most aquatic plants a good chance to thrive.

4 Sprinkle 2 cm (3/4 inch) of sand or fine gravel on top of the pot to keep the soil in place and stop the water from discolouring.

5 Sink the lily into the water a little at a time, lowering it at weekly intervals over about 6 weeks to 45 cm (1 1/2 feet).

6 Blooms appear in less than 6 weeks as a rule and should continue to appear right throughout the summer months.

CLEANING A POND

Your pond should be cleaned annually to remove debris that has accumulated throughout the year. Before cleaning, any beneficial creatures, such as water snails, should be placed in a shallow tray of water so that they can be re-introduced to the pond once you have finished.

1 Empty the pond by baling it out with a bucket, or pump the water out by attaching a hose to the pump outlet.

2 Remove any soil, mud and plant debris from the bottom of the pond. Place any pond animals in a tray of water.

3 Using a stiff brush, give the sides of the pond a thorough clean, applying a weak solution of sterilizing agent.

4 Clean the sides and bottom of the pond with a powerful jet of water. Allow the pond surface to dry, then refill.

LENGTHENING THE LIFE OF THE FILTER

A homemade solution to provide extra protection for the water pump and reduce the risk of any damage, and extend the life of the pond filter, is to simply cover the filter intake with a section cut from a pair of old pantihose. The fine mesh of the pantihose will block many of the particles that might otherwise block the filter. Remember, however, that the filter may still need cleaning regularly if the water in your pond gets particularly dirty.

PLANTS FOR PONDS

Aquatic plants
Common nardoo (*Marsilea drummondii*)
Floating fairy fern (*Azolla caroliniana*)
Louisiana iris (*Iris laevigata*)
Sacred lotus (*Nelumbo nucifera*)
Water fern (*Ceratopteris thalictroides*)
Waterlily (*Nymphaea* sp.)
Water poppy (*Hydrocleys nymphoides*)
Water snowflake (*Nymphoides indica*)
Yellow bladderwort (*Utricularia australis*)

Plants for pond edges
Arum lily (*Calla palustris*)
Calla lily (*Zantedeschia aethiopica*)
Canna (*Canna* sp.)
Cardinal flower (*Lobelia cardinalis*)
Marsh marigold (*Caltha palustris*)
Pickerel weed (*Pontederia cordata*)
Purple looseleaf (*Lythrum salicaria*)
Sweet flag (*Acorus calamus*)
Water mint (*Mentha aquatica*)

KEEP PONDS CLEAN WITH AQUATICS

To keep the water clear and clean in your ponds, you keep the sunlight off with a layer of floating aquatics that cover 70 per cent of the surface area. This will stop the algae from growing and keep your fish fed with their greens when you're away. Fairy moss (azolla) and other plants do the job.

BOG GARDENS

In poorly drained areas where the soil is constantly saturated, most deep-rooted shrubs and trees can't get enough air. Some herbaceous plants – such as arum lily, astilbe, canna, *Gunnera* and primula – will flourish here, and look great teamed with ferns, sedges and some bamboos that also thrive in these conditions. Other plants that like damp conditions include alder, birch, bottlebrush, marsh marigold, mountain ash, swamp cypress, tea tree and willow.

It always makes good sense to work with the conditions, so why not create a bog garden? They can look fantastic and display a wide range of flowering perennials that can be difficult to grow in hot dry climates.

Rockeries

A rockery is a garden composed of stones that are arranged both to show off the beauty of the stone and to create a habitat and ecological niche for plants that grow among rocks in the wild, or that require perfect drainage. Rockeries can house specialist collections of desert plants or other arid-zone plants such as cacti or succulents. In cooler climates, prostrate alpine plants are often used.

CONSTRUCT A ROCKERY

1 If you are building on a level or nearly flat surface, start by excavating the desired area, then add a layer of rock rubble for drainage. Cover this with garden soil to create a slightly mounded base.

2 Start from ground level and work upwards, laying each of the rocks at the same angle – in nature rocks follow a single plane. In a natural rocky outcrop generally two-thirds of each rock is buried in the soil.

3 Backfill the first line of rocks with soil, then set the next layer back a short distance to create a slight slope. Repeat this process for each of the outcrops. Allow some of the rocks to protrude from the soil at odd angles; this will give the rockery a more irregular, natural appearance.

4 You can use good garden loam for rockeries, but as most rockery plants need sharp or excellent drainage a special growing medium usually gives better results. A mix comprising equal parts of coarse sand or fine gravel, leaf mould or peatmoss, and good garden loam works best.

SUITABLE PLANTS FOR ROCKERIES

Alpine phlox (*Phlox condensata*)	Pink (*Dianthus deltoides*)
Campanula	Rock cress (*Arabis* sp.)
Echeveria	Rock rose (*Helianthemum* sp.)
Edelweiss (*Leontopodium* sp.)	Rockfoil (*Saxifraga* sp.)
Erica	Snow in summer (*Cerastium tomentosum*)
Gromwell (*Lithodora diffusa*)	Stone cress (*Aethionema* sp.)
Houseleek (*Sempervivum* sp.)	Stonecrop (*Sedum* sp.)

Hedges and screens

High walls cost a lot of money to build properly and they can make a home look and feel like a jail. However, a hedge or living screen has none of those faults. It's relatively cheap and easy to grow, looks beautiful, provides privacy, shade and shelter and improves the general look of your home.

▦ HOW TO PLANT A HEDGE IN FIVE EASY STEPS

1 For a really straight hedge, mark out the run with a string line. Dig a trench at least 60 cm (2 feet) wide and 45 cm (1½ feet) deep.

2 Incorporate lots of well-rotted manure or compost. Now fill the trench back in, which will create a small mound where the trench was.

3 Using a measuring stick, space out all the plants. Dig a hole for each plant, add some slow-release fertilizer and water crystals, and plant, making sure that the soil has not built up around the trunks.

4 Tip-prune all new shoots to encourage branching. Do this for the first few seasons so that a well-branched, thick-to-the-base hedge is developed.

5 Trim to shape. Secateurs allow precise cutting and are suitable for pruning conifers and all informal hedges. They are ideal for the initial shaping of young plants. For larger plants in an informal hedge, use shears: they produce the best shape and leave the foliage unmarked. Shears can also be used to trim formal hedges for a perfect, but time-consuming cut, or you can use electric hedge trimmers in slow even cuts.

Good hedging plants

EVERGREENS

- Box (*Buxus*) to 1.2 m (4 feet)
- *Elaeagnus* x *ebbingei* to 3 m (10 feet)
- *Escallonia* to 2.4 m (8 feet)
- Holly (*Ilex*) to 4 m (13 feet)
- *Prunus laurocerasus* to 3 m (10 feet)
- *Viburnus tinus* to 2.4 m (8 feet)
- Yew (*Taxus baccata*) to 6 m (20 feet)

DECIDUOUS

- *Berberis thunbergii* to 1.2 m (4 feet)
- *Carpinus betulus* to 6 m (20 feet)
- Copper beech (*Fagus sylvatica* Atropurpurea Group) to 6 m (20 feet)
- *Fuchsia magellanica* to 1.5 m (5 feet)
- Hawthorn (*Crataegus monogyna*) to 3 m (10 feet)
- *Rosa rugosa* to 1.5 m (5 feet)

GOOD CHOICES FOR HEDGES AND SCREENS

For clipped, formal hedges, evergreens with small leaves are the best. For informal hedges, which do not have neat outlines – and can be maintained with only one or two clippings a year – plants that are densely foliaged all the way to the ground are ideal. Screens, on the other hand, can be created with any plants that will achieve the desired result. Evergreen shrubs are, generally speaking, the best for screening. However, do remember that even the mass of bare branches on deciduous shrubs can have a dramatic effect and provide some screening, and they let in the wonderful winter sun.

The plants listed below will all make successful hedges and screens.

Formal hedge Cherry laurel, cypress, dwarf honeysuckle, English and Japanese box, juniper, lavender, photinia, rosemary, sasanqua camellia and spindle bush.

Informal hedge Abelia, cotoneaster, firethorn, grevillea, hibiscus, laurustinus, melaleuca, oleander, orange jessamine, plumbago, rhododendron and wattle.

Tropical mixed screen Ashanti blood, calliandra, cardinal's hat plant, Fijian fire plant, flag bush, hibiscus, oleander, red tassel flower and tibouchina.

Temperate mixed screen Abelia, banksia, bottlebrush, Chinese lantern, escallonia, honey myrtle, Indian hawthorn, oleander and olive.

Cool mixed screen Euonymus, holly, Japanese oleaster, mock orange, osmanthus, rhododendron and weigela.

TOPIARY

Topiary is the ancient art of training and pruning plants into specific shapes. Many topiary shapes are geometric, with triangles or pyramids, cones and squares being widely used. Balls and cylinders are other very popular shapes, but plants can be trained to resemble animals and birds or even architectural features – the only thing that will limit you when doing topiary is your imagination!

There is a wider variety of plants that are used for topiary today but even so, the most popular are the traditional plants with fine, dense foliage, such as the dependable cypress and juniper, and small-leaved evergreens such as box, privet and small-leaved honeysuckle.

Top topiary tips

■ Careful and painstaking clipping has to be done throughout the growing season. This input of time and skill is reflected in the high price charged for a good specimen bought from the nursery.

■ If you decide to try some topiary for yourself, choose a young plant in vigorous growth and start with a simple shape. When you need to remove foliage right back to the trunk or stem, young plants will heal their scars less noticeably than older plants. Sometimes unwanted foliage can be simply rubbed off with the fingers, especially if it is young regrowth from a previous cut.

■ At first you will need to do all your careful shaping with secateurs but once you begin to achieve the shape you want, the plant can be shorn over quickly, little and often, using a pair of shears.

■ For your first efforts, try to select a plant that is already vaguely the same shape that you want to eventually achieve. For example, if you would like a triangular or pyramidal shape, look for a plant that is wide at the base and has a natural taper towards its top. For rounded or ball shapes, choose a multi-stemmed shrub that already has a good overall cover of foliage.

■ Don't make your first shaping too severe as you need to see how quickly new growth comes away from the cuts.

■ If you are adventurous enough to try a layered look straight away, you will need to select a tree or shrub specimen that has foliage almost all the way to soil level and which is at least 75 cm (2^1/2 feet) high. Otherwise you won't have enough to work with.

Hedge-pruning tips

- Always prune any sort of hedge so that the top is slightly narrower than the bottom. This gives the lower growth enough light to live. This is especially important with conifers, such as cypresses, because once that lower growth dies, it usually does not regenerate.

- Conifers should be pruned little and often, and never into older wood, as many of them will not reshoot from bare wood.

- With a formal hedge, pruning should begin early in the plant's life. Cut the vertical growth severely as soon as the plant is established. This encourages low branching and you should continue to trim the plants to shape as they grow. It will take several years for them to reach the desired height but if you let them grow to the height you want first, and then start shaping, you may never achieve the density of foliage necessary for good privacy and you will almost certainly have bare branches at the base.

- Even informal hedges and screens should be sheared lightly at least once a year. Begin doing this right from the start and the plant will develop an attractive, thick, bushy habit.

- In mild climates, maintenance pruning can be done at almost any time of year (but remember, quick regrowth is desirable). In frosty areas, don't prune after midsummer – this allows the existing growth to harden off, which means that it will not be damaged by frost.

- Most hedges can be managed with secateurs and sharp hand-hedging shears. If, however, you have big hedges to maintain, a powered hedge clipper will make the job quicker and easier.

Paths and surfaces

Paths are such basic structures, and are so integral to enjoying a garden, that we often take them for granted. Because of their importance, pathways should always be included in your initial garden design process.

Tips for planning and designing paths

- Always keep in mind that paths also have the practical function of providing access from one part of the garden to another.

MOSAICS FOR GRIP
Mosaics of pebbles and ceramics laid in the surface of a path
will create interest and therefore naturally slow you down.

- Paths are also essential for maintenance; for example, they could
  provide access along the back of a shrub border to trim a hedge.

- Often paths are multi-functional; one laid around the edge of a
  lawn provides access to adjacent planting and also negates the need
  for laborious edging. The very same path may also serve as a circular
  bicycle track for young children.

- The style of path can be chosen to match the overall style and mood
  of the garden and this can be achieved by using the same material
  as the patio so that they echo one another.

- As paths lead away from the house, the materials can be spaced with
  gaps for groundcover plants to create a much softer appearance.

- As the atmosphere of the garden changes into a more relaxed
  style with drifts of naturalized bulbs, a mown grass path may be
  introduced or a path of bark chippings through more wooded areas.

- Straight paths give direct access from one point to another although
  introducing a simple turn in the path around a clump of shrubs will
  add more interest without greatly increasing the distance.

- A zigzag path will make a long, narrow garden seem much wider,
  unlike a straight path, which will foreshorten the view to the end.

- A circular path will have a similar effect, allowing you to stroll around
  the garden rather than just take a quick walk to the end and back.

- The surface pattern of a path is another design factor to consider.
  Brick paths laid to a running bond along the length of the path
  accentuate the direction and stimulate quicker movement, while the
  same pattern laid across the path appears to broaden the width and
  encourages a more leisurely walk. This same effect can be created
  with rectangular paving slabs and even with a timber boardwalk.

- Materials used for path surfaces that are not completely smooth
  underfoot, such as natural stone setts or cobbles, will tend to slow

movement down, as will surfaces where groundcover plantings have been allowed to grow into the joints or soften the edges.

- Stepping stones can be used for visual effect but must be laid close together if they are to be walked on.

- Other types of paving with a textured surface may be laid through shaded areas or on slight inclines where extra grip is needed.

- The width of a path will vary to suit its use. A broad path is often used where a slower pace is anticipated and 1.2 m (4 feet) is needed for two people to stroll comfortably side by side. Narrower paths are fine for quick access, while a single line of bricks may be laid to create a visual rather than practical link.

Choice of surface materials

There is a wide choice of paving materials available today, not just in garden centres but also from specialist stone suppliers, brick manufacturers, builders' merchants and from salvage yards. Of course you do not have to limit yourself to one type of material: consider using combinations of those listed below.

STONE Stone is the most expensive material, but also the finest. Sandstone is probably the most suitable stone for garden paving; it has a warm colour that mellows with age and it associates well with brick, timber, gravel and garden plants. Limestone is usually too soft to be used as paving, but slate on the other hand is a very dense, hard-wearing material and can look terrific in a crisp, geometric design. Granite, which is a hard rock, is usually seen as setts. Its uneven surface, however, means that it is not ideal for seating, but it does provide a firm grip when laid on slopes.

PRE-CAST CONCRETE SLABS Concrete is a mimic, capable of imitating other, more expensive surfaces. There are many types to choose from in all colours, shapes and sizes. The subdued stone colours look better in the garden than more gaudy varieties. Textured slabs are excellent for a non-slip surface and look great laid in bands. Imitation stone slabs are also available.

BRICKS It's best to choose clay rather than concrete bricks as the soft colour of clay bricks is more suited to a garden. They work well for straight or for curved paths, as a trim to other paving materials, or arranged in patterns such as running bond, basket weave and herringbone.

COBBLES AND PEBBLES These are smooth, round stones, which range in size from 2 to 10 cm (3/4 to 4 inches). Cobbles and pebbles can be laid loose for a beach effect or bedded in mortar to form a pathway. They can make intricate mosaic patterns and are often bordered by bricks or tiles.

GRAVEL Pale gravel reflects light, especially in shady areas. It can also be a good intruder alert as it is noisy when trodden on. Loose aggregate, like gravel, is an excellent material that is available as crushed stone or shingle from gravel pits. The size of gravel for surfacing ranges from 1–2 cm (3/8–3/4 inch) and the depth of the surface need only be approximately 2 cm (3/4 inch).

TIMBER Timber is a versatile material that looks good in informal settings. Log slices can be laid down for stepping stones, or bark chippings used to dress a pathway, while timber decking forms a superb sitting area in a sunny aspect.

GROWING FRAGRANT PLANTS IN PAVING

Many smaller fragrant plants can be grown in the cracks and crevices of walls or paving. Suitable plants are fleabane (*Erigeron*), chamomile, *Oenothera triloba*, thyme and violets. If you are laying a new path or patio, you can leave gaps in the paving where the plants can be positioned. In areas already surfaced, you will need to chip out some sand and mortar from the joints of the paving in order to create pockets for planting. How much sand and mortar is taken out will depend on the technique that was used to lay the paving and the type of base beneath, which must be broken through to allow adequate drainage for the plants. Soil may need to be dug out of the joint as well, but again, this depends on the method used when the paving was first laid.

1 Using a small chisel, carefully chip out the mortar from the joint in the paving where the plant is to be positioned, taking great care to minimize disturbance to the surrounding hard surface.

2 With a pointing trowel, carefully scrape out the sand and mortar from the opened joint in the paving.

3 It is important to remove as much rubble as possible to create a pocket for the plant's roots to grow in.

4 Knock the plant from its pot and remove as much soil as possible, gently teasing out the roots. This makes the rootball as small as possible so that it can be lowered down into the planting pocket in the paving.

LAYING PAVING

There are two methods for laying paving stones with mortar: either apply five spots of mortar to the ground beneath each slab and tap it into position or lay a full bed of mortar and place slabs on top. The joints for both methods should be about 10 mm (1/4 inch) wide.

Five-spot method This method supports the slab on all corners as well as in the middle and makes it easy to tap the slab down into position. It does, however, create more of a problem when pointing up later, as the pointing mix may disappear to fill in the void under the slab when pushed into the joints. There is also the possibility that water can sit under the slabs, resulting in the potential problem in cold climates of the slabs moving due to the effect of freeze-thaw action.

Mortar bed method A full bed of mortar is the strongest method because the whole slab is supported and water is kept out. Spread a layer of mortar about 4 cm (1 1/2 inches) deep over the hardcore base and use a trowel to create ridges and furrows in the mortar so that, when the slab is tapped down, the mortar has a space in which to move and you will end up with a solid bed.

5 Using your fingers, gently insert the plant into the planting pocket. Press it into position and firm it into place. Let the plant sit slightly higher than the surface of the paving to allow for settling.

6 Use a brush to fill the rest of the planting pocket with compost. Tug the top of the plant gently a few times to coax more compost down around the roots of the plant.

7 Water the plant to help settle the compost around the roots. If all the compost washes down into the planting pocket, you may need to add more to the hole and then water it in well.

NATURAL PATHS

Wood shavings, sawdust or fine bark make a soft path for woodland gardens. However, these types of materials will need replacing after 2 years or so because they begin to break down, returning humus to the soil in the process. Paths like this look very natural and are quite pleasant to walk on.

Steps and ramps

The primary function of steps is to provide fast access from one level of the garden to another – in much the same manner as stairs in a house. Outside in the garden though, steps can be an attractive feature: they can be broader and deeper than internal steps and they can meander and zigzag up a slope offering interesting routes from bottom to top.

Designing steps and ramps

You might use steps instead of a low retaining wall at a change of level, allowing one area to flow into another without interruption. The same steps can provide an added attraction if they are used as seating or if they are surrounded with plantings. Low plants can be grown at the side of the steps – these will tumble down and soften the construction as well.

Ramps provide even gentler access than steps from one level to another and of course they are very useful for wheelchairs, strollers (pushchairs) and lawnmowers. However, they are not always attractive and, with a maximum gradient of 1:10, they can take up a lot of room in a smaller garden. Ramped steps require less space because they combine ramps of 1:10 or 1:12 with low bump steps of about 10 cm (4 inches) at regular intervals.

Correct step dimensions

Steps need to be carefully planned. The height of risers and the depth of treads are very important considerations because otherwise the climb up the steps can be awkward, disconcerting and even dangerous.

Generally speaking, the maximum height for a riser should not be more than 15 cm (6 inches), while the minimum height should not be less than 10 cm (4 inches). A comfortable depth for a tread is 38 cm (15 inches), though 45 cm

STEPS OR RAMP?
Steps take up only a quarter as much space as a ramp, but ramps have the major advantage of being ideal for moving wheelbarrows and other equipment uphill. Steps can be built on a gradient as steep as 1:2, whereas the gradient of a ramp should not be more than 1:8.

(1¹/₂ feet) is commonly used to fit the unit size of a paving slab. There is also a ratio of riser height to tread depth to consider, which means that the shallower the riser, the deeper the tread should be and, conversely, the steeper the riser, the narrower the tread should be. A useful rule of thumb to remember is 2 x riser + tread = 65 cm (26 inches), although this can vary slightly.

Fences

A fence gives order to the garden landscape. It can direct, contain and divide sections of your garden. Fences can also provide security and privacy, and screen out unwanted views.

Tips for planning and designing fences

- A fence can be a backdrop for plantings, serving to show off a specimen plant or enhance a pretty bed of perennials.

- Remember to consider seasonal changes. Winter can bring a fence into greater prominence as deciduous trees lose their leaves.

- A fence can be a blank background on which to hang garden ornaments such as plaques, wall pots or wall sculptures.

- Choose fence materials that will complement the style of the house.

- Often a fence doesn't need painting. If the right materials are used it can simply be allowed to weather or be treated with wood stain.

- A dark coloured fence tends to recede into the background whereas a lighter colour will make it dominate much more in the landscape. For example, if you have an undistinguished fence you want to hide, a dark olive green will make it disappear almost entirely.

PAINTED WALLS

In some places solid walls divide neighbouring properties, and these too can be treated as a fence. The modern trend is for masonry walls to be a feature in their own right, often splashed with colour. Limewashes are often used for walls, in shades ranging from French blue to terracotta, ochre, muddy purple and bright crimson.

THE GARDEN GATE

A gate can have a highly individual style which will affect the whole mood and feeling of a garden. First impressions count, and the gate is one of the first parts of the garden a visitor will see. Its condition and style can put your personality on show, so remember that the best impression is one that conveys welcome and friendliness. Of course, as it will be in constant use, it must also be strong and sturdy.

- A solid paling fence painted black is more obvious than an open fence of timber slats or metal railings painted in the same colour.

- A white painted fence becomes an imposing structure that draws attention away from the garden.

- Do remember that a fence doesn't have to be overstated to keep unwanted visitors from straying into a private yard. Even a very low picket fence or brick wall, a chain attached to pillars or simply a single line of brick or stone edging will do the job.

- Privacy can be attained by combining a fence with some plantings. A fence may not hide your garden from distant apartment blocks or houses, but tall shrubs and trees definitely will.

Fence materials

Usually fences are made of timber, but metal, stone brick and concrete are also commonly used.

TIMBER Timber is the most versatile of materials because it can be stained, painted or left to weather naturally. Picket fences are perfect for cottage or country-style gardens. Logs make a good fence where a more rustic look is desired. The common paling fence can easily be dressed up with the addition of coping, cappings and cross-beams.

STONE AND MASONRY Stone and masonry fences are solid and permanent. Suitable for modern, Mediterranean and traditionally designed houses, stone and masonry are versatile materials which are open to various stylistic interpretations. Often this type of fence is composed of stone or brick pillars with attractive timber or metal railings connecting them.

METAL Metal is another permanent material, whether it is a solid aluminium fence or one made from old-fashioned iron railings. The latter requires maintenance and painting, however, there are modern powder-coated aluminium copies which last for years with no painting.

Pergolas

It's probably easiest to think of a pergola as a series of arches. Like an arch, the structure is associated with transition from one area to another. Strictly speaking, a pergola is a free-standing structure, but the term is often used to describe a covered gallery – usually supported by pillars – that is attached to a building.

Pergola hints and tips

- Pergolas need to be sturdily constructed, especially if heavy climbers, such as roses or wisteria, are to be grown over them. Remember that a simple design is frequently the best design.

- Posts should never be positioned directly in front of windows. Pergolas should be high enough to allow plants to hang down and still be comfortable to walk under – a good height is about 2.1 m (7 feet).

- For pergolas close to the house, dressed timber and treated pine are the best materials to use.

- Rounded poles of treated pine are more rustic and look much better located some distance from the house – based on the very handy principle of using less refined construction materials the further away you move from the house.

VIGOROUS CLIMBERS FOR PERGOLAS

Actinidia deliciosa (kiwi fruit)
Campsis x *tagliabuana* 'Madame Galen'
Jasminum officinale
Rosa 'Bobbie James', *R. filipes* 'Kiftsgate', *R.* 'Rambling Rector'
Vitis 'Brant', *V. coignetiae*, *V. vinifera* 'Purpurea'
Wisteria floribunda, *W. sinensis*

■ On a small surburban block, square posts of 13–15 cm (5–6 inches) and cross beams of 10 cm (4 inches) are usually quite sufficient for building a sturdy pergola.

■ Don't wind roses around the posts of a pergola – they need annual pruning, and cutting out twisted canes can be a nightmare. Tie the canes to heavy-gauge wires attached to the piers or supporting posts.

Arbours and arches

An arch is used over a path, marking the transition from one area to another. An arbour, on the other hand, is a cocoon-like structure, backed by lattice or a dense hedge or climber. Warm and cosy, it provides the ideal location for an inviting seat or some other focal point.

Planning and designing arbours and arches

■ Arbours and arches are both prominent features and will be clearly seen. It could be a waste of time to include one in your garden if it doesn't look like it belongs, or if it has no reason for being there.

■ Arches and arbours can be included in your garden design to add a sense of arrival to the landscape, and they are often used over a front gate or at an entry point.

■ Arches create views. When choosing a location, look at a view from all possible angles to judge the best position for an arch.

■ Arches do more than frame views, they mark a passage from one section of the garden to another. They are particularly useful for marking the point at which style or function changes. Good locations for arches include the passage from the flower garden to the vegetable garden or from the lawn to the swimming pool. Other suitable points are the change from an informal living space, such as a patio attached to the house, to a more formally laid out section of lawn.

■ If you only have a small garden, one where the separation of the garden into sections is inappropriate, an arbour may be the answer. Arbours can be placed against walls or situated at the end of a view.

■ The ideally located arbour is warm in winter but cool in summer, so positioning is important. A sunny-facing position, possibly on a wall,

CARING FOR WOODEN SURFACES

In addition to keeping plants in good shape, you need to keep hard wooden surfaces in good condition. Any softwood in the garden needs to be protected against the ravages of the weather and occasional new coats of preservative will be required. For most pre-treated woods, linseed oil offers an efficient form of protection, as it conditions the wood as it preserves it. A good time to treat the wood is in early winter, on a fine, reasonably warm day, after the autumn's gardening tasks have been completed. The wood will then be protected against the winter rains and frosts.

Wooden decks, particularly in wet climates, will need occasional scrubbing with a stiff-bristled brush and an algicide to remove any accumulated (and slippery) green slime. Hardwood decks need not be treated, but softwood will need treating with preservative once a year.

suits the winter-sun requirement, but in summer the same position can be too hot for comfort. The solution is in the planting. Choose loose-stemmed shrubs as well as climbers to provide shade and interest. Deciduous vines are ideal.

▪ Arches and arbours are usually constructed of timber or masonry. However, they can also be constructed of stainless steel, iron or even glass bricks. Rustic structures may be composed of twigs, rough branches or treated pine logs. Trellis is excellent for creating a traditional look, whereas dowels or straight, vertical slatted lathes will suit an oriental design.

Lighting

One way to enjoy the best of the garden from inside your home is to install some exterior lighting and transform your after-dark garden from a black hole to an extension of your indoor rooms. Diffuse outdoor lighting will allow you to enjoy the courtyard or the whole garden area at night – in the warmer months for outdoor living, and in winter as illuminated views. So, if you want lighting, use a dormant time in your garden to lay the wiring.

Lighting can either be decorative, such as uplighting in trees or wash lighting in a pond, or functional, lighting up driveways and paths, or perhaps making your home more secure. Carefully placed lights will accentuate any features in your garden, such as stonework, a statue or a wall plaque. Sometimes picking out small details can make all the difference to the ambience.

The advent of low-voltage garden lighting in recent years has made the job of installing lighting safe and a lot of fun. First, select the areas that must be lit, such as paths and accessways, and then add some imaginative touches. Some light here for effect, a pool of colour there for impact, but don't overdo it. Less lighting always works better. Finally, always employ a licensed electrician to install an all-weather powerpoint outdoors.

Furniture and ornament

A garden seat is a pleasurable thing. From your garden seat you can relax, plan your next endeavour, note the combinations of texture and colour that work well and keep a garden diary with notes and ideas for next year.

Well-chosen garden furniture can provide an extra dimension to a small garden. In tight spaces it is unlikely that you'll have room for more than one seat, so siting that chair or bench is worth some careful consideration.

Decide whether you want to sit in the sun or in the shade then use your seating as accent points – tucked into a corner, set against a wall or hedge or sheltering under an arbour where you'll have some cover. Try to 'anchor' furniture with background shrubbery and pots of trailing plants around their base.

What lies beneath your seating can be just as important but is often forgotten. Try to position your garden furniture on a solid level surface of pavers, bricks or compacted gravel. Grass might look idyllic, but the charm will soon wear off after you've spent a few weekends lugging a heavy bench out of the lawn-mower's path, or when you have to remedy a muddy patch in front of it.

Select furniture that matches the style and feel of your garden, as well as your lifestyle. For example, wicker furniture might look great, but if you don't have a veranda for weather protection, it won't last. One of the most durable of materials is stone or reconstituted stone. Its classic look is rarely out of place, it will never date and it lasts forever in all weathers.

Timber has long been popular, with the classic teak bench remaining the 'benchmark' by which others are measured. Not all timbers weather as well though, and will probably need sanding back and oiling at least every few years. If your garden has a rustic, cottage feel to it, furniture made from rough-hewn logs would complement it well.

Iron and iron–timber combinations, such as the classic railway bench, last well, although the iron may need repainting every few years to keep it free from rust. Iron and glass furniture has become very popular, but if you're considering this option, ensure the glass is double-laminated and positioned in a sheltered part of the garden, such as a courtyard.

It is important to remember that garden furniture can be made from just about anything you like. In the right spot even a couple of planks of wood placed on brick bases can work, so use your imagination.

Cleaning garden furniture

- Furniture made from sealed wood should be wiped down with a damp sponge that has been dipped in a detergent solution. When you do this, make sure you keep an eye on cracks in the sealer and renew it regularly to maintain effective protection.
- Give unsealed wood a protective coat once a year by rubbing in a mixture of 4 parts raw linseed oil and 1 part turpentine.
- Wash cane furniture with warm salty water and leave it to dry in the sun. Protect cane pieces by painting them with an outdoor lacquer.
- Wash canvas furniture just as you would wash canvas awnings.
- Lubricate metal hinges regularly using oil or petroleum jelly.
- Use a chamois cloth to wipe over metal frames. Also, liquid wax polish will help prevent the metal from rusting.

FINE DETAIL

Adding small finishing touches such as decorative tap tops, wall plaques and plant stands can really make a garden attractive and interesting, so keep your eye out for those small details that will help you to complete the picture.

Problems

Prevention is better than cure. With the best will in the world there will be problems in the garden. Pesky pests, diseases and weeds will always be around to enjoy and try to destroy your garden. However, there is no need to be downhearted as this chapter is packed with brilliant hints and tips to help you combat every kind of problem.

Healthy plants deter problems

First, the more healthy a plant is, the more resistant it will be to pest and disease attack. Insect pests are attracted to the weakest, most stressed plants in a crop. Improving soil structure and fertility with organic matter makes for healthier soil and this in turn makes for strong, healthy crops – and minimal crop damage. Organic gardening techniques also produce plants that grow steadily rather than rapidly, as is the case with chemical fertilizers. The plants therefore do not become soft and sappy and prone to attack.

Avoid problems with good garden housekeeping

Many diseases and plant pests can be eliminated from the garden simply by good housekeeping practices. Dealing with garden problems as they arise will ensure fewer pests and disease problems.

- Garden waste should be composted. If material is infected, it should be put in the centre of the compost where high temperatures will kill spores. Infected prunings, however, should be burned, if possible.

- A thorough clean-up at the end of summer or early in autumn can do much to prevent pests and diseases in the next growing season. Digging the garden over at this stage not only aerates the soil but can also expose overwintering larvae of various pests.

- Make sure that no vegetables are left on the ground. Any mummified vegetables should be burned if possible.

BEING GREEN

If you are making the effort to minimize exposure to chemicals inside your home, it makes sense to extend the same care to your outdoor areas too. Reducing the use of harsh chemicals to control insects and other pests is better for you and better for your home. You will also be doing the wider environment a favour. You may need to experiment with alternative methods and some of them may need more frequent application than strong chemical pesticides, but the rewards are a safer place for you and your family and a much more welcoming environment for all the local wildlife.

▓ After pruning deciduous trees, check for the presence of borer and destroy any you find by poking a wire into any holes. Use a wire brush to remove any loose bark, which often shelters overwintering pests.

Choose your plants wisely

With some forethought you can create a garden that automatically needs less chemical help. For instance, some plants are bred for resistance to attack by particular insects or to a disease. Ask the staff at your local garden centre when buying plants and seeds.

▓ Lawns are big users of water as well as chemicals such as herbicides and fertilizers. These chemicals tend to leach off the lawn during rain, potentially polluting water systems. You could decide to reduce your lawn area or forget it entirely.

▓ Some plants help keep bugs away. These include chrysanthemums and pyrethrum daisies, and herbs such as chives, garlic and nasturtiums. Many gardening experts recommend companion planting to reduce pests – for instance, planting nasturtiums among tomatoes and brassicas (the cabbage family) is said to protect against whitefly. It's certainly worth trying.

▓ Planting groundcovers rather than leaving soil bare not only reduces moisture loss, it also leaves less room for weeds to grow, reducing the temptation to use herbicides in the garden.

▓ Choose plants that are best suited to your soil and local conditions rather than struggling on with unsuitable plants, which are more likely to surrender to fungal or bacterial disease or pest infestation.

Beneficial insects and animals

To prevent pests getting out of control, call in a natural army of parasites and predators. Many pests have natural enemies that, if encouraged, can keep them in check. Beneficial garden insects include ladybird beetles, wasps, assassin bugs, predatory mites, stick insects, praying mantises and lacewings.

Other wildlife to encourage are birds, frogs, lizards and spiders. One of the disadvantages of using insecticides, particularly broad spectrum ones, in your garden is that you may kill off these helpers too.

Conversely, controlling ants will assist in aphid and mealy bug control, as ants protect both of these pests in return for the honeydew they excrete.

Local organic gardening clubs or even your local garden centre may be able to advise on methods that work for your area.

Pest-repelling plants

Planting a garden to help deter pests is so much nicer than using chemicals. Five favourites are described below.

TANSY This very pretty and hardy perennial, with its tiny button-like flowers, was once grown in monastery herb gardens to repel common pests. When planted near fruit and nut trees, vegetables and berry fruits, it discourages ants, aphids, beetles and fruit fly. If grown near cabbages tansy will repel cabbage moth and cabbage white butterfly. Dried tansy flowers can be sprinkled on pantry shelves to discourage flies.

CORIANDER Also known as cilantro or Chinese parsley, this pretty aromatic herb has a strong pungent scent that discourages aphids. Bees and other beneficial insects are attracted to the umbels of tiny white flowers.

RUE A sturdy evergreen herb with metallic blue, feathery leaves, rue is useful as a disinfectant and as an insecticide. Plant it by doors and windows to repel mosquitoes, flies and other insects, in the garden to discourage beetles and slugs, and rub it over pets to help reduce fleas.

WORMWOOD This is one of the most bitter herbs known, and for centuries it has been used to repel insects, including fleas, flies and moths. It was once

THE IMPORTANCE OF BEES

Bees are very important in the garden. Without them there would be no flower seeds for next year and many fruit and vegetables will set much better crops after being visited by bees. Most bees are busy during the warmer part of the day. To avoid wiping them out, the best time to spray insecticides is either early morning or early evening when bees are less active. Some insecticides such as dimethoate are highly toxic to bees and should not be used when plants are in flower.

TIPS FOR MINIMIZING MOSQUITOES

Eliminating their breeding sites is the key to reducing annoying mosquito populations.

■ Check the garden, daily if necessary, for small pools of water. Mosquitoes breed in the tiniest amounts of water, such as in plant saucers, paint cans, empty pots or plastic sheeting.

■ Stock your pond with frogs and fish, which feed on mosquito larvae and help keep them under control.

■ If you're in the garden after dusk, protect your skin by wearing long sleeves and long trousers.

■ Flyscreens are the best way of keeping mosquitoes out of the house.

■ Coils that burn allethrin repel mosquitoes to some degree.

■ The oils from citronella and lavender may be used as mosquito repellents with some success.

used as an ingredient in ink to stop mice eating old letters. Strangely, it is also a major ingredient in apéritifs and herb wines, such as absinthe and vermouth. Legend has it that as the serpent slithered out of Eden, wormwood sprang up in the impressions left by its tail on the ground, and it has been used ever since to keep away evil spirits. Pick wormwood leaves for drying in summer, and mix them with some dried mint and lavender in sachets to keep your clothes fresh-smelling and free of moth holes.

MINT There are many species of mint, including apple mint, spearmint, eau de cologne mint, pineapple mint and pennyroyal. Mint repels most pests, especially fleas and beetles which dislike the smell. Dried mint sachets in the wardrobe will freshen clothes and keep moths at bay. Fresh mint in the pantry will deter ants. Rub fresh mint leaves on your hands, neck and face to protect your skin from mosquitoes. Plant mints around a dog kennel or strew leaves near animal cages to repel flies. Rub fresh mint around the eyes and mouths of horses or cows to discourage pesky flies. Mint is the perfect companion plant for cabbages and tomatoes because it repels aphids, cabbage white butterflies and whiteflies – all insects that can ruin your crop.

Companion planting

Companion planting is an effective way to protect plants from the unwanted attentions of pests and diseases. A number of plants give off strong odours that can confuse the olfactory senses of pests. Many herbs are useful for this purpose, including basil, lavender, rosemary, rue, thyme, chives and garlic. For them to be effective, you should plant them throughout the garden.

However, companion planting is much wider in scope than just confusing an insect's sense of smell. In its broadest sense, it includes any plant that is beneficial in some way to another plant. Think of companion plants as being your plants' 'good neighbours'.

Good and bad companions

GOOD COMPANIONS

These plants have long been regarded as good companions:

- Basil with apricots, asparagus, beans, fuchsia, grapes and tomatoes

- Beans with potatoes and sweet corn

- Chives with carrots, cucumbers and tomatoes

- Cucumbers with potatoes

- French marigolds (*Tagetes* sp.) with beans, potatoes, roses and tomatoes

- Horseradish with potatoes

- Hyssop with cabbages and grapes

- Leeks with celery

- Lettuce with carrots, onions and strawberries

- Melons with sweet corn

- Mint with cabbages and other brassicas and peas

- Nasturtiums with apple trees, cucumbers, squash, and zucchinis (courgettes)

- Onions with carrots, kohlrabi and turnips

- Peas with carrots

BAD COMPANIONS

Some bad combinations to watch out for include:

- Apples with potatoes

- Beans with garlic

- Cabbages with strawberries

- Gladioli with beans, peas and strawberries

- Sunflowers with any vegetable but squash

- Wormwood with almost everything

REDUCE NEMATODES WITH MARIGOLDS

Nematodes (eelworms) cause reduced growth, low yields and wilting in a variety of vegetable crops. When they are infected, a plant's roots appear to have tiny gall-like growths over the surface (gardeners often mistakenly attribute these effects to drought or poor soil fertility). However, nature has produced a powerful nematicide, a biomolecule produced to some degree in the roots of all species of marigolds (*Tagetes* sp.). The dwarf French marigold (*Tagetes patula*) is particularly useful to use as barrier plantings around garden beds. If the brilliant golden or orange flowers don't go with your garden colour scheme, simply shear the heads off.

It may be a simple matter of one plant shading another or modifying the humidity. One plant's roots might aerate the soil, or help drain excess water. And some plants can protect others as much as themselves by virtue of defence mechanisms such as thorns and stinging hairs, or by producing compounds that are poisonous to insect pests. Other plants offer benefits to their neighbours by attracting or housing desirable insect predators, or by exuding odours that attract insect pollinators.

SHOO FLY!

Place fly-deterrent plants at doorways, on verandas and so on. These plants include basil, bay, chamomile, lavender, lemon verbena, mint, rosemary, sweet woodruff and thyme.

Weed control

They are not just unsightly, but weeds also take space, light, water and food from your chosen, and wanted, plants. They can also harbour pests and diseases. Your garden will never be free of weeds, but they're easier to control if you adopt the approach of 'a little weeding often'.

Manual control methods

HAND-PULLING Hand-weeding is preferable for those small spaces in your garden, especially places where weeds have sprung up among your wanted plants. A garden fork and trowel will help you effectively remove the whole of the root system. Always hand-weed when the ground is moist.

HOEING A Dutch hoe is a useful tool with a long handle and flat blade. How it works is that the blade cuts off weeds just below the surface of the soil and so the tops die off and provide mulch for the garden. A sharp hoe is one of the best cultivators for small gardens. Early and frequent hoeing will control most weeds in flower beds and vegetable gardens.

CHIPPING This is a fast way to remove weeds in lawns, paving, walkways, fencelines and garden beds. A chipper is a thin, narrow blade on a long pole. It works with a slicing action and you don't have to bend down to use it.

Mulching

Mulching is an excellent way to keep your garden free from weeds. When applied thickly, mulch will smother and kill most weed seedlings and any that do manage to poke through can easily be cut down. Should you pull a large weed from the mulch, make sure you re-cover any exposed soil.

Groundcovers

As all weeds need light to live, an easy way to suppress them is to cover them with thickly foliaged, evergreen plants. Small shrubs that are densely leafy to the ground are ideal. Plant them so that when mature, they form a complete cover over the soil. Any weeds that germinate underneath will struggle to live in the very low light. A few may survive but, as long as the shrubs are taller than the weeds, you won't see them and the weeds definitely won't thrive.

WEED FERTILIZER

Here is a handy way to use your dug-up weeds. You can replace nitrogen in the garden by making liquid fertilizer from them.

1 Almost fill a plastic garbage bin with weeds.

2 Cover the weeds with water and replace the lid.

3 In warm weather it will take a few weeks for the weeds to break down. Dilute the fertilizer 10:1 with water and then pour it directly onto the garden.

SOLARIZATION

Solarization is a technique that will totally clear a weed-infested area. This traps the heat from the sun and raises the soil temperature by several degrees, thereby killing weed seeds, roots and bulbs in the ground. It will also eradicate soil nematodes (eelworms) and some diseases, such as verticillium wilt. Solarization only works during hot, dry weather when temperatures are above 25°C (75°F). It involves stretching a sheet of clear or black plastic over soil that has first been stripped of weeds and then dug over. The soil must also be deeply moistened before covering. Ensure that the edges of the plastic are sealed down with soil and that the plastic covers the whole soil surface. For maximum effect, try to keep the plastic on for at least 4 weeks – and pray for continuous hot, sunny weather. As soon as the plastic is removed you can plant directly into the treated soil.

Weed mats

Woven weed mats are made of a plastic mesh which is similar to shade cloth, and are very effective at controlling weeds while still allowing air and water to penetrate to the soil and root zone. The weed mat can be worked around existing plants but is most effective when spread over an unplanted area. You can set new plants in the ground through holes cut in the weed mat. The mat can then be hidden with a topping of organic mulch.

Using herbicides

Before deciding to use a herbicide in your garden, it is important to identify the weed you want to kill and to make sure that the chosen herbicide will kill it.

Most herbicides that are sold for home-garden use are based on the chemical glyphosate. This is absorbed through the leaves and then circulated through

ACT FAST!
On cultivated land you will inevitably find a fresh crop of annual weeds when warmth and rain combine to encourage weed seeds to germinate. Tackle weeds promptly to remove them before they start to flower and set seed.

the sap so that the entire plant dies. A glyphosate herbicide is most effective when applied during the active growing season of the plant. As it is a non-selective chemical, take care not to let it touch your wanted plants. It can either be sprayed on or applied directly to the weed by dabbing or painting. Glyphosate is a relatively safe garden chemical, for both humans and the environment, when it is used according to directions. It is not residual in the ground, but do remember that it will kill or damage anything that it touches. If you are spraying, do so on a still day to avoid spray drift.

SAFETY TIPS FOR HERBICIDES

- Always read the label. It states the product's uses and lists the safety precautions. Mix strictly according to the directions – more product does not necessarily mean more effective and can be damaging.

- Never mix up more than you need right now because the diluted product will not keep.

- To control weeds in lawns, make sure you choose a herbicide that is safe to use on your particular grass. Some grasses will be damaged by any use of herbicide and not all lawn weeds can be controlled by selective herbicides, so you may need to think of another solution.

- While spraying wear shoes, long trousers, a long-sleeved shirt and gloves, and any other protective clothing specified on the label.

- Spray on a still day; this will prevent spray drift, which will damage wanted plants and can be dangerous to other people.

- Keep children, pets and adults out of the area while you spray and don't allow them to return until the spray dries.

- Treat weeds when they are most actively growing (this is usually during the warmer months of the year).

- Wash out spray equipment after use but be careful where you put the waste water – definitely not down drains.

- Don't use the same spray equipment to apply pesticides.

- Store herbicides in a cool place well out of reach of children.

A PINCH OF SALT ON DANDELIONS
You can effectively kill dandelions and plantain weeds by simply dropping a pinch of salt onto them.

There are also selective herbicides that kill only certain types of weeds. They were developed for use on lawns, to kill the weeds without damaging the grass. Some of these are quite toxic so, for general use around the garden, careful application of glyphosate is better. Glyphosate may not kill some woody weeds.

REMOVING WEEDS WITH TAP ROOTS
Many of the most troublesome lawn weeds are those which have a rosette or spreading habit and a long tap root. If you spot them early, remove them with a sharp knife.

1 Start by inserting the tip of the blade into the soil at a steep angle, about 5 cm (2 inches) away from the centre of the weed.

2 Push the blade into the soil towards the weed to a depth of about 15 cm (6 inches). Try not to cut through the root or it will regrow.

3 Lever the blade upwards to remove the weed and root. For soft soil, rest the base of the blade on a block of wood to stop it sinking. Once you have finished removing the weeds, collect them up and dispose of them by placing them in the garbage bin.

DEALING WITH PERENNIAL WEEDS

When you have removed perennial weeds, take them away from the ground you are clearing and carefully dispose of them. Remember, you should never add perennial weeds to the compost heap.

Established perennial weeds can be particularly difficult to eradicate, because even the smallest piece of root has the capacity to develop into a new plant. Use a garden fork to systematically work over an area and gently ease the roots out, making sure that they are not broken. Wear gloves (especially for prickly weeds such as thistles), and pull the weeds out of the soil with as much root as possible.

236 the garden book

Dealing with garden pests

The most important step in pest control is to check your plants thoroughly and frequently and try to combat any infestation fast, before it has time to catch hold. Some insects will cause a measure of damage to only one plant, while others will quickly destroy a whole crop. However, in general it is not in nature's interest to destroy the host plant, so most predator problems can be treated as annoyances rather than catastrophes. You will need to decide whether to treat problems organically or use non-organic, chemical solutions.

Barriers and traps

Among the most useful advances in recent times has been the development of finely woven, transparent cloths to protect vegetables and fruit trees. These allow water and maximum light and air through while excluding insect pests. Floating row covers are ideal for the vegetable garden.

Other relatively newly developed barriers are sticky, non-drying glues that trap insects migrating up the stem or trunk. The glue is placed on a paper collar around the base of the plant. A simple non-sticky collar, made from a cardboard cup with the base cut out, and placed around the base of a seedling, is sufficient to protect it from cutworm damage.

In some areas, carrot fly is a real problem. But the female needs to hover low over the crop in order to detect the odour of the carrots. Erecting a simple,

ATTRACT BIRDS TO EAT PESTS

A home garden is mostly designed for pleasure and one of life's small joys is witnessing a honey-eating bird drawing nectar from a flower or a flock of finches busily extracting insect pests from an old lemon tree.

Birds need gardens and gardens need birds for the control of insect pests. Birds are essential in helping to keep the balance of nature. They can deal with at least half your insect problems, but if you use chemicals they may eat the poisoned insects and die. Birds that eat sprayed insects and survive tend to lay infertile eggs. If you must spray, always use the least toxic chemical available for the job.

FRUIT FLY TRAP

Try this trap for fruit flies. Make a funnel entrance by cutting a plastic 2 litre (70 fluid ounce) bottle in half, then place the top half inside the bottom, with the neck pointing downwards into the rest of the bottle. Try various baits: yeast, yeast extracts, beer or citrus skin. These traps can be hung in a tree or among plants at an angle.

temporary barrier fence of hessian (burlap) around the row will force the female to hover too high to detect the scent and thus leave the carrots alone.

Trap plants

Some plants are particularly attractive to pests – because of their colour, smell or taste – and thereby protect other plants from attack. Bright yellow nasturtiums attract aphids away from cabbages. Zinnias have long been used to lure Japanese beetles. Dill is traditionally used to lure green tomato caterpillar. In themselves, trap plants are not sufficient protection for your garden, but they do contribute towards maintaining healthy crops.

Chemical controls

You may have an infestation of some pest that simply does not respond to preventative measures or natural remedies. You still don't have to resort to highly toxic chemicals. Other relatively low-risk options include the following:

- Pyrethrin, from the pyrethrum daisy, is a broad-spectrum insecticide. But remember that it is also toxic to fish and cats.

- Derris, which is often supplied as a dust made from the derris root, is a broad-spectrum insecticide generally used to protect against caterpillars and beetles and many other crawling insect pests. It is

EARWIG TRAP

Place a hollow piece of drinking straw or a piece of sponge among the earwigs' flower of choice (dahlias or chrysanthemums, for example). Examine the traps each morning and blow any prisoners into boiling water.

moderately toxic and will also kill ladybird beetles, lacewings and other beneficial insects. It is very toxic to fish and pigs as well.

- *Bacillus thuringiensis* (BT) is a bacterial preparation that is toxic to caterpillars but not to other organisms, although it may sometimes kill some butterfly larvae.

- Methoprene and hydropene are insect-growth regulators that keep insects in the juvenile, non-breeding stage. There is no known effect on humans. They are considered an ideal alternative to most other pesticides as they act only on target organisms.

- White oils and other petroleum and vegetable oils work very well in controlling the target pest by suffocating them. It is worth trying these on aphids, azalea lace bugs, caterpillars, mealy bugs, sawflies, scale, spider mites and whiteflies. They are relatively safe for other organisms and humans, although they may kill some beneficial insects if they are sprayed directly onto them.

- Sulphur is toxic to mites, powdery mildews and rust, and it has low toxicity to humans and animals. It may be toxic to some beneficial insects when it is sprayed directly onto them and it may damage some sulphur-sensitive plants.

PERSONAL INSECT REPELLENTS

Available as lotions and sprays, personal insect repellents are designed to keep flies, mosquitoes and other insects away from the body. Ingredients can include Deet (N, N-diethyl-m-toluamide – banned in the United States), di-n-propyl isocinchomeronate, ethyl hexanediol and dimethylphthalate. Some formulas contain pyrethrum and other synthetic pyrethroids.

Natural repellents include essential oils such as eucalyptus, pennyroyal, sassafras and tea-tree – all of which can be toxic in large amounts.

It is always better to try other means of repelling insects first. Try covering up with clothing, for instance. However, if you do use a product, choose a lotion rather than an aerosol as you will be able to apply it more precisely, and therefore use it sparingly.

CAT AND DOG DETERRENT

Chilli and pepper can be sprinkled around the garden as an effective deterrent to cats and dogs, which don't like the smell.

Tips for safe use of pest sprays

- Always read the label carefully, don't take any shortcuts, and follow the manufacturer's instructions exactly.

- Wear a long-sleeved shirt, long trousers, rubber gloves, goggles and any other protective clothing indicated on the label.

- Mix concentrated liquids outside or in a well-ventilated place and avoid breathing in the fumes.

- Mix only as much spray as you need, measuring accurately. Overdosing does not give a better result and can be damaging.

- Don't leave any spills or chemicals around the house or garden while you are spraying. If you should happen to spill the concentrate or the solution on yourself, wash it off immediately with lots of water.

- Choose a cool, calm day when no rain is expected.

- Keep people and pets well out of the way while you are spraying and until the spray has dried. Fish are killed by many pesticides and so ponds should be covered.

- Never smoke or eat while using garden chemicals.

- Do not spray in confined places, such as greenhouses, for any prolonged period. If this is essential, make sure you wear a breathing apparatus that is approved for the job.

- Wash your hands and face immediately after using chemicals.

- Wash out all spray equipment thoroughly when you have finished but don't tip the waste water down the drain.

- Store all chemicals in their original containers, preferably in a locked cupboard, and always well out of the reach of children.

BEER BAIT FOR SNAILS

Beer in a shallow saucer makes an effective trap for snails. Set it up in the evening and empty it out in the morning.

RECIPES FOR NATURAL PEST SPRAYS

With a few basic ingredients you can make a range of non-toxic, economic, effective pest-control solutions to use in the garden. Less toxic methods may need more frequent application – for instance, controlling aphids with soap or garlic sprays may necessitate spraying every 3 days. You may also need to exercise a little more care during the application process – for example, spraying the underside of azalea leaves if they are being attacked by azalea lace bug.

■ SPRAY FOR ANTS

Ingredients
2 cups water
¼ cup kerosene
¼ cup detergent
4 dessertspoons vegetable oil

Method
1 Mix all the ingredients together.

2 Spray this mixture within a 50-cm (20-inch) circle of an ant's nest. Pour ½ cup water into the nest and spray the ants as they leave the nest. This spray can be used in conjunction with ant bait.

■ BAIT FOR ANTS

Ingredients
3 cups water
1 cup sugar
4 level teaspoons boric acid or borax

Method
1 Stir all the ingredients together until they are dissolved.

2 To make a bait, half fill a screw-top jar with cotton wool then pour in about 1 cup of the solution to saturate the cotton wool. Tape the lid on tightly and pierce it with two or three holes in the centre.

3 Place 3–6 baits like this near trails and nests for up to 3 days.

■ SOAP SPRAY FOR SUCKING PESTS LIKE SCALE AND APHIDS

Ingredients
50 g (1¾ ounces) soap
7 litres (245 fluid ounces) water
130 g (4½ ounces) washing soda

Method

1 Grate soap into a bowl.

2 Bring 1 litre (35 fluid ounces) of the water to the boil in a saucepan then remove it from the heat.

3 Add washing soda to the hot water and stir until it is dissolved.

4 Add the soap to the solution and stir this over a gentle heat until the soap has dissolved.

5 Add this mixture to the remaining water. Use undiluted.

■ SOFT SOAP INSECTICIDE

This is an all-purpose garden insecticide for aphids, azalea lace bug, leafhoppers, mites and white fly.

Ingredients

56 g (2 ounces) soft soap (from chemists)
4.5 litres (158 fluid ounces) hot water

Method

Dissolve the soft soap in the hot water and then allow it to cool. Use this insecticide undiluted directly onto plants.

■ GARLIC SPRAY

Use this spray for aphids, mites and small caterpillars. Garlic will also provides some natural fungicide protection.

Ingredients

85 g (3 oz) chopped garlic bulbs
2 tablespoons mineral oil
7 g (1/4 oz) soap
600 ml (21 fluid ounces) water

Method

1 Soak the garlic in the mineral oil for about 24 hours.

2 Dissolve the soap in the water and then carefully, and slowly, add this to the garlic mixture.

3 Strain the spray through some fine gauze, and store it in a ceramic or a glass container.

4 Dilute 1 part mixture to 50 parts water.

Common garden pests

PEST	SYMPTOM
Aphids	Most commonly green, aphids may also be pink, black or grey. All suck sap and feed in large groups, usually on new shoot tips and buds but sometimes on leaves and roots. They cause new shoots to die, distort flowers and can spread plant diseases.
Borers	Borers are caterpillars that attack shrubs and trees, entering at points of injury. They tunnel and leave a mass of sawdust and oozing gum from the wound. Branches or whole trees may be ring-barked. Borers often attack old, weakened or damaged trees.
Cabbage white butterflies	These caterpillars are green with a faint yellow stripe down their back and sides. The white butterflies have three or four black spots on the tips of the wings.
Fruit flies	Fruit flies attack fruits and vegetables. Eggs are laid into the fruit as it ripens and hatch into maggots. When mature, the maggots drop to the ground and emerge as adult flies. Attacks start in spring getting worse through summer. Control is essential.
Leaf miners	The larvae of moths, flies, wasps and beetles tunnel inside the leaves of the plants, leaving narrow, twisted trails.
Mealy bugs	These small, sap-sucking insects are covered in wax threads on the undersides of leaves, in leaf joints and crevices, and roots. They cause wilting on young shoots and attack a range of plants, especially cactus, ferns, palms, succulents, and many trees and shrubs.
Mites	Mites attack a variety of plants. They are often a serious pest of indoor and greenhouse plants. Most adults are not visible to the unaided eye. Their attacks are worst during hot, dry periods when the pest sucks the sap from the leaves.
Nematodes (eelworms)	Microscopic, worm-like nematodes live in the soil and attack roots and bulbs. Some feed on stems and leaves. Bead-like swellings or galls on roots, rot in bulbs, distortions on stems, and brown, dry leaves occur. May exhibit leaf yellowing and stunted growth.
Sawflies	Similar to caterpillars, sawfly larvae feed on plant foliage. They cluster on branches by day and spread out at night to feed. When disturbed they eject a sticky yellow fluid.
Scale	Scale are small bumps on leaves, branches and stems. They suck sap, hiding beneath a protective shield or mealy or waxy secretions. Severe scale can cause weakening and death. Sooty mould may grow on the secretion and affect the vigour of the plant.
Snails and slugs	Most active during spring and autumn after rain, snail and slug numbers can build up fast if not controlled. They feed, mostly at night, by rasping the surface from foliage, leaving a silvery trail of mucus behind.

CONTROL

There are many natural predators of aphids and gardeners can easily squash clusters of the pests by hand or squirt them away with a strong jet of water. Soapy water mixed with white oil is a non-toxic control and the pyrethrum- or fatty-acid based sprays, which are more effective, are among the safest to use.

Scrape away webbing and damaged bark and probe into tunnels with a piece of thin wire. If this fails to bring out the pest, squirt in a few drops of kerosene or methylated spirits (denatured alcohol). Putty the holes to prevent the entry of water, which in turn could lead to problems.

Spray with carbaryl or with *Bacillus thuringiensis* or BT (a disease that affects only caterpillars), or use a contact powder such as derris or cabbage dust.

Collect fruit as it falls and seal it in a plastic bag left in the sun. Don't leave fruit on the ground for more than 3 days and never bury it. Spray fortnightly from fruit set. Splash baits and traps only warn you that the fly is present, they are not a control in themselves.

If damage is minor, remove infected leaves and trash them. It is necessary, if spraying, to use a systemic or penetrant spray such as dimethoate. A weak solution of white oil may help combat citrus leaf miner.

Spray with a systemic insecticide such as omethoate or immerse potted plants in a maldison solution. Ladybird beetles, wasps and small birds are natural predators of mealy bugs, but as the pests secrete themselves in crevices and beneath the soil, chemical control is usually necessary.

Mites have several predators, including ladybird beetles, but the most effective is another mite – the predatory mite. These can be bought and released onto affected plants, but once released, toxic sprays will kill the predators. Miticides are sold but are not always effective.

Root nematodes thrive in light, sandy soils, and are discouraged by high levels of organic matter in the soil. Growing marigolds (*Tagetes*) can clear an area of nematodes which are repelled by an exudate from the plant. In the worst cases, treat soil with a nematicide and in vegetable gardens practise crop rotation.

Large birds feed on the larvae and should keep populations down. Otherwise, remove infested twigs and squash the sawflies underfoot. If spraying is necessary, use maldison.

Small numbers can be washed off with a brush and soapy water. Spray larger infestations with white oil or combinations of white oil and maldison until all the insects have been killed.

Clean up hiding places like under the rims of pots, under bricks and in the folds of leaves close to the ground. Collect on dewy mornings and drop into salty water. Encircle with a band of sawdust or coarse sand. Snail baits are effective but attractive and poisonous to dogs, so scatter thinly, never piled in heaps.

Common garden pests

PEST	SYMPTOM
Thrips	Thrips are tiny insects that grow to around 1 mm ($^1/_{32}$ inch). They cause a silver streaking or blasted appearance on leaves and flowers. They attack vegetables and ornamentals and are most often seen during hot, dry conditions. The eggs of most thrips are laid within the plant tissues and the nymphs and adults shelter within partly opened blossoms.
Whiteflies	These sap-sucking, tiny white flies infest the undersides of foliage, causing yellowing and wilting. Sooty mould will also grow on the honeydew they secrete. When disturbed they rise in clouds, but they quickly resettle. They attack many plants and may be a big problem in greenhouses, especially on ferns and orchids.

Plant diseases and nutrient deficiencies

Plant diseases can be caused by a variety of things, such as bacteria, fungi and viruses. Diseases can be spread by insects, by spores floating through the air, in the soil or in garden debris. Using secateurs, pruning knives and other gardening tools can also spread diseases from one plant to another. Some non-pathogenic diseases may be due to environmental conditions, deficiencies in diet, chemical injuries and the incorrect use of herbicides or fertilizers.

Remove diseased plants quickly

Viral diseases are passed on mainly by sap-sucking insects. As soon as a virus-infected plant is detected, it should be removed and added to an activated compost heap. Or better yet, burn any diseased plant material if possible.

CHILLI AND SOAP SPRAY
Gather together chillies, soap, a grater, a sharp knife and a chopping board. You'll also need a spray bottle and water. Grate soap (or use soap flakes). Add soap to a spray bottle nearly full of water. Chop 8 chillies and add to the bottle. Shake and spray your homemade insecticide onto any plant.

CONTROL

Thrips are often hard to control as they are protected inside flowers or under leaves for most of their lives. Maldison and dimethoate control thrips. After a 10-day interval a second application of the chemical is is recommended.

The parasitic wasp *Encarsia formosa* often keeps the numbers of whiteflies down. If spraying is necessary, use white oil or dimethoate at fortnightly intervals. Commercial, non-poisonous, sticky, whitefly traps are available.

Some symptoms of nutrient deficiencies

SYMPTOMS	DEFICIENCY
Yellowing of older leaves, often with reddish tints; premature maturity; retarded growth; excessive leaf loss	Nitrogen
Stunted growth; blue-green or bronze tonings on older leaves	Phosphorus
Leaf margins scorched; spotting surrounded by pale zones on leaves	Potassium
Patchy yellowing, older leaves with dark green at base and leaf loss	Magnesium
Distorted stems; curling and mottling of older leaves	Molybdenum
Yellowish or light green areas between veins on leaves	Manganese
Yellow young leaves but veins green; leaves small and early leaf fall	Iron
Reduced leaf size; twisted foliage; creamy-white to yellow blotches on young citrus and grape leaves	Zinc
Tip curling, blackening and early shedding of young leaves	Calcium
Yellowing leaf margins; dimpled apples; hollow stems in cauliflower; distorted leaves on beetroot	Boron
Twisted and curling foliage; tips of young leaves wilt and die; leaves darken to blue-green colour	Copper
Yellowing on young leaves that reduce and fail to mature	Sulphur

Common plant diseases

DISEASE	SYMPTOM
Black spot	Black spot is a fungal disease that affects a number of different plants, notably roses, but also apples, pears, plums and quinces. Black spot is usually worst when humidity is high or in tropical and subtropical areas. It causes dark spots on the leaves which wither and fall prematurely. Extensive defoliation can kill a young plant.
Collar rot of citrus (*Phytophthora citrophthora*)	Collar rot usually occurs on the trunk close to ground level causing flaky bark and rotting wood. First, you may notice gum followed by damp, soft bark. Later this bark may get dry and flake off. Badly affected trees fail to produce new growth and will die. Lemons are most susceptible, but all citrus trees can be affected.
Downy mildews	These mildews are a group of fungi that attack a wide range of vegetables, fruits and ornamentals. Small, yellow, pale green or brownish spots appear on leaves and cause portions of the leaf to dry out and die. In humid conditions, greyish downy patches develop on the undersides of the leaves under each spot.
Powdery mildews	The powdery mildews are a group of fungi that coat leaves, young shoots, flowers and fruits with a conspicuous white or pale grey, ash-like film. It occurs on many plants including vegetables and ornamentals. Powdery mildew is more prevalent in warm, humid weather and spreads rapidly from plant to plant by wind.
Root rots	Root rot is caused by fungal diseases. One of the most serious is *Phytophthora cinnamomi*. In hot weather a healthy plant may wilt and die within days. Armillaria root rot spreads through the soil by flat, black cords that resemble shoelaces. Infected trees lose vigour, leaves yellow and branches die back from the tips. Clusters of honey- or gold-coloured toadstools appear at the base of dead trees or from roots remaining in the ground.
Rose canker	Dark reddish lesions and cracking bark on rose canes are symptoms of rose canker. They are caused by a fungus that enters through pruning cuts or wounds. Cankers can encircle stems and cut off the flow of nutrients and water to growth further up.
Rusts	Rusts are recognized as small yellow or orange patches or spots, which appear mainly on the upper surfaces of leaves. On the underside, powdery, raised pustules appear under each spot. This disease can cause leaf fall and seriously weaken plants. Most rusts attack a specific plant or a small group of related plants and will not transfer from one host to another, but there are varieties for a broad range of plants.
Sooty mould	This dark fungal growth forms on the sticky secretions (honeydew) produced by sap-sucking insects. It causes black mould to appear on leaves and stems but doesn't harm plants directly. Occasionally sooty mould will appear on shrubs growing under trees or palms infested with pests as their sugary secretions have fallen onto the leaves below.

CONTROL

Collect all fallen leaves. Cut off and destroy infected leaves. Spraying may also be necessary. A number of fungicides, such as captan, copper oxychloride and mancozeb control black spot. Ensure good air circulation by not overcrowding plants.

Treat by cutting away damaged bark to expose healthy bark and clean wood. Paint with a paste of copper oxychloride to cover the wound.

Do not overcrowd plants and avoid overhead watering. Remove and burn affected leaves. Spray with a fungal spray such as zineb, wetting the undersides, too. If plants are regularly infected, your climate is probably too humid for them.

Grow mildew-resistant varieties where possible. Remove and destroy affected foliage. Avoid overcrowding and overhead watering. At first sign of infection, spray with wettable sulphur or coat with sulphur dust at regular intervals.

Remove dead plants, including their roots. Drench the soil with Fongarid or Ridomil, early application of which can save mildly affected plants. In future, grow plant species that are tolerant of *Phytophthora cinnamomi*.

Prune off and burn diseased canes. Canker can be spread from plant to plant by infected secateurs. Make a neat slanting cut to just above a good outward-facing bud and disinfect secateurs often.

As a preventative measure it is best to grow rust-resistant varieties of plants whenever possible. As different rusts affect a great many plants, the treatment often differs. Spraying with zineb, sulphur or oxycarboxin is effective against most rust fungi. Clear away fallen leaves to prevent a carry-over of the disease.

If you remove the primary infection, such as the aphids, scale or psyllids, the sooty mould will disappear. Hose the plant with a strong spray to assist in the clean-up.

 index